T0272595

Fear AND LOATHING

AT GOODISON PARK

LOU REED FOSTER

Fear AND Loathing AT GOODISON PARK

EVERTON FC
UNDER
DAVID MOYES

First published by Pitch Publishing, 2023

Pitch Publishing
9 Donnington Park,
85 Birdham Road,
Chichester,
West Sussex,
PO20 7AJ
www.pitchpublishing.co.uk
info@pitchpublishing.co.uk

A CIP catalogue record is available for this book
from the British Library.

ISBN 978 1 80150 436 2

Typesetting and origination by Pitch Publishing
Printed and bound in Great Britain by TJ Books, Padstow

Contents

This book is dedicated to my mum and dad, for all your love and encouragement. And for making sure I was born Blue, the greatest gift you have ever given me.

To Lucy, for your endless love and support. And for tolerating my moods when Everton get beat.

And to the Dark House Blues, for being my Everton family.

UTFT

Acknowledgements

MY HUGE thanks to everyone at Pitch Publishing for giving me the opportunity to write my first book. A big thank you as well to both Jim Keoghan and Paul McParlan: two writers of enviable talent who were generous with both their advice and contributions. Once again, a big thank you to my family for their support and encouragement, and to Lucy for helping me to edit the book. Lastly, a special thank you to anyone who buys a copy.

Foreword

I FIRST had the idea to write this book in 2019. I was completing my MA degree in Writing at Liverpool John Moores University, and I'd decided that I wanted to write a book about Everton Football Club, but initially struggled to settle on an era to focus my attention on. After a while, the choice seemed obvious – I decided to write about David Moyes. Firstly, I'd grown up during the period in which the Scot took charge of Everton, and so there are many moments from his era that hold a special significance for me. Moreover, as a decade since his 2013 departure was fast approaching, it seemed like an ideal time to start a project detailing his years at the club.

Although I have always been against Moyes's potential return, the whispers surrounding him triggered a resurgence of memories about that period in the club's history. I found myself contemplating where his tenure sat in the history of Everton Football Club, what it meant to me at the time, and perhaps even more so, what it means almost a decade after his departure. In early 2020, I started to dedicate more time to researching the book, and when the Covid-19 pandemic sent the world into lockdown, I found that the project gave me a focus in a strange and worrying time. In 2021, I began writing and by the end of the year had submitted my proposal to Pitch Publishing.

As the book progressed, I found it interesting just how much I'd forgotten or misremembered, and compiling the research brought back some fantastic memories and, sadly, equally as many that I'd have preferred remained buried. In the 11 years that David Moyes oversaw Everton Football Club, Goodison Park witnessed some highs and lows, as we became a side transformed from relegation fodder to one operating just outside the boundaries of success. Nonetheless, it was a period of stability and at times excitement, and I hope reading this book brings you the joy that writing it gave me.

Introduction

AS A young Evertonian, I came of age under David Moyes's stewardship, and it was a time when my expectations of Everton were formed. The generation prior to my own no doubt grew up with a very different idea of what Everton Football Club represented, having witnessed the glory years under Howard Kendall in the 1980s, followed by the chaotic demise of a club slow to adapt to the changing nature of English football in the 1990s. By the time Moyes arrived at Goodison Park in 2002, Everton had forfeited their place among the elite and had a fanbase largely resigned to the idea of a yearly scrap for Premier League survival.

This loss of status within the game was the result of numerous contributing factors, but by the millennium Everton could no longer be considered anything other than a club that had gone through a significant period of decline. A football club that once set the standard, demoted to the rank of perpetual underdogs and also-rans. Of course, the most successful period in the club's history may have been firmly in the rear-view mirror, but it remained fresh in the memory of most match-going Evertonians. However, growing up in the Premier League era, I have never known Everton to be anything other than a sleeping giant, yet to properly emerge from its slumber.

It is a fair critique to state that David Moyes was ultimately unsuccessful, as he failed to make an addition to Everton's trophy cabinet, even though he was given 11 years to do so. However, what Moyes did succeed in, was reinstating the ambitions of a fanbase who had become far too accustomed to dogfights and great escapes. Once again, Evertonians started to look up the table, and it seemed for a while that the turmoil of late-20th century Everton would soon give way to success in the early part of the 21st.

Of course, it wasn't to be, at least not in the truest sense of the term, but it felt like Everton were once again prepared to fight for their status, despite the club's limited finances when compared to the newly created 'top four'. While many of Everton's Premier League contemporaries, such as Manchester United and Liverpool, had long since sold their souls to the corporate financiers of football, attracting not only substantial financial benefits, but also an affluent and transient tourist 'fan' to the stadiums of working-class cities, Everton's fanbase predominantly remained fiercely local and insular. Marginalised and overlooked by a disinterested media, Everton had fallen off the pace both on and off the pitch, though this only served to intensify the bond between Evertonians and their club.

Moyes excelled at discovering cost-effective talent and built a team Evertonians were prepared to support, a team fans could fall in love with. Recruiting the likes of Tim Cahill, Leighton Baines and Seamus Coleman, to name a few, the Everton boss put together a team filled with fan favourites, and though their inability to bring silverware to Goodison Park may prevent their names being mentioned in the same breath as title- or trophy-winning club legends, there's no question over their place in the 'modern icon' or 'cult hero' categories. David Moyes restored some pride at Everton and while at times it felt as though every step forward was followed by two in the opposite direction, it was an era that could have and probably should have ended with a piece of silverware. It was an era when Evertonians once again started to demand more than merely securing top-flight status.

1

Power to the People's Club

'I AM from a city [Glasgow] that is not unlike Liverpool. I am joining the people's football club. The majority of people you meet on the street are Everton fans. It is a fantastic opportunity, something you dream about. I said, "yes" right away as it is such a big club.' (Beesley, *Liverpool Echo*, 2019.)

Little did anyone know at the time of the press conference from which the above quote is taken that a singular sentence within it would go on to form such a core aspect of Everton Football Club's culture and identity in the years to come. Just as Joe Royle's 'Dogs of War' had defined his mid-nineties stint in the Goodison Park dugout, and the 'School of Science' moniker seeped into the consciousness of fans who bore witness to the majestic Holy Trinity under Harry Catterick, David Moyes's 'People's Club' restored Everton's fractured identity.

Prior to David Moyes taking over as manager at Goodison Park, he orchestrated from the dugout of Deepdale. Preston North End were languishing in the bottom half of Division Two in January 1998 (which was, confusingly, the third tier of English football, and has since been rebranded as the equally bemusing League One). Avoiding relegation in his first campaign, Moyes guided his team to the Division Two play-offs in the 1998/99 season, bowing out to Gillingham in the semi-finals. The following year, Moyes lead the Lilywhites to the Division Two title, securing the promotion to Division One that had so narrowly escaped their grasp 12 months earlier. In his first season in the second tier, the youthful manager guided Preston to the Division One play-offs, losing 3-0 to Bolton Wanderers in the 2001 play-off final, painfully missing out on promotion to the Premier League.

The impressive start that David Moyes had made to his fledgling career in management caught the attention of Everton's board, who dispensed with the services of Walter Smith on 13 March 2002, following a 3-0 defeat to Middlesbrough in the sixth round of the FA Cup. With just one win in the previous 13 league games, the Blues' form had seen them sleepwalk into yet another relegation battle, with only goal difference separating 16th-placed Everton from the bottom three.

On 14 March 2002, Everton appointed Moyes as their new head coach, with the Scot having just 48 hours to prepare for his first game in charge against Fulham at Goodison Park.

The line-ups in front of 34,639 spectators were as follows:

Everton: Simonsen, Hibbert, Weir, Stubbs, Unsworth, Pistone, Carsley, Gravesen, Gemmill, Radzinski, Ferguson

Fulham: Van der Sar, Finnan, Melville, Goma, Brevett, Collins, Legwinski, Malbranque, Boa Morte, Marlet, Saha

It was almost as if Everton had received a jump-start, as David Unsworth's goal with just 27 seconds on the clock got the David Moyes era off to a flier. Goodison Park had not seen this Everton side score a goal for six weeks, but just 12 minutes into the game Duncan Ferguson would add a second, marking his return to the starting line-up with a goal after a seven-week lay-off. In a match where tensions threatened to boil over, referee Graham Barber brandished six yellow cards in the first half; two of them to Thomas Gravesen, who was dismissed after just 28 minutes.

As Fulham laid siege to Everton's goal after the break, Steed Malbranque's strike seven minutes into the second half ensured it would be a heart-stopping finale, but the Blues held on for a 2-1 win and the most precious of three points. 'What's my philosophy? Winning is important, but wanting to win is more important,' said Moyes, after his Goodison Park baptism.

'If I can instil that into my players, we'll be successful. A lot of people in that stadium probably thought: "Who is David Moyes?" If the fans want a hero, I hope it's not the manager but the players. But after all that's happened it feels as if I've been here six months, let alone two days. That was a dream start.' (Fifield, *The Guardian*, 2002.)

Indeed, a 4-3 victory at Pride Park a week later continued the dream start for Moyes, as Everton picked up only their second away win of the campaign in the Premier League. A total of 13 points from the last nine games of the season ensured Everton finished the 2001/02 campaign in 15th, seven points clear of relegation. Brushes with the drop had become par for the course in recent seasons, and it was now David Moyes's responsibility to ensure Everton's yearly dances with death were a thing of the past. Yet, when Moyes referred to Everton as 'the People's Club', he tapped into a zeitgeist among the fanbase. Disregarded and disenfranchised, much like the L4 community surrounding Goodison Park, being a part of the People's Club began to restore Everton's battered pride. It was a moniker that for many was a true recognition and embodiment of Evertonians. An anti-corporate emblem that fans could relate to, one in a sport that was now increasingly marketed as a television programme, geared towards an audience seemingly more concerned with glory-hunting than local pride. Amidst it all, Everton FC were the People's Club.

2

Remember the Name ...

AFTER SECURING Premier League status by a rather precarious seven points just months prior, Everton started the 2002/03 season celebrating the momentous achievement of playing 100 seasons of top-flight football, the first club to do so. Ahead of the opening league game of the season, at home to Spurs, Everton marked the historic occasion by welcoming heroes of seasons gone by on to the pitch, such as Howard Kendall and Alex 'Golden Vision' Young, but David Moyes would hand a debut to a teenage sensation who had the potential to be the club's modern-day equivalent.

At the age of 16 years, nine months and 24 days, Wayne Rooney became the second-youngest player to make a first-team appearance for Everton, falling shy of Joe Royle's 36-year-old record by 15 days. An obdurate opponent for even the most seasoned professional, Rooney's immediate impact suggested a fearlessness and footballing intelligence well beyond his years, earning him a debut assist in a 2-2 draw.

Fellow debutant Richard Wright, arriving in a £3.5 million transfer from Arsenal, had a less-than-ideal start to his Everton career. At fault for both goals, the England keeper offered his apologies to his team-mates at full time, though his new manager had little sympathy.

'I don't feel sorry for him,' Moyes said. 'I told him he should have saved both goals.' There were words of encouragement however from goalscorer Les Ferdinand, having netted his 15th goal in 16 appearances against the Blues. The Spurs striker said, 'I gave him a gee-up at the end, but he's a quality keeper.' (Fifield, *The Guardian*, 2002.)

Wright would make amends a week later, saving a penalty in a 1-0 win at Sunderland, as Chinese international Li Tie, arriving on loan from Liaoning FC in a deal brokered by new shirt sponsors Kejian, impressed in Everton's new-look midfield. Eleven points from the opening nine games left the Blues in 12th place by mid-October. A 3-0 League Cup second round win at Wrexham on 1 October saw Wayne Rooney, still 23 days away from his 17th birthday, become Everton's youngest ever goalscorer, stealing the show with two goals in six minutes to eclipse Tommy Lawton's 65-year-old record. Rooney's rise was already meteoric, but the Croxteth-born teenager's stardom was about to go supernova.

When Everton welcomed Arsene Wenger's side to Goodison Park on Saturday, 19 October, the Blues faced the seemingly impossible task of overcoming league and cup double winners Arsenal, who had continued their unbeaten form from the previous campaign, extending their run to 30 consecutive league games. The line-ups at Goodison Park in front of 39,038 spectators were as follows:

Everton: Wright, Weir, Unsworth, Hibbert, Yobo, Pembridge, Gravesen, Tie, Carsley, Radzinski, Campbell

Arsenal: Seaman, Lauren, Cole, Toure, Cygan, Campbell, Vieira, Silva, Ljungberg, Kanu, Henry

Winning can become habitual, and the champions came to Goodison in insatiable form. In addition to their long unbeaten run in the league, the Gunners had also scored in 48 games on the bounce and took just seven minutes to make it 49 as Freddie Ljungberg finished in typically clinical fashion. Everton looked unfazed however, and restored parity midway through the first half as Lee Carsley's effort rattled off the post before Tomasz Radzinski slotted home the rebound.

The emergence of Francis Jeffers in the second half reminded Evertonians of the last teenage sensation to pass through Goodison Park, the 1998 FA Youth Cup winner replacing Nwankwo Kanu in Arsenal's attack, but it would be the introduction of Everton's £80-per-week youngster with ten minutes remaining that changed the complexion of the game, and indeed the future of English football.

'I was fuming before kick-off because I had played a couple of games before that and I thought I had done quite well and deserved to start,' Wayne Rooney would later recall, in a 2017 interview with *The Everton Show*. 'When I was 16, I was always confident, thought I was good enough to play and that was always part of my character as a football player – not being happy that I wasn't playing.' (*The Irish Examiner*, 2017.)

The phrase 'wonderkid' is so often used to describe a gifted youngster as they progress from academy prospect to first-team Premier League player, placing an inconceivable amount of unnecessary pressure on the shoulders of those not yet old enough to get a round in at their local. However, such superlatives sell papers and generate clicks, with little thought given to how counter-productive the media spotlight could be to a young player's development. I have seen countless youngsters burst on to the scene, only for their potential to go unfulfilled, but at 16 years of age, there was little doubt that Wayne Rooney was simply cut from a different cloth.

Leaving experienced centre-half Sol Campbell for dead mere moments after setting foot on the Goodison turf, it was clear that Rooney was not going to be intimidated by the seemingly invincible opposition. In a ten-minute cameo, he made world-class talent appear ordinary, fearful almost, and as the clock ticked past 90 minutes, the young forward plucked the ball out of the air with consummate skill, before doing what 30 Premier League sides before him had failed to; scoring a winning goal against Arsenal.

'Rooney. Instant control,' said Clive Tyldesley, his commentary almost as iconic as the goal itself. His second touch opened up the space against a retreating Arsenal defence, but few players would have the audacity to shoot from such an unfavourable position. For Rooney though, he may as well have been in Stanley Park, or kicking balls against the shutters of shops on his Croxteth estate. 'Fancies his chances,' Tyldesley continued, as the Everton striker launched an emphatic strike that arced gracefully over a flailing David Seaman, going in off the underside of the bar. 'Oh, brilliant goal! Brilliant goal! Remember the name: Wayne Rooney!'

Dethroning Michael Owen as the Premier League's youngest goalscorer, Rooney's record-breaking strike left Arsene Wenger in a state of disbelief. 'He's supposed to be 16,' the Arsenal manager commented. 'Owen's a complete striker, but I didn't see him play at 16. At that age, Rooney is already a complete footballer. The guy can play. He's the best English under-20 I've seen since I came here [in 1996]. He can play people in, he's clever and a natural, built like a Gascoigne with his low centre of gravity. And he can dribble – I like strikers who can dribble.' (Fifield, *The Guardian*, 2002.)

The win proved that Wenger's Arsenal were human after all, but Rooney's other-worldly talent had kids in Everton tops all over the city trying to recreate the audacious skills on display at Goodison Park. After the 2002 FIFA World Cup in Japan and South Korea, we'd spent the summer pretending to be Ronaldo, or recreating Ronaldinho's spectacular strike for Brazil against England. But after the Arsenal game, it was Wayne Rooney's match-winning effort that we endeavoured to repeat, with both goals coincidentally scored past the ageing David Seaman.

Meanwhile, Rooney's graduation from Everton's academy was put on hold, with the teenager originally due to sign his first professional contract on 24 October 2002, his 17th birthday. However, with the striker agreeing to switch from his existing management company to Paul Stretford's ProActive group, Everton were forced to wait for his signature while the three-year, £1,000-per-week offer was reviewed.

'It's all been made clear by Mr Kenwright this morning that until discussions are completed with his change of management the deal won't be signed,' Stretford said. 'I don't know when it will happen, but it should be in the very near future. We would hope so. Certainly, there is nothing for anyone to worry about – we just have the best interests of the boy at heart.' (Winrow, *The Guardian*, 2002.)

Indeed, Bill Kenwright stated, 'There's nothing mischievous in this but Wayne has just changed agents and his new agency agreement doesn't go through for another few months. I don't think he will actually be signing [with ProActive] until December, but the contract has been agreed – it was agreed several months ago. I am not worried in the slightest. I can assure every Evertonian that Wayne Rooney will sign his full professional contract and will be staying at Goodison Park. Just like me, he is a Blue through and through.' (Winrow, *The Guardian*, 2002.)

As the young man was the subject of both national and international attention, with the likes of *Gazzetta dello Sport* and the *Moscow Times* dedicating their back pages to him, Evertonians could justifiably fear the youngster might soon follow in the footsteps of recent departees Michael Ball and Francis Jeffers, though manager David Moyes was adamant that there would be no such repeat.

'When I came here, I spoke to the board and I understand fully the financial situation,' the Everton boss said, perhaps naively. 'I want to lay some foundations here which won't be knocked away. I am confident now that if I want to keep someone, the board will back me, and we won't see a repeat of the sales in the past.' (Winrow, *The Guardian*, 2002.)

3

Teenage Riot

A RUN of six consecutive league wins between October and November 2002 earned Everton their best winning streak since the 1986/87 season, when Howard Kendall's side won five on the spin. With only one goal conceded during the run, as five of the wins were 1-0 victories, David Moyes's early-season priority of plugging the defensive gaps of previous years began to pay dividends.

Wayne Rooney's continued impact up top earned the Blues their first win at Elland Road for 51 years, an individual moment of brilliance from the youngster in the 80th minute the difference between the two clubs. Interestingly, it was a year to the day since Paul Gascoigne had scored his first and last goal in an Everton shirt, when the heir apparent to English football's enigmatic genius stole the show with a moment of brilliance worthy of Gazza himself.

Picking up the BBC Young Sports Personality of the Year award in December 2002, Rooney's rise from schoolboy to household name continued at breakneck speed, with the teenager scoring the winner in a 2-1 home victory over Blackburn Rovers six days later, shortly followed by his first career red card, in a Boxing Day 1-1 draw at Birmingham City.

By January 2003, Everton were in fifth place in the league and welcomed Manchester City to Goodison Park for a New Year's Day encounter billed as the 'Chinese Derby', as an estimated 350 million viewers tuned in from the Far East to watch two of their most celebrated footballing exports. Both national and provincial Chinese broadcasters screened the meeting of Everton's Li Tie, and Manchester City's Sun Jihai into the early hours, as the two fought out a 2-2 draw.

Everton were planning to capitalise on such a lucrative commercial opportunity with a pre-season tour of China in 2003, as part of the club's partnership with telecommunications company Kejian. The plan was to take part in a four-team tournament alongside Aston Villa and Chinese sides Shenzhen and Shandong, and it could have been a potentially rewarding visit for a club eager to expand its revenue streams, but an outbreak of SARS in the region prevented the Blues from travelling. The two-year sponsorship deal with Kejian contractually required Everton to visit China as soon as feasibly possible. The club could have easily rescheduled and capitalised on the Chinese market as soon as SARS was under control in the area, yet the Everton board failed to see the lucrative side of such a decision. Indeed, an alternative trip could have been arranged in conjunction with Manchester City, in light of the interest in the New Year's Day fixture between the two clubs. However, the trip was never re-scheduled and the opportunity passed the club by.

Meanwhile, on Saturday, 18 January 2003, Wayne Rooney finally put pen to paper on his first professional contract with Everton Football Club, signing a £13,000-per-week three-year deal, the maximum time permitted for a 17-year-old. 'I think everyone knows that me and my family are Everton mad,' Rooney said. 'For as long as I can remember, I have dreamed of playing for the club and to actually be appearing in the first team is fantastic. I'm really enjoying my football at the moment, and I love training with the rest of the lads, though I honestly cannot find the words to describe the feeling I get when I run out at Goodison Park wearing that blue shirt.' (Fifield, *The Guardian*, 2003.)

Meanwhile, Rooney's continued development earned him his first international cap on 12 February 2003; a half-time substitute in a friendly against Australia at the Boleyn Ground, the Everton forward became the youngest player to feature for the England international team, aged 17 years and 111 days. Interestingly, ex-Everton striker Francis Jeffers also made his international debut that night and scored his first and last goal for his country in a 3-1 defeat to the Socceroos.

A 2-1 win over Southampton after the international break, thanks to a 92nd-minute winner from Tomasz Radzinski, kept Everton firmly in contention for a European spot, with the Blues in fifth place in the league. As the business end of the season gathered pace, Rooney contributed a further three goals, including a last-minute winner against Aston Villa, with Everton maintaining a top-six position from November 2002 until the final game of the campaign on 11 May, when they would end the day in seventh place, missing out on Europe at the final hurdle.

'There are winners and losers,' sighed a dejected David Moyes in his post-match discourse. 'This has been a good season for Everton but there's no consoling us. We just didn't have enough to get over the finishing line.' (Fifield, *The Guardian*, 2003.)

The Premier League table at the end of the 2002/03 season

Team	Pld	W	D	L	GF	GA	GD	Pts
Man United	38	25	8	5	74	34	+40	83
Arsenal	38	23	9	6	85	42	+43	78
Newcastle	38	21	6	11	63	48	+15	69
Chelsea	38	19	10	9	68	38	+30	67
Liverpool	38	18	10	10	61	41	+20	64
Blackburn	38	16	12	10	52	43	+9	60
Everton	38	17	8	13	48	49	-1	59

To miss out on Europe by a solitary point on the final day of the campaign was gut-wrenching, though falling short due to goal difference, as we would have done had we finished level on points with Blackburn Rovers, would have been even more frustrating. David Moyes's first full season in charge at Everton exceeded expectations, though the Blues would end the campaign as the only team in the top nine not to qualify for Europe, as eighth-placed Southampton qualified as losing FA Cup finalists, and ninth-placed Manchester City earned a European spot via the UEFA Fair Play rule, as the best-behaved team in the league not already in a European competition.

Kevin Campbell finished the season as Everton's top scorer, with 12 goals in all competitions, with Tomasz Radzinski contributing 11 and Wayne Rooney eight. Indeed, by the end of Rooney's debut season, there was no doubt of his pedigree among the best young players in Europe, though the Everton forward would be overlooked for the PFA Young Player of the Year award, losing out to Newcastle United's Jermaine Jenas, an even more bemusing decision almost 20 years later.

Indeed, the 2002/03 season was an early indicator of the long-term progress that the club would make under David Moyes, and no doubt most Evertonians felt that the campaign could provide a springboard for a stable future, following a roller-coaster period in the club's history. However, it should not have been a season that warranted an official DVD release by the club titled *The Magnificent 7th*, an embarrassing and ill-advised piece of merchandise that exemplified Everton's diminished status and ambition. It reeked of small-time thinking and is still the butt of jokes from those across the park to this day. There is nothing magnificent about finishing seventh.

4

125 Years of Everton FC

WITH SOME on-the-pitch pride restored at Goodison Park, the 2003/04 season began with an optimism that Everton were starting to move in the right direction after many years of decline. Celebrating the club's 125th anniversary, David Moyes looked to build on the stable foundations he had lain the season before, with shrewd acquisitions in the summer transfer market, such as the versatile Kevin Kilbane arriving for around £1 million from Sunderland, and Scottish forward James McFadden joining from Motherwell for £1.25 million.

Indeed, David Moyes was already showcasing his ability to operate with limited financial means, creating a team far greater than the sum of its parts. Francis Jeffers made a surprise return to the club on a season-long loan, having failed to make an impression at Highbury, though the signing of the summer was the experienced goalkeeper Nigel Martyn, who joined for a nominal fee from Leeds United. An injury to Richard Wright, who hurt his shoulder in a freak accident by falling out of his loft while packing away suitcases after a family holiday, ruled the ex-Arsenal keeper out for Everton's pre-season fixtures, prompting Moyes to look for someone who could provide both cover and competition.

'I'm pretty confident that I can get myself back quickly,' Wright said. 'I spoke to the specialist and he was positive. I'm not superstitious, but the accident was on Friday the 13th [of June] and I am going to be careful now what I do on certain dates.' (BBC Sport, 2003.)

Fortune must have favoured the maladroit keeper, recovering in time for the start of the campaign. However, just six games into the season, Wright would sustain a knee injury in a 2-2 draw with Newcastle United, ruling him out for the remainder of the year. The injury to Wright saw Martyn take his spot as Everton's first-choice keeper, with the veteran England international keeping hold of the number one jersey for the next two years, his consistent performances prompting comparisons to the legendary Neville Southall.

Meanwhile, the 2003/04 season had begun in earnest, as the Blues got off to a less than ideal start, with just three wins out of the opening 14 league games. Back-to-back victories over Portsmouth and Leicester City in December earned Everton their first consecutive wins of the campaign, the triumph over the Foxes ensuring the Blues celebrated the 125th anniversary of the club's first ever fixture with all three points. A goal for Wayne Rooney in each match, followed by a 28 December winner over Birmingham City, took his tally to four for the season.

Indeed, Rooney's continued influence saw the teenager linked with a move to everyone from Real Madrid to newly cash-rich Chelsea, with the south London club under the new ownership of Russian oil billionaire Roman Abramovich. Though reports suggested a £35 million deal could be lined up to take the teenager to Stamford Bridge, any speculation was swiftly dismissed by Everton's deputy chairman Bill Kenwright, in a somewhat contradictory statement.

'Wayne Rooney is going nowhere,' Kenwright said. 'David Moyes and I sing from the same hymn sheet and always said any club would have to pay a king's ransom for a player like Rooney. He is part of the fabric at our football club. A talent like Wayne's comes along once in a lifetime. We are only concerned at his progress in the blue shirt of Everton. He is a Blue and wants to remain a Blue.' (*The Guardian*, 2003.)

Everton boss David Moyes was quick to rebuke the transfer rumours and reiterated his stance on wanting a final say on player departures, stating, 'The story is complete rubbish. There is no truth in it as far as I know, and as the manager I would expect to know about something like that if it was happening. As people know, when I joined the club, I made it clear to the board that if they haven't got the money to spend, then don't give me any – but do not take away my best players. Nothing has changed.' (*The Guardian*, 2003.)

Everton's apparent stance on Rooney's future notwithstanding, media speculation surrounding the teenager continued apace, and as David Moyes's side struggled to repeat the consistent form of the 2002/03 season, the club's end-of-year objective was to maintain Premier League status, fuelling a narrative that in order to fulfil his potential, the prodigious talent must leave Goodison Park.

Back-to-back victories over Aston Villa and Portsmouth in February and March saw Moyes's side travel to Leicester City's Walker's Stadium on Saturday, 20 March looking to make it three on the spin for the first time in over a year, with just six points separating 14th-placed Everton from the Foxes in 17th. Wayne Rooney scored his fourth goal in as many games to open the scoring for Everton, his man-of-the-match display only blemished by picking up a tenth yellow card of the season, earning him a one-game suspension. A Marcus Bent equaliser in the final minute denied Everton all three points, though the game is possibly mostly remembered for Duncan Ferguson's first-half act of self-destruction. Picking up a caution for a foul on Nikos Dabizas, the Scot would find his name in the referee's notebook for a second time just three minutes later, this time for grabbing German international Steffen Freund by the throat, leaving referee Barry Knight with little option but to dismiss Everton's ill-tempered forward.

A suspension for both Rooney and Ferguson would leave David Moyes short on attacking options, with Jeffers having failed to register a single league goal since his return. Still, the now-iconic image of the big man ferociously gripping the throat of a terrified-looking Freund does make a great t-shirt.

Despite just one win out of the final ten fixtures of the campaign, Everton would finish the 2003/04 season six points clear of relegation in 17th place. Nine goals each for Ferguson and Rooney saw the two finish as joint-top goalscorers, and the contribution of the Everton teenager in particular was difficult to ignore. Of the nine league victories, the 17-year-old scored in four of them. Three out of those four strikes were winning goals, with Rooney also finding the net five times in 12 draws. Selected as part of Sven-Goran Eriksson's England squad for the 2004 European Championships in Portugal, it would be a summer of intense speculation as David Moyes sought to retain the services of his generational talent.

The Premier League table at the end of the 2003/04 season

Team	Pld	W	D	L	GF	GA	GD	Pts
16. Man City	38	9	14	15	55	54	+1	41
17. Everton	38	9	12	17	45	57	-12	39
18. Leicester **(R)**	38	6	15	17	48	65	-17	33
19. Leeds **(R)**	38	8	9	21	40	79	-39	33
20. Wolves **(R)**	38	7	12	19	38	77	-39	33

5

Once A Blue ...

'THIS IDEA that Wayne has suddenly developed beyond Everton's level is just laughable nonsense,' David Moyes stated in an interview on 3 July 2004. 'Wayne certainly hasn't outgrown Everton Football Club. Don't anyone tell me that he should move on because Everton aren't big enough for him. This is a big club with a big tradition, and he has plenty to achieve here. He has become a top-class international at Everton, so the club can't be all bad.' (*The Irish Examiner*, 2004.)

Indeed, Wayne Rooney had become a top-class international while at Everton. Briefly holding the record as the European Championships' youngest ever goalscorer (his record lasted four days, before it was topped by Swiss midfielder Johan Vonlanthen), Rooney scored four goals in four games for England, reaching the quarter-finals and earning himself a place in UEFA's Team of the Tournament. At just 18, Rooney's international tournament debut was electric, no doubt increasing his market value should Everton receive a legitimate offer.

However, on 8 July, Everton boss David Moyes insisted that his summer spending plans were based on the assumption that Rooney would still be an Everton player at the start of the 2004/05 season. With a £50,000-per-week, five-year deal on the table, Everton Football Club offered the 18-year-old the most lucrative contract in the club's history.

'Whatever happens, Wayne's here and we hope he remains and, really, it's not crossed my mind about any other scenario,' said Moyes. 'Everton have made Wayne a terrific offer and I'm pleased the club have really pushed the boat out, and for an 18-year-old player I think it's a good deal. He's got two years to go on his contract; we'd like to extend it and make it five years. Hopefully Wayne and his advisors feel this is the right place for his continued development.'

The Everton boss continued, 'Wayne's a great young player, one of the best in Europe; hopefully, one day he might be one of the best in the world. Everton probably need a little bit of the credit for keeping him going. We've not made him the player – he and his family have done that – but we've given him those opportunities at Everton and hopefully we'll get repaid for that in the chance to keep him on for a couple more years at least. If we can get a successful team here and build a side which can be in the Champions League then this would hopefully be his home for a long, long time.' (Fifield, *The Guardian*, 2004.)

A feeling, however, not shared by forward Tomasz Radzinski who, prior to a move to Fulham in a £1.75 million deal in July 2004, felt it necessary to wade into the Rooney debate. The Canadian forward, whose departure from the club saw Everton bring in Marcus Bent for £450,000 and Tim Cahill, who signed from Millwall for a fee of £2 million, told BBC Sport: 'I hope Wayne Rooney goes somewhere where he can improve and grow as a player.'

Meanwhile, off the pitch, club chief executive Trevor Birch resigned from his post after only six weeks at the club as Everton's summer descended into a soap opera. With a £40 million debt looming over Goodison Park, Birch had been brought in to assist the club in resolving the precarious financial situation, following his success in similar roles at Chelsea and Leeds United. However, Birch was thought to have grown frustrated that his advice to find an external investor was ignored, and ultimately decided he could no longer work effectively with majority shareholders Bill Kenwright and Paul Gregg. Few could blame Birch for retreating from a boardroom on the brink of civil war, with

Gregg allegedly lining up investment from a Thai consortium, following the £1.5 million one-year shirt sponsorship deal with Thai beverage company Chang Beer, with Kenwright vehemently opposing the idea of such a takeover. The two founding members of True Blue Holdings, who took control of Everton in 1999, remained at loggerheads over the direction in which to take the club, though Kenwright retained the backing of True Blue's third director, Jon Woods.

With Everton lacking the requisite funds to compensate for a £40 million debt, Rooney's departure was inevitable, despite weeks of rhetoric regarding their determination to keep hold of the player. On the morning of 25 August 2004, Wayne Rooney told Everton of his desire to leave the club, subsequently submitting a written transfer request. 'This has been one of the hardest decisions of my life,' Rooney told *The Guardian*. 'But I feel the time is now right for me to move forward with my career. The Euros were a fantastic experience for me, it made me realise I could play at the highest level. To do that I need to be with a club that is playing in Europe every year. I hope the Everton fans can come to understand my decision and I hope the transfer fee Everton Football Club will receive will help the club move forward. The Everton fans have always been fantastic in their support of me. I hope they respect my decision and I also hope that someday in the future I could be welcomed back to watch the team I have supported since boyhood.'

A £20 million bid from Newcastle United quickly followed and was just as swiftly rejected, as was a bid of equal value from Manchester United. 'We don't want to lose Wayne, but if we do the only way is at the top price and the value we want,' David Moyes said. 'I would like to quote Bobby Robson's words: "You're talking about buying the most exciting, brilliant young player in Europe." If that is what Sir Bobby thinks then he has got to pay the most exciting and brilliant price because his current valuation is well short. Didier Drogba went to Chelsea for £24 million so Wayne's price should be well more than that. He is English and if you want to buy English you have to pay a higher premium.' (*The Guardian*, 2004.)

Meanwhile, Bill Kenwright appeared to publicly shift the responsibility for Rooney's imminent departure on to unsuspecting manager David Moyes, stating, 'Whatever happens with a sale, if it happens, the manager makes all the decisions about the players at our football club.' (Fifield, *The Guardian*, 2004.)

Understandably perturbed, Moyes refuted Kenwright's suggestions that he would make the final call on Rooney's future. 'I am the manager of the club, but decisions have to be made at clubs and I am sure that one of the biggest transfers ever seen is not just down to the manager,' reiterated Moyes. 'Whatever has been said, it was my idea to give Wayne the biggest contract in the club's history ... I told Bill Kenwright that was what to do and the club backed me up on that. But if people are not happy and don't want to stay, it becomes difficult. At the moment he is staying because we have not had an offer that is acceptable. We don't want unhappy people because that does not work but I want to make sure we get the right price for Wayne.'

Moyes continued, 'So many people felt it was better for Wayne to leave to improve his future. I have always felt it was better for his future to stay at Everton. We have given him his opportunity here, we put him in the team very early and I hoped he would see that through. I have always said I want to build a team, not sell one, and if that was ever taken away from me, I would consider things. But he is not being taken away from me – he has stated he wants to go because mainly he wants to play European football and we cannot offer that to him at the moment at Everton.

'He wants that opportunity, two clubs in Europe have come in for him and he sees his future at one of those clubs.' (*The Guardian*, 2004.)

With bids of £20 million and £23.5 million from Manchester United and Newcastle United already turned down, rumours circulated that Manchester United were prepared to offer French striker David Bellion as a makeweight in their offer. Manchester United manager Sir Alex Ferguson stated, 'It is as it was yesterday. David Gill [United's chief executive] is in dialogue with Bill Kenwright. It only takes a second to say yes. The difficulty is getting the medicals but at the moment it is not at the stage where we are talking about it. We are waiting for an agreement before doing anything else.' (*The Guardian*, 2004.)

Meanwhile, Newcastle United chairman Freddie Shepherd claimed that the north-east club were confident of securing Rooney's signature before the transfer window deadline. 'I'm always confident,' said the Magpies' chairman. 'I think Wayne Rooney will be in another club by Tuesday, and I would like to think he will be wearing a black and white shirt. Our bid is in, and it's confidential, it would not be fair to Everton to disclose it. They have had the bid and have to decide which way to go. He's their player, he's not our player and it's up to them to say yes or no. One thing we're not at Newcastle is shrinking violets, put it that way. But I would put my house on it all being sorted out before the transfer deadline.' (*The Guardian*, 2004.)

Eventually, on Tuesday, 31 August 2004, Everton accepted a bid of £20 million, plus a further £7 million in additional fees, from Manchester United, with Wayne Rooney signing a five-year deal. It was the first time I remember being heartbroken by the sale of an Everton player, and though it is a feeling I have become very accustomed to over the years, I doubt I'll ever truly get over Wayne Rooney's departure. Without question the finest English talent of his generation, perhaps of all time, and he was ours, until he wasn't.

6

Time For Heroes

IT WAS hard not to feel as though Everton had been robbed of a modern icon with the departure of Wayne Rooney in the summer of 2004, but as the 2004/05 campaign kicked off, David Moyes's summer signings of Tim Cahill and Marcus Bent wasted little time in settling into life at Goodison Park. Five wins from the opening seven games of the season saw Everton off to a flying start, the pair scoring two goals apiece before the end of September.

A 1-0 win at Manchester City courtesy of Tim Cahill on 11 September, saw the Australian attacker become the first player in top-flight English football to be sent off for lifting his jersey over his head, in what referee Steve Bennett called an 'over-exuberant celebration'. Recent changes to the guidelines for players celebrating a goal stated that a player would receive a booking for removing their shirt. Despite Cahill's caution in only lifting his shirt over his face, and therefore not fully removing it from his body, he still found himself in Bennett's notebook for the second time that afternoon and was dismissed with an hour gone.

Everton, quite rightly, argued that the rule change outlined that the player in question should only face a booking if the shirt was removed fully, appealing to the FA that Cahill's one-match suspension should be overturned. The club even received support from then FIFA president Sepp Blatter, who said, 'A referee should never expel a player just because he pulled his shirt over his head, he should just have a word with him. If you take off your shirt and wave it over your head that's a different matter.' (*Liverpool Echo*, 2004.) However, Sepp's surprising words of support fell on deaf ears, as did the club's protestations, and Cahill's one-match ban stood.

Meanwhile, Everton had unveiled Keith Wyness as the club's new chief executive on 9 September, replacing the outgoing Trevor Birch. 'My ambition is to make Everton one of the best-managed clubs in the Premiership,' Wyness said. 'We need viability and stability. Changes need to be made and I want to instil a culture of innovation and be open to change. I will roll my sleeves up and get stuck in and I will do everything to support the chairman and the board.' (BBC Sport, 2004.)

By December, Everton had won nine of their opening 15 Premier League fixtures and sat in third place in the table. This was a team that a galvanised Goodison crowd could get behind, a team that didn't seem to know when it was beat. A Radhi Jaidi own goal on 4 December sparked wild, frenetic celebrations as the Blues earned a dramatic 3-2 victory over Bolton Wanderers, with Everton twice coming from behind to secure a late win. It was a game that left a mark on me as a young Evertonian, witnessing 'fortress Goodison' in full swing.

Without a win in the Merseyside derby in five years, Everton welcomed Liverpool to Goodison Park on 11 December, nine points clear of Rafael Benitez's side. David Moyes had yet to record a victory over Liverpool since his arrival in March 2002, but with his side in such fine form, it was an opportune time for the Scot to break his derby duck.

The line-ups at Goodison Park for the 200th Merseyside derby were as follows:

Everton: Martyn, Hibbert, Stubbs, Weir, Pistone, Carsley, Osman, Gravesen, Cahill, Kilbane, Bent

Liverpool: Kirkland, Josemi, Carragher, Hyypia, Riise, Diao, Hamann, Gerrard, Kewell, Sinama Pongolle, Mellor

The game began as most derbies do, with a predictably fierce exchange of tackles. The in-form Cahill headed wide from six yards out after 21 minutes, with Marcus Bent providing a pinpoint cross that the Australian attacker would usually eat for breakfast. At the other end, Neil Mellor's header from six yards forced Nigel Martyn into a point-blank save, as Alan Stubbs cleared the rebound to safety.

Goalless at the interval, though it felt unlikely to end that way, the second half began as the first had ended, with both sides searching for an opening. As the clock ticked on, the match began to take on a 'next goal wins' feel, and with 22 minutes remaining, Leon Osman found Republic of Ireland international Lee Carsley in space 20 yards out, the midfielder almost passing the ball past an awkwardly positioned Chris Kirkland in front of an erupting Street End. Dragged to the ground in celebration, Carsley was swamped by his team-mates, a homogeneous pile of blue with Cahill's raised arm at the forefront, forever captured in a now iconic still.

Liverpool's John Arne Riise was forced into a goal-line clearance moments later as Everton went for the kill, with Tim Cahill coming close to opening his derby account. Duncan Ferguson replaced the tireless Marcus Bent with 15 minutes to play and almost immediately flattened Sami Hyypia with his chest, getting a booking for his trouble. At full time, a jubilant Goodison Park celebrated the first derby day win for five years, with Lee Carsley's effort the difference between the two sides.

'I think the blue half of Merseyside will have a very good night,' the Everton boss said at full time. 'But it is not just the three points today, it's the other 33 points we got before today which are important. We are up to second and that says we are moving on when really a lot of people didn't think we could do so. We've got a real honest group of lads who are doing everything that is asked of them. They have got great confidence, great self-belief at the moment and that is helping us win games.'

Moyes continued, 'The reason I'm most excited is for the fans. If we are in second place, we have got to be in with a shout of the title, haven't we? I think if it was any other club, people would say we were in the mix, but there seems to be a doubt that we have the resources to keep it up. We'll have to see about that. We certainly haven't got the finances to match Chelsea, but by hook or by crook we are trying everything else to bridge that gap.' (Kay, *Liverpool Echo*, 2022.)

Victory in the derby took the Blues into second place, just four points off league leaders Chelsea. For me, this was the game when the David Moyes era truly kicked in.

7

Fortress Goodison

A 2-1 Boxing Day win over Manchester City, with Cahill and Bent on target for the Blues, took Everton's points tally to 40 for the season, already one point better than the whole of the previous campaign. Indeed, as Moyes stated, 'plucky little Everton' had to be considered title contenders as the midway point of the season approached.

As the January transfer window opened, it afforded the Blues the opportunity to reinforce a threadbare squad and provide David Moyes with the resources he needed to 'bridge that gap'. On 4 January, Everton spent a club record £6 million on Southampton forward James Beattie, with the 26-year-old turning down a more lucrative wage offer from Aston Villa to join the Blues.

'He's coming into his peak years as a centre-forward. If he's banging in goals for Everton and we're near the top of the table, then people will be clamouring for him to be back in the England squad,' said Moyes of his new signing, in reference to Beattie's omission from England's Euro 2004 party. 'This club has had some great centre-forwards and for me James might be a mix of Andy Gray and Graeme Sharp,' the Everton boss continued, perhaps a little too optimistically. (*The Guardian*, 2005.)

Meanwhile, the club also bade farewell to heroic forward Kevin Campbell, who joined West Bromwich Albion on a free transfer, as well as cult midfielder Thomas Gravesen, who made the surprise switch to the Bernabeu as Real

Madrid snapped him up for a fee of £2.5 million, the Danish international only having six months left on his contract. 'It's not a question of Thomas wanting to leave,' said Gravesen's agent, John Sivebaek. 'He's happy there, but this is Real Madrid we're talking about. This type of opportunity might never come again.' (Fifield, *The Guardian*, 2005.)

Indeed, Gravesen had been in fine form for the Blues in the first half of the 2004/05 season, his marauding runs from midfield offering support to Everton's attack, but while La Liga was the destination of a departing player, it too provided David Moyes with a replacement as Mikel Arteta joined on an initial five-month loan deal from Real Sociedad on 1 February, with Liverpool duo Xabi Alonso and Luis Garcia providing an assist. 'I asked Xabi [Alonso] about coming here and he told me to do it because Everton are playing really well this season and they have passionate supporters,' recalled Arteta of his countryman. 'Luis Garcia said the same.' (Fifield, *The Guardian*, 2005.)

The cultured midfielder wasted little time in settling into life on Merseyside as he looked to get his stalled career back on track after a challenging time in San Sebastian. A James Beattie strike four minutes into a 2-2 draw at Southampton got the Blues' record signing off to a decent start, as he inevitably marked his return to the south coast with a goal. By mid-February, Everton's lofty title ambitions had slipped away, but Champions League qualification was well within reach. However, as David Moyes's side welcomed league leaders Chelsea to Goodison Park on 12 February, new signing James Beattie would earn himself a three-match ban for headbutting French defender William Gallas, twice.

Down to ten men after just eight minutes, Everton fell to a 1-0 defeat to Jose Mourinho's side, but with trips to Villa Park and Anfield approaching, alongside the visit of Blackburn Rovers to Goodison Park, Beattie's moronic assault would see him miss three challenging fixtures in the pursuit of a top-four finish. No doubt vexed, the Everton boss stood by his player, stating, 'I was a centre-half in my playing days, and

I would have been embarrassed to go down the way Gallas did. What has happened to big, tough defenders? John Terry wouldn't have reacted like that. It wasn't a sending-off. I've seen it, and it's just not possible to headbutt somebody from behind. I think James had been blocked to start with and was then simply running with his head down and collided with Gallas.' (*Daily Mirror*, 2005.)

Moyes's comments prompted a strong reaction from the sporting press, with the *Daily Mirror* referring to the Scot's defence of Beattie as 'astonishing and ridiculous', saying it 'simply took the breath away'. Amidst a media maelstrom, Moyes U-turned, telling the Everton website, 'Having had some time to reflect and, perhaps more significantly, having now had time to carefully study video recordings of Saturday's game, I believe that I should set the record straight by conceding that the dismissal of James Beattie was right and correct. My comments on Saturday came immediately after the final whistle and at a point when I had only had the opportunity to see one, very quick re-run of the incident.'

The Everton boss continued, 'Although the incident was totally out of character – James has never even been suspended before in his career – his actions were unacceptable and, self-evidently, had a detrimental effect on his team-mates. James did issue a formal apology to myself, his team-mates and to the Everton supporters immediately after the game and that was the right thing to have done. He will now be subjected to the normal club discipline. He is a competitive player, but a fair player, and I know how upset he is by what has happened. However, I must say that I do still believe the Chelsea player in question did go down too easily.' (*Daily Mail*, 2005.)

Out of character it may have been, but Beattie struggled to adapt to life at Everton, despite his promise. Meanwhile, three defeats out of the next four games, including a 2-1 loss at Anfield, meant Everton's five-point advantage over fifth-placed Liverpool in February 2005 was reduced to a solitary point by April. Everton needed to come up with a response, but with four out of the remaining seven games to be played at home, fortress Goodison still had its part to play.

The Premier League table on 3 April 2005

Team	Pld	GD	Pts
1. Chelsea	31	+50	80
2. Arsenal	31	+39	67
3. Man United	31	+31	67
4. Everton	31	+2	51
5. Liverpool	31	+13	50

A 4-0 win over Crystal Palace at Goodison Park on 10 April saw David Moyes's side pick up their first three points since the end of February. A Mikel Arteta free kick inside ten minutes, followed by a Tim Cahill double early in the second half had the points wrapped up before the hour mark, allowing 16-year-old James Vaughan to make his debut as the club's youngest post-war player, beating Joe Royle's long-standing record by 12 days.

In a glowing cameo, Vaughan hit Everton's fourth of the afternoon, making him the youngest goalscorer in Premier League history at 16 years and 271 days, dethroning Leeds United's James Milner, as well as eclipsing Wayne Rooney's record of Everton's youngest goalscorer. Four goals and a four-point gap restored, following Liverpool's 1-0 defeat at Manchester City, promised a buoyant end to the weekend, though no doubt young James Vaughan celebrated harder than most following his record-breaking performance.

The visit of Manchester United to Goodison Park on 20 April for a midweek game under the lights saw Duncan Ferguson roll back the years with a vintage performance as the totemic Scot terrorised a panicked United defence. The Blues had welcomed Sir Alex Ferguson's side only two months prior in the FA Cup, as Wayne Rooney made his first return to L4 since his departure the previous summer. A tame Everton had fallen to a 2-0 defeat in the cup, though there would be no repeat of that insipid display here.

The line-ups were as follows:

Everton: Martyn, Hibbert, Yobo, Weir, Watson, Carsley, Bent, Arteta, Cahill, Kilbane, Ferguson

Man United: Howard, G Neville, Ferdinand, Brown, Heinze, Fletcher, Keane, Scholes, Ronaldo, Rooney, Van Nistelrooy

Without a league victory against United for a decade, Everton's record in this fixture left little room for optimism. A Duncan Ferguson goal had been the difference the last time Everton beat United in the Premier League in 1995, and the talismanic Scot looked in the mood from the first whistle this time, provocative in his harassment of the opposition. Greeted by jeers and boos with every touch of the ball, Wayne Rooney was in an equally precocious mood, and tested Nigel Martyn after six minutes with a 20-yard drive, though the Everton keeper was equal to it.

A series of collisions between Tim Cahill and Roy Keane set the tempo in a combative midfield, as referee Phil Dowd prepared himself for a busy evening. As Cahill continued to make a nuisance of himself, the Australian attacker almost gave Everton a first-half lead with a spectacular overhead kick, only for Wes Brown to clear on the line. A Cristiano Ronaldo effort moments later forced Martyn into another save as the game swung from end to end.

Everton's veteran keeper produced yet another fine save early in the second half, this time denying Paul Scholes. As tensions boiled over, Duncan Ferguson thwarted Tim Howard's attempt to release the ball early by bundling the American to the ground, receiving a verbal warning from Dowd. The Scot earned himself a caution moments later as a late challenge on fellow countryman Darren Fletcher ignited an already defiant crowd.

The energy from within the stands seemed to overflow on to the pitch, reaching its crescendo on 55 minutes in a manner reminiscent of that famous old Howard Kendall quote from his team-talk at the European Cup Winners' Cup semi-final against Bayern Munich in 1985: 'Get the ball into the box and the Gwladys Street will suck it in.'

Ferguson was playing like a man possessed, chasing down every ball as United's usually composed backline cheaply conceded possession with panicked and rushed clearances. As the Blues pressed, Steve Watson won a free kick in front of the Family Enclosure and as Mikel Arteta stood over the ball, the anticipation in the ground was palpable, his pinpoint cross meeting the diving head of Duncan Ferguson to fire Everton ahead. A trademark header from Ferguson, followed by a trademark celebration, as the Scot ran the length of the touchline with his arm exultantly raised, an Everton sweatband visible beneath his long-sleeved shirt. It was a triumphant performance from Big Dunc emphasized by a wall of Goodison Park noise swelling into an ear-splitting crescendo.

A measure of United's frustration was indicated by a close-up shot of Paul Scholes on that evening's episode of *Match of the Day*, as the Salford-born midfielder could be seen muttering expletives to himself after a rash attempt on goal. Scholes would earn himself a sending-off for two bookable offences before the evening's end, alongside Gary Neville, who received a straight red for kicking the ball at a member of the crowd.

As Everton held out for a 1-0 win, the significance of this victory couldn't be underestimated. Ending a decade-long wait for a league victory over Manchester United was a measure of the new-found belief within the squad, and a glance at the league table at full time reinforced this conviction with Champions League football within Everton's grasp.

The Premier League table on Wednesday, 20 April 2005

Team	Pld	GD	Pts
1. Chelsea	33	+50	82
2. Arsenal	33	+40	71
3. Man Utd	33	+28	67
4. Everton	33	+7	57
5. Liverpool	34	+13	54

A 1-1 draw at home to Birmingham City saw Duncan Ferguson on target once again, this time rescuing a late point for the Blues. 'We obviously would have liked three points rather than one, but we are happy with our return of seven points from our last three home games,' Moyes confirmed. 'We know we are close to making European football and it would be nice if that happens and we also know we will still be fourth after all the games are played. Emotionally the win against Manchester United took a lot out of us, but we kept going and Duncan got the equaliser. We told the players to re-focus on the Birmingham game right after the win in midweek, but they're only human and it's very difficult.' (BBC Sport, 2005.)

A 2-0 defeat at Craven Cottage, with a goal from former Everton loanee Brian McBride, saw the Blues endure some worrisome form as the season entered the final weeks, but Liverpool failed to capitalise on Everton's dropped points, falling to a 1-0 defeat at Selhurst Park, before grinding out a 1-1 draw against Middlesbrough at Anfield. As Everton welcomed Newcastle United to Goodison Park on Saturday, 7 May, a win for the Blues would guarantee Champions League football, should Liverpool lose at Highbury 24 hours later.

With 40,438 spectators packed into Goodison Park, there was a cautious optimism within the stands as Everton started the game on the front foot, Mikel Arteta's free kick coming close after seven minutes. However, Newcastle quickly settled into the game and it was only the poor finishing of the visitors that kept the score at 0-0, with Patrick Kluivert somehow missing the target from point-blank range.

Everton were probably the more eager side to hear the referee's half-time whistle as the game progressed, so when veteran centre-half David Weir headed the Blues in front from an Arteta free kick, it began to feel like it was going to be our day. A Shola Ameobi sending-off early in the second half intensified this belief, and it wasn't long before Moyes's side made use of their numerical advantage, attacking Shay Given's goal with purpose and precision. A second assist of the day for Arteta exemplified his creative influence, though there was an element of fortune as the Spanish midfielder's shot inadvertently found itself at the feet of Tim Cahill, whose composed finish ignited wild celebrations in even the most sedate sections of the stadium.

The pubs of Walton will have no doubt done a roaring trade at full time, and as Liverpool stumbled to a 3-1 defeat to Arsenal on Sunday, 8 May, guaranteeing Champions League football at Goodison Park for the 2005/06 season, many a hangover will have been cured by the sight of the Premier League table. Securing fourth place with two games remaining was an astonishing achievement, especially as David Moyes's side had avoided relegation by just six points a year before, compounded by the loss of Wayne Rooney. However, with the arrival of Tim Cahill, who finished the year as top scorer with 12 goals in all competitions, Rooney's departure became little more than a footnote. Goodison Park had a new hero.

The Premier League table at the end of the 2004/05 season

Team	Pld	W	D	L	GF	GA	GD	Pts
1. Chelsea	38	29	8	1	72	15	+57	95
2. Arsenal	38	25	8	5	87	36	+51	83
3. Man Utd	38	22	11	5	58	26	+32	77
4. Everton	38	18	7	13	45	46	-1	61
5. Liverpool	38	17	7	14	52	41	+11	58

8

Back to Where
We Once Belonged

THE EXCITEMENT in the summer of 2005 was profound. Everton had unfinished business with the European Cup, unable as they had been to compete in the competition following the title-winning years of 1985 and 1987, as a consequence of the blanket ban on English clubs following the Heysel Stadium disaster. The injustice of automatic disqualification from UEFA competitions until the eventual lifting of the ban in 1990 is still felt to this day, especially among fans old enough to have seen Howard Kendall's team in action: no doubt the greatest in the club's history.

Indeed, the European Cup is the benchmark by which we now measure big club status, and if this was Everton's invitation to rejoin the party, the club had to grab it with both hands. As the Blues would be entering the competition at the third qualifying round, the date of the draw, 29 July 2005, was written on the calendar of every Evertonian, as we eagerly waited to discover who our opponents would be for the August fixture.

With the likes of Ajax, AS Monaco and Internazionale in the pot, conversation turned to who our preferred opposition would be, with fans of a certain vintage suggesting Panathinaikos would be their ideal choice as it would afford us the opportunity to settle an old score, as the Greek giants had eliminated Everton at the quarter-final stage of the 1971

European Cup, with their away goal in a 1-1 draw at Goodison Park the deciding factor. Indeed, the prospect of a few days basking in the Athenian sunshine was an alluring one, though it wasn't to be.

Instead, Everton would face La Liga outfit Villarreal. Relative minnows historically, the Yellow Submarine, as they are affectionately nicknamed due to their flamboyantly yellow kit, were not to be underestimated going into the game. Having finished third in La Liga the previous year, behind champions Barcelona and second-placed Real Madrid, Villarreal lost only nine league games throughout the whole campaign and were unbeaten at home.

Historic status notwithstanding, underestimating them would be an unwise decision. As Everton's new £2 million signing Mikel Arteta offered: 'If I could have chosen who we'd play, I'd never have chosen them. They like to play good football and played the best stuff in Spain along with Barcelona last year. They have great players like Juan Roman Riquelme, Diego Forlan, Juan Pablo Sorin – international players – so we'll have to be at the top of our game to beat them. Jose Reina was there last year and has since gone to Liverpool, so I'll ask him about them as well. I'll see if he can offer us any kind of advice about how to beat them. I'll do my best to use my knowledge of playing in Spain and try to tell everyone about how they play and identify their weaknesses. But we just have to have confidence in ourselves. It could have been tougher, if we'd drawn an Italian team maybe, but this is so tough as well.' (Fifield, *The Guardian*, 2005.)

Indeed, Chilean coach Manuel Pellegrini, who would of course go on to lift the 2013/14 Premier League trophy with Manchester City, had in his first season in Spain guided Villarreal to their highest ever league position, making the La Liga club's El Madrigal stadium a fortress in doing so. The shrewd acquisition of Diego Forlan from Manchester United ensured that Villarreal had a top-class focal point in their side, with the Uruguayan international finishing his debut campaign in Spain as the league's top goalscorer, finding the net 25 times in 38 games.

Furthermore, Argentine international Juan Roman Riquelme was fulfilling his unquestionable potential after his career had stalled during an unsuccessful spell at Barcelona. Following an initial loan spell, Riquelme made the permanent switch to El Madrigal, establishing himself as one of the finest playmakers in Europe. Finishing the 2004/05 campaign with a career-best 15 goals in 35 games, the Argentinian international earned a nomination for the 2005 FIFA World Player of the Year award and was presented with the title of La Liga's Most Artistic Player by Spanish newspaper *Marca*. Should Everton have ambitions to progress to the Champions League group stages, there was little doubt that limiting the influence of the former Boca boy would be a priority for David Moyes's side.

With Everton having the home advantage for the first leg of the tie, I couldn't wait to get to the ground to experience European football for the first time. Hearing Tony Britten's Champions League anthem on the Goodison Park sound system was a measure of how far Everton had come in the short time since David Moyes's arrival in 2002, with the Scot sharing in the excitement of the occasion.

'It feels like Christmas Eve and I'm opening up all my toys,' the Everton boss said. 'This is so important for the supporters. They missed out on Europe all those years ago because of other situations. Everton were at the top of British football and the troubles in the game had nothing to do with them, but they suffered. There's no way of knowing how much damage was done to this football club by the European ban, but that's history. We can make our own history now.'

He continued, 'This is a step upwards and its importance to this club is huge, but it's not boom or bust. There is a rebuilding job on at Everton which will take longer than two qualifying games in the Champions League to complete. But with the financial implications of getting through and, if we do qualify for the group stage, we will have earned it. The draw just made us realise what the Champions League actually means. Any Spanish team would constitute a difficult tie, though I doubt Villarreal will be too pleased to have drawn a side from the Premiership. We are the underdogs, but we know we've got a lot of character. We know we'll be fighting and scratching for everything, and that won't change over the two games. We showed last year we were resilient, and we never give up. We've come a distance. If someone had told me a year ago, we'd be playing Villarreal in the Champions League, then Manchester United in the league, I'd have kissed him.' (Fifield, *The Guardian*, 2005.)

With a starting place for new signings Simon Davies and Phil Neville, the line-ups at Goodison Park on Tuesday, 9 August 2005 were as follows:

Everton: Martyn, Hibbert, Yobo, Weir, Pistone, Cahill, Arteta, Neville, Davies, Kilbane, Beattie

Villarreal: Barbosa, Rodriguez, Quique Alvarez, Javi Venta, Arruabarrena, Riquelme, Josico, Senna, Sorin, Forlan, Figueroa

Kick-off was met with a thunderous wall of noise around the stadium, as Moyes's side were inspired into a lively opening to the game, stifling Villarreal of time and space. Seizing the impetus, Alessandro Pistone linked up well with Kevin Kilbane down the left as the Irish international found James Beattie with a threatening cross, only for the forward's tame effort to be comfortably saved by Mariano Barbosa.

However, it wasn't long before Villarreal gained a foothold in the game and punished Everton for failing to take advantage of their early momentum, as former Birmingham City striker Luciano Figueroa ran on to a sublime Marcos Senna pass and confidently finished past Nigel Martyn. A stunned silence descended on Goodison Park, as the Blues fought hard to regain their purchase on the game, Tim Cahill's far-post header almost restoring parity.

As the interval approached, some fine work from new signing Simon Davies saw Mikel Arteta find Phil Neville in space. His whipped cross into the penalty box found Beattie, who could do little more than lob his initial header into the air. Reacting quickest, the forward prodded the loose ball past a helpless Barbosa, providing the finish to his own assist and sending Goodison Park into raptures.

However, the celebrations would be short-lived. Slick passing from Riquelme in midfield found Juan Pablo Sorin in space down the right flank, and his cross was met with a bullet header from Josico, leaving Nigel Martyn with no chance. Once again, Goodison was left stunned and as referee Tom Ovrebo blew for half-time, Everton were left to contemplate the enormity of the next 45 minutes.

Shooting towards the Gwladys Street for the second half, the volume and intensity of the noise around the stadium swelled. Playing with urgency, Everton earned a flurry of corners early in the second period, though Villarreal's defence remained resolute. Despite the pressure, the Blues struggled to create a genuine opening, with keeper Barbosa well protected by his backline. Indeed, the best opportunity of the second half fell to Diego Forlan, but the Uruguayan's uncharacteristically tame header was comfortably blocked by Alessandro Pistone.

The introduction of fresh legs in the form of Duncan Ferguson and Marcus Bent gave Everton's forward line renewed momentum, laying siege to Gabriel Barbosa's goal in the dying stages of the game, though the visitors remained firm, holding out for a first-leg 2-1 win. With a fortnight to prepare for the return fixture, David Moyes had to find a way of motivating his players after a dispiriting night at Goodison Park.

9

The Collina Conspiracy

EVERTON'S START to the 2005/06 season didn't get any easier, as the Blues welcomed Manchester United to Goodison Park for the opening Premier League game of the season. From 1-0 down at half-time, courtesy of a Ruud van Nistelrooy strike on 43 minutes, Everton went into self-destruct mode seconds after the restart, as Joseph Yobo inexplicably passed the ball across his own 18-yard box, straight to the feet of Wayne Rooney. Doubling United's lead, the ex-Everton youngster didn't hold back in celebrating his first Goodison goal since leaving the club, as the Blues' week went from bad to worse.

'I've not been ranting and raving because the performance was good,' Moyes said at full time, following the 2-0 defeat. 'The first thing a centre-half learns is you don't play square across the box, you do that in Sunday League teams. I'm disappointed because the goal made it a long way to come back from.' (BBC Sport, 2005.)

Indeed, it was a less than ideal start to the campaign for his side, but as we flew out to Villarreal's neighbouring city of Valencia, the anticipation of a European away game was palpable. Setting up in the Plaza de la Reina, Valencia's beautiful central square, Everton flags were draped over the nearby bell towers as a saxophonist earned a small fortune playing 'Z-Cars' on repeat. Spirits were high, as were a small contingent of Evertonians, who'd sat for the best part of the day snorting certain substances with such nasal strength that it seemed plausible for the table to follow the suspect powder up their powerful noses. Every pub in the vicinity was drunk completely dry, symbolic of a fanbase that was now thirstier than ever.

As we arrived at the ramshackle El Madrigal the following evening, you could be forgiven for thinking that we were the home side, such was the presence of Evertonians. With a capacity of 23,500, the Estadio de la Ceramica, as it is now known, is a compact but atmospheric ground, capable of accommodating roughly half of the population of the city of Villarreal. It is a stadium that is the beating heart of its community, its 2017 name change done in recognition of the historic ceramics industry in the area. It had the feel of a proper football ground, like something from a bygone era, not unlike Goodison Park in that respect.

So limited were the facilities at El Madrigal, that a series of renovations had to take place in advance of the game, in order to comply with a number of UEFA-imposed prerequisites for any stadium hosting Champions League football. Yellow tiles were added to the façade of the stadium, to improve the aesthetics, and a number of alterations had to be made to changing facilities for players and officials. Arbitrarily, the club also had to expand the area that separates the pitch from the stands by one metre and ensure that the advertising system was computerised, which tellingly indicates where UEFA's priorities lie.

The noise prior to kick-off was deafening, and there was little doubt that if Everton were to overturn their first-leg deficit, the fans as well as the players would need to be in top form.

The teams lined up as follows:

Villarreal: Barbosa, Rodriguez, Arruabarrena, Forlan, Josico, Riquelme, Figueroa, Sorin, Quique Alvarez, Javi Venta, Senna

Everton: Martyn, Hibbert, Yobo, Weir, Neville, Arteta, Davies, Cahill, Kilbane, Bent, Ferguson

Villarreal started the game on the front foot, dictating the pace of the play as Everton struggled to gain a measure of control in the opening exchanges. Referee Pierluigi Collina, who had been granted permission to defer his retirement despite reaching the required age, booked Kevin Kilbane two minutes into the game for a foul on Javi Venta, which forced Manuel Pellegrini into an early substitution, with Jan Kromkamp replacing the Spanish right-back on 14 minutes.

Luminous yellow jerseys appeared to outnumber those in blue, as Villarreal showed their quality, though Everton muscled their way into a goalscoring opportunity as Phil Neville's throw-in found its way to Tim Cahill via a Duncan Ferguson flick-on, but the Australian failed to muster enough power to beat the relieved Barbosa. It was a chance, and one you would have bet your house on Cahill converting, and within five minutes the significance of the miss would be underlined, as Juan Pablo Sorin's deflected shot extended Villarreal's aggregate lead to 3-1.

At 2-1 Everton already had a mountain to climb, but 3-1 expanded the mountain to a whole range, with Everton now needing two goals without a reply just to take the game to extra time. Indeed, Everton seemed likely to puncture Villarreal's backline, but it looked doubtful that the Blues would not concede another, with Nigel Martyn's heroics keeping his side afloat either side of the interval.

With 20 minutes remaining, the game was ebbing away from Everton's grasp, until Mikel Arteta's beautifully caressed free kick handed the Blues a lifeline. The goal galvanised Everton, with Barbosa now called up to perform heroics of his own as Ferguson forced the keeper into a remarkable save at the expense of a corner with minutes left to play. As Ferguson rose again from the subsequent set piece, the Scot headed home what looked to be the aggregate equaliser as El Madrigal momentarily erupted in blue euphoria. Ecstasy quickly turned to agony, however, as Collina spotted an infringement, awarding Villarreal a free kick. Protests fell on deaf ears, and moments later the club's exit from Europe's premier competition was all but confirmed as Diego Forlan converted to finish off a Villarreal counter-attack in the dying minutes of the game.

'I was really frustrated with Collina,' said Mikel Arteta after the game. 'Duncan did nothing wrong. I asked him why he disallowed the goal, but he just said: "Walk away, walk away." Afterwards he said he had spotted a foul before the corner but then why didn't he blow before I took the corner? The goal was absolutely perfect, there was nothing wrong with it and we should have won 2-1 in normal time. But our confidence has not been affected because we have shown that we can play against the top teams.'

Arteta added, 'We need to get over this as quickly as we can. We know other teams have bought very well this summer and it is going to be very difficult to qualify for the Champions League again. People don't expect us to finish fourth again, but I believe we can. We have been thinking about being in the Champions League all summer and now we are not there. We feel we should be, but we need to forget about it. We can take confidence from the way we played. That will stand us in good stead for the UEFA Cup. If we can get into the group stages there, it will be another good achievement and I think we will.' (Fifield, *The Guardian*, 2005.)

Defending his decision to disallow the goal, Collina confirmed he had noticed a foul committed by Marcus Bent off the ball, telling Sky Sports, 'It was because I've seen a foul made by another player – Bent. Away from the ball, during a free kick or corner kick, in the penalty box, there are several couples of players. The referee cannot follow all of them, but your attention is on some of the players. Sometimes you can see things happen as well as you cannot see at other times. If you're looking at another couple of players, you're not able to see the other part of the box. At that time, I was looking at those players – Bent and his Spanish opponent – and I've seen something that probably television didn't show. Clearly, Duncan Ferguson didn't make any foul, but I didn't punish him for a foul. I punished Bent's foul.'

Collina's inadequate and ambiguous explanation only sought to intensify theories of a UEFA plot to ensure Everton failed to progress to the Champions League group stages. Indeed, the Italian referee's retirement just days after the game raised further eyebrows, especially as the season had only just begun.

Everton's qualification had come as a surprise, and at the expense of the 2005 holders, Liverpool. A subsequent rule change stating that the holders gain automatic qualification regardless of their final league position was swiftly implemented, meaning an unprecedented five English teams would potentially enter the group stages, much to the consternation of UEFA.

Whether or not you subscribe to such theories, a Champions League qualifying game between Villarreal and Everton seemed an odd match for such a high-profile official to bow out with. The original celebrity referee, Collina's striking features were world famous, featuring on video game covers and Vauxhall Motors adverts. He'd officiated a UEFA Cup Final, Champions League Final and a World Cup Final, not to mention Soccer Aid. A household name no doubt, the deferring of Collina's retirement by a matter of days for such a low-key encounter, unbefitting of his illustrious career, sparked what has perhaps become the most infamous conspiracy theory in Everton's recent past.

In 2012, Everton boss David Moyes would discuss the seismic impact the defeat against Villarreal had, controversially reinforcing claims of a conspiracy. 'It was a defining point for us,' Moyes said. 'Villarreal went on to the semi-final. The draw we got was a stinker. I always think it was the "hot balls" in the bag that day. We went away and Duncan scored to make it 2-1 [to Everton] on the night to take it to extra time and Pierluigi Collina chops it off. That could have changed what we did at Everton, if we had got into the group stages with the money that was available. Everyone knows the previous season Liverpool had won the European Cup so deep down I didn't think they [UEFA] wanted five British teams in the group stages. I am sure they were all delighted when we were knocked out.' (Carroll, *Liverpool Echo*, 2019.)

The peculiar circumstances of Collina's eventual retirement notwithstanding, Villarreal were simply better than Everton over two legs, and their subsequent run to the semi-finals of the 2005/06 Champions League exemplified the quality at their disposal. However, had Ferguson's goal stood, it could have changed the course of Everton's modern history.

10

Pedestrian At Best

THE CHAMPIONS League exit had knocked Everton for six, and the season's disastrous start was compounded by their immediate elimination from the UEFA Cup, the Blues' second European exit in as many months. They had dropped into Europe's secondary competition, with a two-legged tie against Romanian outfit Dinamo Bucuresti standing between David Moyes's side and a place in the group stage. A 5-1 capitulation in eastern Europe all but settled the tie in 90 minutes, with Everton's 1-0 win in the second leg achieving little more than moderately curbing an embarrassing aggregate score.

'This is my lowest point ever as a manager; it's as bad as I can remember but we did a good job in the first half,' said Moyes, after the 5-1 drubbing in Romania. 'We were probably in control of the game but then in the second half we just made it far too easy for them to score. We have made a terrible start to the season, but I'm the manager so it's my responsibility. I'll take the blame.' (Taylor, *The Guardian*, 2005.)

Indeed, it was about to get worse, as Everton's European hangover overflowed into their Premier League form, losing seven out of the opening eight fixtures leaving Moyes's side in 20th place by mid-October. What was more worrying, was Everton's failure to register a single goal in any of the defeats, with Marcus Bent's finish at Bolton Wanderers a standalone strike. With 20 goals conceded in the opening 12 games in all competitions, Everton's early form in the 2005/06 season was worrisome.

A 1-0 defeat at home to Middlesbrough in the League Cup third round on 25 October saw Everton eliminated from three competitions in three months. It would be the end of November before the Blues climbed out of the relegation zone, with a slight upturn in fortune. However, a seasonably generous Everton shipped eight goals in two games in December, as £5 million signing Per Kroldrup suffered a humiliating debut at Villa Park in what would be his only league game for the club.

'If you go to the parks on a Sunday morning you will not see goals as bad as the ones we conceded,' Moyes bemoaned after a 4-0 defeat to Bolton Wanderers. 'We had a mad ten or 15 minutes. I will take responsibility because I work and coach the players, but it is very difficult to take responsibility for those goals. We have lost by four goals at home, and it is very embarrassing for us. I don't feel very good after that.' (BBC Sport, 2004.)

The New Year brought about a much-improved run of form, with six wins and one draw between 31 December and 11 February, with the Blues keeping five cleans sheets along the way. A 1-1 draw at Wigan Athletic's JJB Stadium saw Duncan Ferguson earn his eighth Premier League red card in a seven-minute cameo in which Pascal Chimbonda was dumped on to the turf by the Scot moments after he entered the pitch, before Ferguson left Paul Scharner crumpled in a heap courtesy of a blow to the gut. As a melee erupted, with Everton defender David Weir apoplectic at the behaviour of his team-mate, Wigan's Jimmy Bullard made the grave mistake of trying to wind up an incensed Ferguson.

'I get pulled up all the time on this,' Bullard would confess to *The Football Show* in April 2020. '*Soccer AM* were the first to play this clip as this was a midweek game. He'd only been on the pitch for a bit! I was telling him to calm down, but he'd gone. He'd lost the plot. I always want to get involved if there's a bit of drama. I loved it as a player. I knew James McFadden and I asked him if Dunc was alright. He told me not to say anything. But what you don't see on the video is, Mike Dean gives him the red card, and as he's walking away, I told Dunc

I'd see him in the tunnel, for a bit of banter, but that backfired. Lee McCulloch and McFadden told me that was a bad idea. It was a disaster as he was waiting in the tunnel and there was still 15 minutes to play. It was the worst 15 minutes I've ever had, as I kept looking over thinking he was going to punch me.' (Jones, *Liverpool Echo*, 2020.)

With only a solitary league defeat since December, Everton climbed to ninth place in the league by mid-March, but inconsistent form throughout the remainder of the campaign hindered any further progress up the table as they finished the season in 11th place. A season that promised so much but ultimately delivered very little as David Moyes's side struggled to recover from their European heartbreak. The 2005/06 campaign would also be the last in an Everton shirt for the talismanic Duncan Ferguson, announcing his retirement at the end of it, no doubt to the relief of Jimmy Bullard, Steffen Freund and the many other adversaries accumulated by the Scot throughout his career. Scoring on his final appearance at Goodison Park in a 2-2 draw with West Brom, Ferguson's tally was 60 league goals in 239 games over two spells for the club.

11

The Andy Johnson Derby

AS REFERENCED by David Moyes many times during the campaign, 2005/06 was a season in which goals did not come easily for Everton, as they scored a meagre 34 times in the league. Consequently, the Everton boss sought to bolster his attacking options, placing a club record £7.25 million bid for Crystal Palace's Andy Johnson – but the Blues faced competition for the in-demand forward. On 24 May 2006, Palace accepted an offer of £8.5 million from Wigan Athletic, with fellow Lancastrians Bolton Wanderers matching the bid 24 hours later, leaving the final decision on his destination with the player himself. Despite his indication that Goodison Park would be his preferred choice, Everton looked set to miss out on the England international, until they eventually upped their bid to a record £8.6 million on 30 May, setting a double record of both Everton's most expensive signing and Crystal Palace's most expensive sale.

Looking to the Championship once more, Moyes sought the signature of promising defender Joleon Lescott from Wolverhampton Wanderers, in a deal delayed by several weeks as Everton had requested extra medical checks to be completed. Following the reconstruction of the defender's knee during surgery, Lescott had been unable to participate for the duration of the 2003/04 Premier League season for Wolves, a campaign which saw the Midlands club relegated. Having only been promoted the previous year, Lescott's absence for the entire season meant that the versatile defender missed out on representing his boyhood club in the Premier League, his unfortunate omission no doubt influencing his desire to compete in the top flight.

Named in the Championship PFA Team of the Year, Lescott's impressive 2005/06 campaign at Wolves did not go unnoticed, with Moyes keen to sign the 23-year-old, stating, 'Joleon is someone we have watched for quite a long time, and fortunately this time we have been able to get our man.' (BBC Sport, 2006.) Indeed, after some toing and froing, Everton secured Lescott's signature, with an up-front payment of £2 million, followed by a further £2 million to be paid in instalments and an additional £1 million, contingent on appearances.

Everton's business was not yet done, however: with veteran goalkeeper Nigel Martyn announcing his retirement from football, a replacement stopper was a must before the beginning of the new campaign. Martyn, who made 100 appearances in all competitions in a blue shirt, keeping 37 clean sheets, was no doubt one of the club's best acquisitions of the modern era, with Moyes himself describing him as his 'greatest ever signing'. Instrumental in Everton's 2004/05 Champions League qualification, the former England international remains exceptionally highly thought of at Goodison Park, with his nickname 'Big Nige' a play on Neville Southall's 'Big Nev' moniker. Certainly, among Evertonians, there is no higher praise than a comparison to the great Neville Southall.

With this in mind, David Moyes had quite a challenge on his hands in finding an adequate replacement, especially with limited funds at his disposal. Shrewdly, and perhaps out of necessity, Moyes utilised the loan market, bringing in United States goalkeeper Tim Howard from Manchester United on a 12-month loan on 9 May. Howard, who had arrived at Old Trafford in 2003 from MLS side MetroStars, had lost his place in United's starting XI upon the arrival of Edwin van der Sar in the summer of 2005, but at Everton had an opportunity to establish himself as one of the Premier League's most consistent goalkeepers.

The arrival of Howard at Goodison Park all but ended the Everton career of the once-promising Richard Wright, with his often calamitous injuries leaving Moyes less than impressed. Not only did the ex-England stopper fall out of his loft in 2003, injuring his shoulder, he twisted his ankle during the warm-up of a 2006 FA Cup fourth round replay at Stamford Bridge by falling over a sign advising players not to practise in the goalmouth. Everton lost the tie 4-1.

With all incoming transfers taken care of, the Blues began the 2006/07 Premier League campaign at home to Watford, with Andy Johnson wasting little time introducing himself to the Goodison crowd, opening the scoring 15 minutes in after controlling the ball well with his chest and unleashing a superb left-footed effort. Everton were in control for much of the game, though there were chances at either end, with both sides hitting the frame of the goal.

With less than ten minutes remaining, Mikel Arteta stepped up to double Everton's lead from 12 yards out after the Blues were awarded a dubious penalty for an alleged Chris Powell handball. An Alan Stubbs own goal in the 90th minute ensured a nervous finale, but the Blues held on to secure all three points on the opening day of the new campaign.

'Andy was always a threat and I hope that is the first of many goals for us,' Moyes stated after the game. 'The fans were delighted when we signed him – he has a proven record in the Championship and the Premier League. His goal was excellent, along with all his work. Watford gave us trouble, but we made it difficult for ourselves.' (BBC Sport, 2006.)

With an opening day victory, followed by a point at Ewood Park thanks to a late Tim Cahill equaliser, Everton had made a decent start to the season. A tricky visit to White Hart Lane followed, and with the Blues having failed to win a league game away at Spurs since 1985, the odds of returning to Merseyside with three points were not in Moyes's favour. A Kevin Kilbane sending-off on 32 minutes for a second bookable offence made life difficult, with the Irish international's dismissal his final act in an Everton shirt, as he departed the club for Wigan Athletic for an undisclosed fee five days later.

Despite the numerical disadvantage, Everton began the second half brightly, as Spurs struggled to cope with the pace and work-rate of Andy Johnson, who continued to demonstrate why the club were prepared to spend a record amount for his services. An Arteta free kick, won by the unplayable Johnson, was flicked on by debutant Lescott and turned into his own net by the helpless Calum Davenport to give Everton a 1-0 lead on 53 minutes. The in-form Johnson made it 2-0 13 minutes later, finishing well from Phil Neville's low cross into the penalty area.

'That might just be the best performance I have been involved with at Everton,' Moyes declared after the final whistle. 'We were tremendous, but it is only what I have been saying about how we were playing in pre-season. Our passing was nothing short of fantastic. Andy Johnson was also tremendous. If England are looking for a striker to score goals, he's the man. He's a great player to play with and was a constant threat.' (BBC Sport, 2006.) Indeed, Johnson had made a bright start in Everton blue, but he was about to take a shortcut to cult hero status.

Two wins and a draw had got the 2006/07 season off to a flying start for David Moyes, his new recruits settling into life in L4 with little fuss. Andy Johnson in particular had enjoyed a dream start to his Everton career, but a derby day brace for the club's record signing in a 3-0 victory over Liverpool guaranteed a successful initiation for the 25-year-old. Ecstasy enveloped Goodison Park, with such victories occurring just once in a generation. Indeed, it was Everton's biggest win over Liverpool since the 4-0 victory at Anfield in 1964, and the biggest at home since the 5-0 drubbing in 1909.

The line-ups at Goodison Park for the 204th Merseyside derby on 9 September 2006, were as follows:

Everton: Howard, Hibbert, Yobo, Lescott, Naysmith, Osman, Neville, Carsley, Arteta, Cahill, Johnson

Liverpool: Reina, Finnan, Carragher, Hyypia, Aurelio, Gerrard, Alonso, Sissoko, Luis Garcia, Fowler, Crouch

The game started in manic fashion, with the visitors creating an opportunity inside ten seconds, as Tim Howard saved well from Robbie Fowler's effort. Despite the early scare, Everton soon settled into a confident rhythm, with Johnson, Carsley and Arteta combining well, allowing Tim Cahill to open the scoring. One goal to the good, the noise from the Goodison crowd was deafening and as Liverpool searched for a response, the industrious work of Andy Johnson up front began to stretch their defence and the England forward was out for blood. Capitalising on a Jamie Carragher error, with the Liverpool defender unable to cope with Johnson's pace and movement, the opportunistic forward finished at the near post in composed fashion to double Everton's lead ten minutes before the interval.

Liverpool continued to struggle in the second half; uncertain as they were about how to deal with the in-form Johnson, their indecision about whether or not to sit deep or attempt to take him out higher up the pitch only led to further opportunities for Everton, as Cahill and Arteta looked to expose the space in behind. Meanwhile, a spell of Liverpool possession saw Tim Howard produce a fine save from substitute Dirk Kuyt around the hour mark. Howard was equal to almost everything thrown his way, with the frame of the goal rescuing the American on two occasions, as Steven Gerrard twice struck the post in the second half.

With Everton 2-0 up with a matter of minutes remaining, Liverpool looked frustrated, perhaps even taken aback by Everton's attacking intent as an exasperated-looking Rafael Benitez on the touchline enriched an already memorable afternoon. It was about to get even better for the Blues however, with Johnson getting his second goal of the day in the 90th minute to put an emphatic exclamation point on proceedings.

A swerving Lee Carsley effort appeared to catch Liverpool keeper Pepe Reina off guard, the Spanish international misjudging the shot and parrying the ball wildly into the air before palming it directly on to the opportunistic head of

Andy Johnson, who gratefully headed home. In the weeks that followed, I must have heard B.J. Thomas's 1969 hit 'Raindrops Keep Fallin' on My Head' countless times, with the lyrics cleverly changed to 'Reina Drops Keep Fallin' on My Head', in reference to the Liverpool keeper's comedic error. The now iconic image of Johnson celebrating in front of the Park End by holding up three fingers on his right hand and making a 'zero' symbol with his left forged an instant bond between Everton's new record signing and the supporters, as Goodison marched to the tune of Andy Johnson's drum.

'Maybe nowadays you need to pay that sort of money to sign a player who'll make a difference,' said Moyes, when discussing Johnson's club record fee. 'The board did brilliantly to come up with the money, but everyone can see what we've bought. He's a team player. We have to work hard until we get to a certain level, and we can change our formula, but Andy must be a dream. He makes ordinary passes look good. Andrew Johnson is an unbelievable striker and is going to get goals. He fought hard and showed character and now he knows what it means to be a Blue. We always said Andrew would score goals but for his second he said, "I'm going to gamble here." We are pleased to have him.' (Fifield, *The Guardian*, 2006.)

It takes more than just scoring goals for Evertonians to truly take to a centre-forward. Gary Lineker scored 30 league goals in 41 games in his solitary campaign with the club during the 1985/86 season, though was never adored in the same manner as Andy Gray or Graeme Sharp. Equally, in more recent times, the prolific Romelu Lukaku divided opinion, with the attitude and commitment of the Belgian international called into question on a regular basis. Andy Johnson's goals no doubt enhanced his profile among Evertonians, but his selfless endeavour and work-rate, similar to that of Marcus Bent prior to his January 2006 departure, endeared the England forward to the fanbase.

'I'm grateful to the manager for taking a chance on me,' said the centre-forward. 'Not many players come out of the

Championship for the big fee I did, and people thought it was a bit of a gamble. I knew my own abilities, and I didn't think I had something to prove by coming here, but it was a big risk for the gaffer. I'd like to think I'm repaying him now.' (Fifield, *The Guardian*, 2006.)

Indeed, while the 3-0 victory over Liverpool is remembered for Johnson's bustling performance, Tim Howard at the other end of the pitch equally rose to the occasion. 'I made my first save inside of ten seconds,' Howard recalled in his 2014 autobiography, *The Keeper: Achieving Goals and Saving Them*, 'and I made every one after that. We won the game 3-0. We crushed Liverpool. It was Everton's biggest victory over their neighbours for 42 years. The crowd went absolutely bonkers.'

12

Sticks and Stones

MOYES'S SIDE continued through September 2006 unbeaten, though three consecutive draws at home to Wigan Athletic and Manchester City, and away to Newcastle United respectively, limited Everton's points total to 13 out of a possible 21 in the opening weeks of the campaign. Andy Johnson's goalscoring exploits enabled Everton to maintain their unbeaten status for seven weeks with strikes against Wigan and Manchester City taking his tally to six goals in his first seven Premier League games for the Blues.

The first defeat of the season came on Saturday, 14 October, against Middlesbrough at the Riverside Stadium, as the Blues slumped to a 2-1 defeat to Gareth Southgate's side, perhaps unfairly. Everton's five-man midfield dominated possession in the opening period, though it was the home side who struck first, as Yakubu was brought down in the box by Tim Howard, the Nigerian international picking himself up and scoring from the spot. Everton could have had a penalty of their own as the game progressed, as Emmanuel Pogatetz bundled Andy Johnson to the ground inside the penalty area, only for referee Mark Halsey to wave play on.

Frustratingly, Middlesbrough were then awarded their second penalty of the game, this time due to a supposed handball by Joleon Lescott. With Yakubu stepping up once more, Howard atoned for his earlier indiscretion by saving 'Boro's second spot-kick of the day, no doubt keeping Everton's hopes of getting something out of the game alive. However, the home side would double their lead moments later, as Mark Viduka finished a Jason Euell through-ball from eight yards out. A superb solo effort from Tim Cahill, which saw him nutmeg German international Robert Huth before firing past a helpless Mark Schwarzer, halved Everton's deficit with 13 minutes to go, though an equaliser was not forthcoming despite a late siege on the opposition goal.

'The penalties they were given were justified,' Moyes agreed after the game. 'But for me, either of the two challenges on Johnson or Cahill should have been given in light of the two that were given against us. I don't think we deserved to lose and were worth at least a point.' (BBC Sport, 2006.)

A return to winning ways, courtesy of a 2-0 victory at home to Sheffield United, followed by a 1-1 draw at the Emirates Stadium left Everton in sixth place by the end of October, though managerial comments following each encounter would see the integrity of an Everton centre-forward called into question. 'I don't blame Johnson for going down,' Sheffield United manager Neil Warnock said following Everton's 2-0 victory. 'I don't think it is anything like a penalty. The referee blew too early.' (*Metro*, 2006.)

Indeed, Warnock's accusatory comments were hastily picked up by Arsenal manager Arsene Wenger prior to Everton's visit to north London, with the Gunners' coach stating, 'If he [Johnson] gets penalties, he gets them, and it is for the referee to judge. Eight out of ten are genuine penalties and two he gets he makes more of it. But he does not look to me to be a cheat.' However, following the 1-1 draw, Wenger stated that Johnson was 'Very clever in the box,' and it was a label that unfortunately stuck. (Prentice, *Liverpool Echo*, 2011.)

A frustrated Everton left Craven Cottage a week later as a fortuitous Fulham goal gave Chris Coleman's side a 1-0 win, but it was the denial of a penalty for the second time in three weeks that incensed David Moyes, with Andy Johnson quickly becoming the victim of an unfair reputation. Defending his team-mate, centre-half Alan Stubbs, who'd made his return to Goodison Park in January 2006, stated, 'It was a stonewall penalty. A certain manager's comments have put all the referees on alert and I've no idea why the referee never gave it. That decision probably summed up his performance.' (*Metro*, 2006.)

Everton boss David Moyes also came to the defence of AJ. 'Andy is honest as the day is long,' Moyes said in support of his record signing. 'Maybe some referees are watching too many television programmes. Andy nicked the ball away from the defender who went to ground without making contact with the ball.' (Eurosport, 2006.)

Unfortunately, this would be a consistent theme throughout the remainder of the campaign, with Arsenal involved for the second time in little over a week. Arsene Wenger's side made the trip to Goodison Park on 8 November, for the last 16 of the Carling Cup (League Cup). At 0-0, Andy Johnson was denied another blatant penalty, with referee Graham Poll unconvinced that the Everton forward had in any way been impeded. James McFadden's protestations earned him a red card for dissent, while Emmanuel Adebayor's header with five minutes remaining saw Everton fall to a 1-0 defeat as Goodison Park erupted into a chorus of 'cheat, cheat, cheat …' when Graham Poll made his way off the pitch at full time.

Notwithstanding the injustice of certain refereeing decisions, some of the early-season optimism swiftly began to evaporate by November, as Aston Villa recorded their first win of the campaign in a 1-0 victory at Goodison Park, with veteran centre-forward Chris Sutton opening his goalscoring account for the Villans. Indeed, it was a miserable afternoon for the Toffees, compounded by the loss of the influential Tim Cahill, who suffered knee ligament damage after an accidental clash with team-mate Lee Carsley.

'We looked pretty flat from the start,' Moyes stated in his post-match comments, 'and never really got going. There are no excuses. No one could say they were better than us, but they got the goal and we missed our chances. We've not scored in our last three matches, which is a bit worrying because we think we are making lots of chances.' (BBC Sport, 2006.)

Meanwhile, the Andy Johnson witch-hunt continued at full speed, with Chelsea boss Jose Mourinho weighing in following his side's 3-2 win at Goodison Park on 17 December. When the Everton forward jumped out of the way of Chelsea keeper Hilario in an attempt to avoid a collision, Mourinho accused Johnson of being 'a dangerous kind of opponent', who 'chased penalties'. Waving an imaginary yellow card in a heated touchline tete-a-tete with David Moyes, Mourinho claimed he had been 'embarrassed' by Johnson's conduct. 'You cannot trust him,' he said. 'A great player but too much of that.'

The incendiary comments sparked outrage at Goodison Park, prompting the club to write a letter of complaint to the Football Association, and seek legal advice regarding the defamation of Johnson's character. 'To publicly question the integrity of a player of Andrew's professionalism and honesty is not only wholly unacceptable and quite possibly defamatory but also, in our opinion, highly damaging for both club and player,' an Everton statement read. 'We would urge the footballing authorities to look closely at Mr Mourinho's comments and then, perhaps, seek a formal explanation.' (Fifield, *The Guardian*, 2006.)

Indeed, the incident against Chelsea came just a matter of weeks after goalkeeper Petr Cech sustained a skull fracture following a collision with Reading's Stephen Hunt. With this in mind, Andy Johnson's reluctance to collide with Chelsea's Hilario is perfectly understandable, with the Everton forward himself confirming that Mourinho had perhaps misread the situation. 'I believe the incident which was highlighted by Mr Mourinho was badly misinterpreted by him,' Johnson said. 'I feel greatly disappointed that my integrity has been unfairly questioned in this way. I hope the Chelsea manager will retract his statement.' (Fifield, *The Guardian*, 2006.)

Just 24 hours later, Mourinho would do just that, in a move perhaps considered out of character for the Portuguese antagonist. 'First I would like to say I have the utmost respect for Everton Football Club, David Moyes and their players,' insisted Mourinho. 'That's why I love to play them, and especially at Goodison Park where the atmosphere is magnificent. Secondly, after the match I was clear and said Andy Johnson is a great player and I never used aggressive words, like some managers did against my players in previous seasons, or like some others recently said about him and [Cristiano] Ronaldo. I never used the word "cheat".' (*The Guardian*, 2006.)

The Chelsea boss continued, 'After seeing it again on the video, [the referee] Mr [Mark] Halsey did wonderful work and both decisions for penalties were correct. Did Andy Johnson try to avoid a collision with my goalkeeper? It seems now the answer to that is yes so Everton, his manager and he deserve my apologies.'

13

Operation Goodison Exercise

BY NEW Year, Everton occupied eighth place in the league, firmly in contention for a European spot and for the visit of Reading to Goodison Park on 14 January 2007, the Blues would have a special guest in their corner, as Sylvester Stallone was welcomed to L4. The guest of Robert Earl, the founder of restaurant chain Planet Hollywood, who'd purchased a 23 per cent stake in the club in October 2006, Sly was visiting England to promote his new film, the sixth instalment of the *Rocky* series, and took the time to see Everton come back from a goal down to secure a 1-1 draw.

'It is going to be quite an occasion,' said chief executive Keith Wyness in the lead-up to the game. 'Of all the film stars around today, there are not many you can take on to the pitch at a sporting occasion and have some relevance. But Sylvester – and his part as Rocky – has a special place in the hearts of sports fans.' (Walker, *The Guardian*, 2007.)

Indeed, while Stallone offered some Hollywood glamour to an otherwise insipid display, the return of Tim Cahill to the side following two months in the treatment room was no doubt welcome news to David Moyes as the business end of the season gathered pace. Making the trip across the park for the Merseyside derby, Everton were buoyed by the surprise inclusion of Andy Johnson in the starting line-up, as the forward declared himself fit from an ankle injury sustained in a 2-0 win at Wigan Athletic a fortnight earlier. The team selections at Anfield on 3 February were as follows:

Liverpool: Reina, Finnan, Carragher, Agger, Riise, Pennant, Alonso, Gerrard, Bellamy, Kuyt, Crouch

Everton: Howard, Hibbert, Yobo, Stubbs, Lescott, Carsley, Neville, Cahill, Arteta, Osman, Johnson

Everton went into the game chasing a Merseyside derby double having already secured a 3-0 victory over Liverpool earlier in the campaign. Playing a 4-5-1 formation with Johnson a willing runner, David Moyes's side were happy to concede possession of the ball, looking to exploit the space in behind on the break. A man-of-the-match display from Alan Stubbs saw the 35-year-old roll back the years with a superb defensive performance, making the ungraceful Peter Crouch look awkward and cumbersome. With comparatively few fireworks for a Merseyside derby, a relatively forgettable 90 minutes concluded in a 0-0 draw. However, the inflammatory post-match comments would live long in the memory of Evertonians.

'I'm really disappointed,' Liverpool coach Rafael Benitez insisted. 'One team wanted to win and the other only wanted not to lose. They put nine players behind the ball and defended deep and narrow, but that's what small clubs do when they come here. When you play against a big club, a draw is sometimes a good result.' (Wilson, *The Guardian*, 2007.)

Everton's David Moyes stated, 'We've taken four points off Liverpool this season, so we must be doing something right. There's a difference of about £100 million in spending between the two clubs, but we are doing our best to bridge the gap. I would have liked to come here and put on a bigger show, but it's not an easy place to get a result and we've not done bad. We could even have won the game with a bit more luck.' (Wilson, *The Guardian*, 2007.)

While Benitez's comments reek of sour grapes, Moyes was indeed correct in his assertion that Everton may well have walked away with all three points, having created the best chances of the game, despite their defensive approach. A better finish may well have been expected of Andy Johnson, as having bypassed Jamie Carragher with ease, the England forward found Pepe Reina equal to his effort.

Four years after Benitez's incendiary comments, in a 2011 interview with the *Independent*, the former Liverpool manager, having recently parted ways with Italian giants Internazionale, elaborated on his disrespectful description of Everton, insisting that he was referring solely to David Moyes's unambitious tactics. 'I don't want to be disrespectful to the club. I was talking about the way they were playing, not the club,' said the Madrid-born manager. He continued to backtrack many years later, in a 2019 interview with the *Liverpool Echo*, stating, 'I made a mistake when I said it was a small club. What I wanted to say was they are a small team because in this game I remember they had one chance. Liverpool fans, they were happy and the Evertonians were upset. But I didn't want to say they were a small club, I wanted to say they were a small team.'

Interestingly, Benitez's insistence that he misspoke after the 2007 Merseyside derby began to gather pace when the Spanish manager was linked with the oft vacant position in Everton's dugout, as the club embarked on a merry-go-round of managers post-Moyes. With outdated tactics and a diminished pedigree, Benitez's limited opportunities in Europe resulted in the former Liverpool man taking charge of Chinese Super League side Dalian Professional (formerly Dalian Yifang) in 2019. It was no secret, however, that a return to the Premier League was high on Benitez's agenda and, after terminating his contract with Dalian Professional by mutual consent in January 2021 (citing concerns over the Covid-19 pandemic), the now unemployed manager was to be linked with Everton with increasing regularity.

Within six months, after the departure of Carlo Ancelotti for Real Madrid, Rafael Benitez would become Everton's manager, signing a three-year contract on 30 June 2021. Only the second person to manage both Everton and Liverpool, after William Edward Barclay in the 1890s, Benitez's appointment was subject to protests from Evertonians, with a banner left near his Wirral home, reading 'We know where you live. Don't sign'. After six and a half-months in charge, with the Blues in 15th place in the Premier League, six points above the relegation zone having lost nine of the previous 13 games, Benitez was relieved of his duties on 16 January 2022, and is widely considered to be the worst managerial appointment in the club's history.

Meanwhile, back in 2007, and the Spaniard's inflammatory comments intensified the animosity felt between the two clubs, as Everton's chief executive Keith Wyness stated that Benitez was 'in a minority of one in believing Everton is, in any respect, a small football club'. No doubt, while it can be said that Moyes's tactics were indeed unambitious at times, the comments made by Rafael Benitez were intentionally provocative, and that of a manager who had failed to register a goal against Moyes's side during the 2006/07 season, conceding three. In a forthright response to Benitez's jibe, Everton's Alan Stubbs countered, 'You're going to be bitter when you've not had a result. You can always turn round and say you're misquoted or whatever but, at the end of the day, you know what you're talking about.' (Fifield, *The Guardian*, 2007.)

A week after the well-deserved point at Anfield, Everton's push for Europe continued, with a 1-0 victory over Blackburn Rovers at Ewood Park, as Andy Johnson celebrated his 26th birthday with the winning strike inside ten minutes. Debutant Manuel Fernandes, on loan from Benfica, shone in midfield, the Portugal under-21 star having arrived at Goodison Park on a six-month loan deal on 31 January.

'It was a very pleasing win,' Moyes stated after the game. 'We have struggled all season to build runs of results, but we have beaten Wigan, drawn at Liverpool, and beaten Blackburn. It is a vital time of the season to grind results out and that is what we have done. I thought we played very well, especially in the first half. Andy Johnson took his goal very well. It was his birthday today and I told him beforehand I expected a brace from him, and he might have got it. He had three or four goal attempts. I thought Manuel Fernandes played well – he was important to us, especially in the first half.' (BBC Sport, 2007.)

However, a 2-1 defeat at home to Spurs put a dent in the Blues' European ambitions. Notably, Moyes was without Andy Johnson for the fixture, ruled out with a knee injury, though new signing Manuel Fernandes once again impressed in midfield. Interestingly, with the game poised at 1-1, Moyes felt the full fury of the Goodison Park crowd due to a negative substitution with five minutes remaining, replacing the influential Fernandes with defender Tony Hibbert. A Jermaine Jenas strike moments later sparked fury in the stands, as did the belated introduction of forward James Vaughan, as the victory for Spurs took them to within three points of eighth-placed Everton.

A chance to make amends quickly presented itself however, with a trip to Vicarage Road four days later, with Moyes able to recall the fit-again Johnson to the starting XI. Romping to a 3-0 victory, Everton redeemed themselves with a fine away performance, with Johnson and Fernandes once again the pick of the bunch. The on-loan Portuguese star opened the scoring with his first goal for the Blues, on 23 minutes, prodding home a loose ball after Watford keeper Richard Lee fumbled a Tim Cahill header. Andy Johnson doubled Everton's lead two minutes later from 12 yards, with Mariappa DeMerit's infringement on the influential Johnson giving referee Lee Mason little choice but to award a penalty. A stunning Leon Osman finish in the dying seconds of the game rounded off a comfortable win on the road for the Blues.

Meanwhile, with rumours circulating that Bedford-born Andy Johnson was struggling to adapt to life on Merseyside, with the England international reportedly homesick and eager to force a move to a club in the south of England, the Blues' record signing responded emphatically, declaring, 'If I could sign here for the rest of my career, I would do it tomorrow. I am more than happy here, I love the club, the fans, and the lads in the dressing room. I am sure the fans can see how much I love it here in my football. I want to make it clear there is no truth in this report. I am loving being an Everton player and I regard it as a great honour to put that blue shirt on every week.' (Thompson, *Liverpool Echo*, 2007.)

Indeed, it was clear to see that AJ was enjoying his football at Goodison Park, as he and the rest of David Moyes's side discovered a fine run of form at just the right time, with the win over Watford sparking a seven-game unbeaten run from 24 February to 15 April.

With 15 points out of a possible 21 taken during this period, Everton's push for a European place was given a significant boost, with the Blues demonstrating on more than one occasion the grit and determination to grind out results for which Moyes's Everton became known. A dramatic stoppage-time winner at home to Arsenal courtesy of Johnson rounded off a superb performance from the forward, whose persistence and industry caused Arsene Wenger's side problems all afternoon.

A torrential downpour of rain assisted in creating an atmospheric Goodison with minutes remaining, and as Arsenal failed to clear a corner, Johnson reacted quickest to his own flick-on and angled a low drive past a helpless Lehmann, no doubt to the forward's satisfaction following Arsene Wenger's defamatory comments earlier in the campaign.

'That is four points we have taken from Arsenal this season and hopefully that shows signs of progress,' Moyes said. 'I think we deserved to win, and credit goes to the players. Our keeper had to make saves and fortune favoured us. This is a terrific group of lads. It's going to be tough for the rest of the season but hopefully we'll give our supporters something to shout about.' (BBC Sport, 2007.)

A 1-1 draw at Villa Park followed by a comfortable 4-1 home victory over Fulham extended Everton's unbeaten run, lifting the Blues to fifth place in the table. Everton travelled to the Reebok Stadium in the top five for the first time since the previous October, three points behind fourth-placed Bolton Wanderers. In a fiercely contested match, Wanderers started the brighter of the two sides, taking the lead on 17 minutes, thanks to a moment of criminal defending from Joleon

Lescott, who remained rooted to the spot as his team-mates raced out of the box, trying to catch Bolton's attackers offside from an Ivan Campo free kick. With Kevin Davies played onside by the Everton left-back, the unmarked forward had time and space to control the ball with his chest, before firing home a right-footed volley.

Bolton failed to capitalise on their opener however, and a moment of hesitant defending from the home side gifted James Vaughan the chance to level the scores on 33 minutes, the 18-year-old calmly slotting underneath an on-rushing Jussi Jaaskelainen.

As both sides pushed for a winner, a combination of poor finishing and tireless defending ensured the points were shared at full time, though a draw favoured neither side in the race for Europe.

Having dropped back into sixth place, three points adrift of fifth-placed Bolton, Everton welcomed Charlton Athletic to Goodison Park and as Darren Bent cancelled out Joleon Lescott's opener, the points looked set to be shared, until James McFadden stepped up and produced perhaps the most audacious finish I have had the pleasure of witnessing. With the frenetic energy of a cup tie, Everton pushed for a stoppage-time winner, and as the visitors half-cleared a hopeful Gary Naysmith cross, McFadden intercepted the loose ball by flicking it over the head of Madjid Bougherra before gracefully striking it on the volley as it dropped, leaving Scott Carson with no chance. 'McFadden's produced a great bit of skill,' Charlton boss Alan Pardew conceded at full time. 'How do you defend against that?'

'I think we deserved it,' exclaimed Moyes, no doubt relieved at his side's late display, 'but I've got to say that Charlton have been doing very well lately and we always knew, right up until the end, it would be tight. Credit to them for coming back when they did as well, and at that point I probably would have taken a point, but luckily, we had that extra bit of quality to win it. We've relied on Andy Johnson and Tim Cahill too much for goals this season, but now we're getting goals from all over the park and that is exactly what we need.' (BBC Sport, 2007.)

With just four games remaining, Everton suffered back-to-back league defeats for the first time since December 2006, losing 1-0 to relegation-threatened West Ham at Upton Park, before throwing away a 2-0 lead over Manchester United, conceding four goals in the final 30 minutes of the game. The penultimate fixture of the season came at Goodison Park as Harry Redknapp's Portsmouth travelled from the south coast, and Moyes's side cruised to a 3-0 victory despite the absence of top scorer Johnson, with the teenage partnership of James Vaughan and Victor Anichebe leading the line.

'I think we are in Europe now,' Moyes confirmed after the game, 'but we can't say for definite, and I could end up with egg on my face. However, I'll take a place on goal difference because we have earned that this season. I have to pay tribute to the supporters today. They acted like supporters of a proper football club – they were nothing short of magnificent and made as much of a difference as the players. We didn't play well in the first half, but we were terrific after the break.' (BBC Sport, 2007.)

With both FA Cup finalists (Manchester United and Chelsea) and the winners of the League Cup (Chelsea) securing Champions League places, their UEFA Cup spots would be reassigned to the sixth- and seventh-placed teams at the end of the 2006/07 season, while the fifth-placed side would gain automatic qualification. Everton went into the final game of the season sitting in fifth place on 57 points. Sharing the same points tally as the Blues were Spurs in sixth, with Everton's superior goal difference keeping them above the north London club. In seventh was Sam Allardyce's Bolton Wanderers with 55 points. As all three UEFA Cup spots guaranteed qualification for the first round of the competition, there was no advantage in terms of final league placement, though no doubt all three teams aspired to finish the campaign in the highest possible position.

Eighth-placed Reading were also in contention for a European spot going into the final game of the season, with the Berkshire club on 54 points, a solitary point behind Bolton and three behind Everton, though only a freak set of results on the last day would see the Blues finish lower than seventh, with Moyes's side 21 goals better off than Steve Coppell's Reading.

Everton's trip to Stamford Bridge was by far the most challenging of the final day fixtures for those in contention for Europe, with Mourinho's side unbeaten at home for 62 consecutive league games. Spurs would welcome Manchester City to White Hart Lane while Bolton hosted mid-table Aston Villa. European hopefuls Reading travelled to Ewood Park.

After an insipid first-half display from both sides at Stamford Bridge, the game burst into life early in the second half as James Vaughan rounded off a superb Leon Osman run by coolly slotting past Petr Cech to put Everton 1-0 up. The young forward could have had a second moments later, but a world-class save from the Chelsea keeper prevented Vaughan's acrobatic attempt from doubling Everton's lead. A Didier Drogba strike seven minutes later restored parity, though a clear foul on Mikel Arteta by Paulo Ferreira in the build-up should have seen the goal ruled out.

An outraged David Moyes remonstrated with the officials but was sent to the stands for his trouble. As Chelsea stepped up a gear, Tim Howard was forced into action, but was equal to everything the south London club threw at him. Everton believed they had won it right at the death, as substitute James McFadden scored from close range, though the linesman wasted little time in raising his flag, as fellow substitute James Beattie had strayed into an offside position.

'This is disappointing,' a somewhat downbeat Moyes stated after the 1-1 draw. 'We thought we were going to finish fifth. We were incensed by the decision not to award a foul against Paulo Ferreira in the build-up to their goal. It was a terrible decision, and it was wrong. You have to work really hard for what you get at Chelsea and Petr Cech made a great save when we were 1-0 up. But we played really well today.' (BBC Sport, 2007.)

A 2-1 Spurs victory over Manchester City ensured that Martin Jol's side secured fifth place, two points clear of David Moyes's Everton. Had Chelsea's equaliser been ruled out for foul play, or McFadden's late goal stood, the Blues would have finished in fifth place, due to a superior goal difference. However, the final league position notwithstanding, David Moyes had secured European football for the second time in three years, as the progress made under his stewardship became tangible.

The Premier League table at the end of the 2006/07 season

Team	Pld	W	D	L	GF	GA	GD	Pts
1. Man Utd	38	28	5	5	83	27	+56	89
2. Chelsea	38	24	11	3	64	24	+40	83
3. Liverpool	38	20	8	10	57	27	+30	68
4. Arsenal	38	19	11	8	63	35	+28	68
5. Spurs	38	17	9	12	57	54	+3	60
6. Everton	38	15	13	10	52	36	+16	58
7. Bolton	38	16	8	14	47	52	-5	56

14

Buy the Ticket, Take the Ride

THE SUMMER of 2007 was an exciting time to be an Evertonian. Establishing themselves as one of the most consistent teams in the league, Everton were not easy to beat. However, David Moyes's side offered much more than just a resolute defence, with the 2006/07 campaign a turning point for a squad now looking to play with an attacking intent.

The 2006/07 season was the first since Moyes's arrival at Goodison Park in March 2002 in which his Everton side scored more than 50 league goals (52), with the Blues finishing the campaign with a positive goal difference (+16) for the first time since 1999/2000. The influence of midfield maestro Mikel Arteta was paramount, with the Spaniard's contribution reflected in a Player of the Season award.

Indeed, Andy Johnson's goal contribution also assisted in ensuring Everton had an attacking outlet, alongside the continued efforts of Tim Cahill. The Everton coach was starting to build a squad capable of playing consistent, attractive football and in the summer of 2007, Moyes's shrewd eye for a bargain ensured the Blues had quite possibly their best transfer window of the modern era.

Heading to Bramall Lane was Gary Naysmith in a £1 million deal, alongside the once promising James Beattie, who had become an increasingly peripheral figure at Goodison Park, having struggled to meet expectations. Making the switch to Sheffield United in a £4 million transfer, a record fee for the Blades at the time, Beattie left Everton with a record of

13 league goals in 76 games. Heading in the other direction, Everton signed promising defender Phil Jagielka for £4 million, the highest transfer fee for a Sheffield United player.

Joining Jagielka in Everton's new-look backline a little over a month later was Leighton Baines, who arrived from Wigan Athletic on 7 August, for an initial fee of £5 million, with an additional £1 million to be paid in add-ons, dependent on appearances. The deal for the Kirkby-born left-back was a fantastic piece of business by Moyes, especially as Wigan had already accepted a £6 million bid from Sunderland, leaving the decision up to the player. As Roy Keane, who was the Black Cats' manager at the time, wrote in his autobiography, *The Second Half*, 'I met Leighton at a hotel in Sunderland. He was leaving Wigan. We'd made an offer and it had been accepted. The first thing he said to me was, "Roy, if Everton come looking for me, I'll be moving to Everton, because I'm an Evertonian." And I went, "Okay." I appreciated it.'

With two smart additions to Everton's defence, Moyes sought to bolster his attacking options, with South African international Steven Pienaar joining the club on a season-long loan from Borussia Dortmund. A skilful left-winger, also capable of playing as an attacking midfielder, Pienaar arrived at Goodison Park looking to revitalise a stalling career, after struggling to adapt to life at BVB following his 2006 move from Ajax.

Cult hero Thomas Gravesen, who'd departed the club for Real Madrid in 2005, returned to Goodison Park on loan from Celtic and Everton broke their record transfer fee for the second consecutive summer, signing Nigerian forward Yakubu Ayegbeni on a five-year contract from Middlesbrough on 29 August for a fee of £11.25 million. Shunning the number nine jersey, available due to James Beattie's departure, Yakubu requested the number 22, setting this number as his goalscoring target for the season. Indeed, it was a summer of exceptional business for Everton, but there was one club announcement that truly set pulses racing among the fanbase.

On Monday, 2 July 2007, at 11.30am, Everton Football Club's official website announced that David Moyes's side had captured Argentinian star Juan Roman Riquelme on a three-year deal from Villarreal, after rumours of a swoop for the gifted playmaker had been circulating online for many months. It was a signing that had the potential to catapult Everton's creative output into another stratosphere; a genuine world-class acquisition that would send a message to the rest of the Premier League.

If only it were true. In fact, Everton had not signed Riquelme, as a club spokesperson embarrassingly explained, 'During the process of uploading the new home page designs for the website, some test data was displayed for a very short period of time and was immediately removed after it had been identified. Example data had been used during the testing process and this was unfortunately missed by our appointed web development company during the final upload. We have since spoken to our suppliers to convey our complete dissatisfaction at the way in which this misinformation appeared and they have apologised to the club and any Everton supporters who may have read the test article.' (Prentice, *Liverpool Echo*, 2015.)

The phrases 'typical Everton' and 'Everton that' have crept into the lexicon of Evertonians over the past couple of decades, and you have probably muttered them yourself if you have followed the club's fortunes over the years. Indeed, their common usage among the fanbase is an indicator of our limited expectations of a club that has consistently let us down, forcing us to embrace disappointment. Announcing the signing of such a sought-after player, only for it to be untrue, was a very 'typical Everton' moment – especially during what was an otherwise successful transfer window.

The 2007/08 season began on 11 August with the Blues facing Wigan Athletic at Goodison Park in front of a crowd of 39,220. New boys Phil Jagielka and Steven Pienaar were left on the bench for the opening day fixture, while Leighton Baines was unable to face his former club due to a hamstring injury.

A looping Leon Osman header gave Everton the lead after 26 minutes, with Mikel Arteta's creative flair causing his former Everton team-mate Kevin Kilbane all manner of issues. Pienaar replaced goalscorer Osman to make his Everton debut on 73 minutes, and the Blues' lead was doubled within a matter of minutes as Andy Johnson's selfless endeavour allowed Victor Anichebe to finish from six yards out. Wigan substitute Antoine Sibierski pulled one back with ten minutes remaining to ensure an anxious finale, but Moyes's side held on for an opening day victory.

'I thought we played well,' Moyes stated afterwards. 'It was a good performance – I told the players I wanted a solid start and a win, and we got it. Leon Osman's header was terrific. He was very clever in heading it in the only place he could score. When it was 2-0, I thought it would have been a case for us getting a third rather than Wigan pulling one back, but you have to give them credit for battling on.' (McNulty, BBC Sport, 2007.)

A 3-1 victory over Spurs at White Hart Lane three days later saw the Toffees make it two wins out of two, before a disappointing 1-0 defeat at Reading ended Everton's 100 per cent start to the season. A late James McFadden strike rescued a point in a 1-1 draw at Goodison Park against Blackburn Rovers a week later. Yakubu opened his Everton account in a 2-1 win at Bolton Wanderers, with Thomas Gravesen, making his second debut for the club, the architect in Moyes's midfield.

'Thomas Gravesen made a massive difference to us when he came on,' Moyes said. 'He brought a calmness to us and made us play better. He's lacking a bit of fitness, but he made some killer passes that helped us win the game. It was great for Yakubu to get off the mark, but huge credit must go to Andy Johnson – that was a real strike-partnership goal.' (McNulty, BBC Sport, 2007.)

However, one player who had not returned to the club was the precocious Andy van der Meyde, who had failed to report for training in the days prior to the victory at White

Hart Lane and was subsequently suspended for one week and handed the maximum possible fine. 'Andy has had numerous warnings about this type of thing, and we won't tolerate it any longer,' said David Moyes. 'I will make a decision about the player's future next week.' (*The Guardian*, 2007.)

Signed for £2 million in August 2005, Van der Meyde was a gamble that was not paying off, with the Dutch winger's lifestyle a constant issue for both player and club. A hospital admission in August 2006 for breathing problems following a night out prompted questions about his off-the-field behaviour, though he claimed that his drink had been spiked while at a nightclub in Liverpool. Van der Meyde's unquestionable potential notwithstanding, he was a player whose ego was always in inverse proportion to his ability, and one who squandered the opportunity to rebuild a floundering career at a club willing him to rediscover his hunger.

Meanwhile, the much-anticipated UEFA Cup draw approached, with Everton set to discover their opponents on 31 August, as the Blues entered the competition at the first-round stage, alongside fellow Premier League clubs Tottenham Hotspur and Bolton Wanderers. With 45 potential opponents, including the likes of Villarreal, Ajax and Bayern Munich, Everton were drawn against Ukrainian outfit Metalist Kharkiv, with the first leg scheduled to take place at Goodison Park on 20 September and the return fixture pencilled in for 4 October.

Though relatively little was known about Metalist Kharkiv, Everton could ill-afford another European embarrassment, with the humiliation in Romania back in 2005 still fresh in the memory. Indeed, a repeat of such an ignominious exit from Europe was something David Moyes was keen to avoid. 'We need a good run in Europe, and we need to put the voodoo of Bucharest behind us,' said the Scot. 'The real disappointment was not getting through to the Champions League, and the nature of that game against Villarreal, a mistake by the referee, was the most galling aspect of all. But that is all water under the bridge now.'

Indeed, it was a sentiment echoed by Everton captain Phil Neville. 'There has been a turnaround of players since then,' Neville said. 'A more positive outlook, a freshness about the squad, and I don't think there is a fear about the place that there was two years ago. Maybe when we finished fourth, we didn't believe that we should have been in the Champions League. We got the hardest possible draw when we got Villarreal and the shock of going out meant we started the league season poorly and went to Bucharest with a large injury list and to a country where no one had any experience of playing. It was a real eye-opener.' (Hunter, *The Guardian*, 2007.)

The starting line-ups for Everton v Metalist Kharkiv in the first round of the UEFA Cup on Thursday, 20 September at Goodison Park in front of 37,120 spectators were as follows:

Everton: Wessels, Hibbert, Yobo, Lescott, Baines, Osman, Carsley, Neville, McFadden, Johnson, Yakubu

Metalist Kharkiv: Goryainov, Bordiyan, Babych, Gancarczyk, Obradobic, Guie, Slysir, Valiaev, Devic, Nwoha, Rykun

With kick-off delayed for an hour due to a ticketing issue, the well-oiled patrons of L4's alehouses arrived at Goodison Park in full voice, eager for a European night under the lights. Once the game eventually began, any feelings of complacency were quickly extinguished as Metalist, third-placed finishers in the Ukrainian league the season before, almost took a shock lead with their first move of the match, forcing Stefan Wessels into action to tip Serhiy Valiaev's 30-yard rocket over the bar. The visitors continued to demonstrate that they would be no pushovers, as they quickly managed to fashion a second opportunity of the game, with Olexandr Rykun volleying over the bar from 15 yards out.

Everton soon settled into the fixture, however, and began to dominate possession. With their first sight of goal, David Moyes's side opened the scoring after 24 minutes, as Joleon Lescott rose to head home a floated James McFadden corner, with the relief around the ground almost audible. However,

Kharkiv continued to frustrate Everton, limiting clear-cut opportunities to a minimum, allowing an anxiety to creep into the stands at Goodison.

Midway through the second half, the game burst into life, with Austrian referee Fritz Stuchlik at the centre of the action. Awarding Everton a penalty for an Oleksandr Babych foul on the increasingly influential Joleon Lescott, Stuchlik proceeded to show Seweryn Gancarczyk a second yellow card for his over-zealous protestations. As Andy Johnson rifled the resulting spot kick into the roof of the net, Moyes's side could breathe easy; two goals to the good against a deflated ten-man opposition. Stuchlik, however, insisted that the penalty should be retaken, due to encroachment, much to the frustration of the crowd. The Blues forward stepped up for a second time, only for Kharkiv keeper Goryainov to deny Johnson his first European goal, to keep the score at 1-0.

A chorus of boos rang around Goodison Park, directed at the pedantic Stuchlik for his insistence on a retake. Everton's frustrations would be compounded with 12 minutes remaining as a Metalist counter-attack saw substitute Hitcham Mahdoufi find fellow sub Zeze in space, allowing the Ivorian to calmy slot past Wessels. Everton substitute Victor Anichebe had a penalty appeal turned down as he earned himself a booking for his frantic protests.

The young forward continued to cause the Kharkiv defence issues, and with a minute remaining, a desperate Babych wrestled him to the ground, and this time Stuchlik did point to the spot. Johnson once again picked up the ball and confidently placed it on the penalty spot, as a rare opportunity to atone for his earlier miss quickly presented itself. As Goodison held its breath, the Everton forward stepped up in front of the Gwladys Street and blazed his wild spot kick over the bar to a soundtrack of exasperated groans.

'If he gives a foul for people entering the box, he should do it again,' said a perturbed Moyes at full time, in reference to the referee's insistence on a retake due to encroachment. 'For the first one there were more Metalist players in the area than Everton, so to punish us seemed harsh. In the end we lost a sloppy goal and that puts us under a lot of pressure.' (Stevenson, BBC Sport, 2007.)

Indeed, if they failed to get a positive result in Ukraine, Everton would face an early exit from Europe for the second time in two years, and this time there could be no excuse. While Evertonians could understandably feel hard done by for the refereeing decisions against Villarreal, and a hangover from this match could perhaps explain, though certainly not justify, the subsequent capitulation against Dinamo Bucuresti, nothing less than a win in Kharkiv would be good enough.

15

A European Tour

KHARKIV IS a post-industrial city in north-eastern Ukraine with a fascinating history. It was in fact the first capital of an independent Ukraine between December 1919 and January 1934, after which the honour was given to Kyiv. Driving into the city centre from the airport, the skyline was dominated by cumbersome tower blocks, built during the Soviet era, with the bottom of every tree painted white in the absence of lampposts. Swathes of the city appeared to be under redevelopment ahead of hosting a number of games for the 2008 European Championships, co-hosted by Ukraine and Poland.

Arriving at Freedom Square, the architectural gem at the heart of the city, flags were already on display throughout. 'WHEN TONY HIBBERT SCORES, WE RIOT' and 'SUPERMAN WEARS TIM CAHILL PYJAMAS' were my personal favourites, along with: 'COMBAT GLOBAL WARMING – STOP KOPITES FROM FLYING TO HOME GAMES' and 'SCOUSE BLUES GO THE MATCH – SCOUSE REDS GO THE PUB'. At 15 years of age, I was having the time of my life. I should have been sitting a French mock GCSE at school, and while my mates were filling out a multiple-choice exam on the differences between the masculine and feminine nouns of the Gallic language, I was singing Everton songs with pint after pint of cheap Stella. I still managed to pass with a C, for the record.

We made our way to the stadium, which was under partial redevelopment, with one whole side of the ground yet to be rebuilt, reminiscent of the Park End's regeneration in the 1990s. Sensationalist stories in the media regarding Eastern European football hooliganism had been doing the rounds in the weeks leading up to the game, with fans of Metalist Kharkiv reportedly a keen proponent of this particular pastime. Consequently, Everton's travelling contingent were left to wonder what kind of welcome we could expect when we arrived at the Metalist Oblast Sports Complex.

However, any apprehensions regarding fan safety or the possibility of violence were completely unfounded. The Metalist fans were more eager to swap memorabilia than punches, or at least the ones I encountered were. I swapped my Everton scarf with a Metalist fan who was roughly my age, and we had our picture taken together outside the stadium. I'm not suggesting that the issue of hooliganism is not still prevalent throughout Europe, but it emphasised to me at a young age the influence the media can have and its perception of football fans.

Once inside the stadium, the atmosphere was electric. A deafening crescendo of 'Metalist, Metalist' welcomed the players to the pitch, and as the home side dominated much of the early proceedings, Kharkiv's vocal support grew even louder. Everton were struggling to get a foothold in the game, with Tim Howard forced into action numerous times before Brazilian midfielder Edmar opened the scoring.

Everton needed a quick response and whatever David Moyes said to his players at half-time reaped immediate dividends, with Joleon Lescott latching on to Steven Pienaar's deflected shot to score his fifth goal of the season three minutes into the second period. After a pedestrian display, Everton were fortunate to be level, but it would only take four minutes for Kharkiv to regain control, as Olexandr Rykun's curling effort ricocheted off the inside of the post, falling kindly for Hicham Mahdoufi to smash in the rebound.

The home crowd could sense that a famous victory was within reach, but as our hopes of exorcising our last UEFA Cup outing looked to be improbable, Everton suddenly increased the tempo, creating a succession of chances. The Metalist players, composed all evening, now appeared to be afflicted with nerves as a spectacular James McFadden effort gave Everton a much-needed lifeline. With an aggregate score of 3-3 and a matter of minutes remaining, Victor Anichebe took advantage of a rare defensive lapse and, twisting this way and that, the teenager eventually hammered the ball home, as Everton's travelling fans erupted into pandemonium.

'I didn't mention it to the players, but Bucharest was in my thoughts,' admitted Moyes, no doubt relieved to have secured passage to the group stages. 'I just want to have a run in Europe. I'm delighted for the players and myself as this is something I really want to do. Metalist proved once again that they are a very good team tonight. They made it hard for us and we are just delighted to have got through. Metalist were a very, very good side. It was always difficult for us, and we had to change things round three or four times. They gave us loads of problems with their technical ability, but we are through and sometimes the first rounds are the hardest.' (Taylor, *The Guardian*, 2007.)

Indeed, there is little question that Everton's qualification into the 2007/08 UEFA Cup group stage was a watershed moment in the trajectory of David Moyes's team. Losing both the Champions League and the UEFA Cup qualifying games back in 2005/06 resulted in a hangover that the club took months to recover from and rendered the achievement of the 2004/05 fourth-place finish redundant. Metalist Kharkiv were no doubt a tricky opponent and overcoming this banana-skin of a tie demonstrated the progression and guaranteed that this time, our European adventure would not be quite so brief.

Taking place on Tuesday, 9 October in Nyon, Switzerland, the draw for the 2007/08 UEFA Cup group stage saw Everton placed in Group A. With a total of eight groups, consisting of five teams in each, Everton would face four opponents, two at home and two away. Visiting Goodison Park would be Greek side AEL (Larissa) and Russian giants Zenit St Petersburg, while the Blues would travel to German outfit FC Nuremberg and AZ of the Netherlands.

However, Everton would first welcome Liverpool to Goodison Park for the Merseyside derby on Saturday, 20 October. Though Everton went into the game in tenth place, a win for David Moyes's side would see them go level on points with fourth-placed Liverpool.

The line-ups that day were as follows:

Everton: Howard, Hibbert, Yobo, Stubbs, Lescott, Arteta, Jagielka, Neville, Osman, Yakubu, Anichebe

Liverpool: Reina, Finnan, Carragher, Hyypia, Riise, Gerrard, Mascherano, Sissoko, Benayoun, Voronin, Kuyt

The notable absentees, Tim Cahill and Fernando Torres, meant both managers were without an influential figure, with James Vaughan and Thomas Gravesen also unavailable for David Moyes.

Chances at either end of the pitch in the early exchanges set the tone, with Everton taking the lead on 38 minutes as Sami Hyypia put one past his own keeper. A penalty to Liverpool early in the second half provided the visitors with an opportunity to draw level, as Tony Hibbert was dismissed for a foul on Steven Gerrard. Controversially, referee Mark Clattenburg initially appeared to be reaching for a yellow card, before Gerrard intervened, and the official brandished a red card instead. To add insult to injury, Liverpool's equalising penalty-taker, Dirk Kuyt, should have already been sent off for a reckless lunge on Phil Neville.

As the half progressed, Yakubu came within an inch of restoring Everton's lead with a stunning 30-yard effort, though Liverpool soon began to exploit the space created due to their numerical advantage. With 20 minutes remaining, midfielder Lucas Leiva was brought on to replace a stunned-looking Gerrard, and in the 90th minute, a shot by the Brazilian international was palmed away on the line by Phil Neville, and Clattenburg awarded Liverpool their second penalty of the afternoon. Hibbert was joined for an early bath by his team-mate.

Kuyt stepped up once more and put Liverpool 2-1 ahead, but with seconds remaining the Blues had a penalty appeal of their own waved away as Jamie Carragher hauled Joleon Lescott to the ground, in clear view of Clattenburg, as the Durham-born referee looked on, disinterestedly.

'Decisions happen, that's football,' a visibly frustrated Moyes stated after the 2-1 defeat. 'But in the last seconds there's the chance for it to be corrected and it would have been a result we deserved. We deserved that penalty and if the other penalties were more blatant than that, then I am in the wrong game. I seem to see football differently. If the ref doesn't see that, you ask why.'

Unsurprisingly, Liverpool manager Rafael Benitez held a different perspective of the events, stating, 'People talk about a penalty they could have had, but last season we lost here 3-0. Two of their goals were fouls and nobody complained then. I always feel that in England, players should not be rewarded with penalties for diving. I felt both penalty decisions were right, and I also agree with the yellow card for Kuyt and not a red.' (McNulty, BBC Sport, 2007.)

In 2021, Mark Clattenburg was a guest on Jamie Carragher's *The Greatest Game* podcast and spoke at length about his refereeing performance during the 2007/08 Merseyside derby, his last appearance at Goodison Park until 2014.

'I was out of my depth,' Clattenburg claimed. 'I don't know why I was refereeing it. I'd just done the Manchester derby and the London derby, so it was my third derby in three or four weeks. I had underestimated it – the working-class derby.

'The other two were different derbies, this one was brutal. Some derbies are different in certain stadiums. Sunderland–Newcastle is more intense at Sunderland and Everton–Liverpool is more intense at Goodison. There was always more intensity. I remember the first half, I did okay, but in the second half I had an absolute nightmare. I listened to my assistant referee for the Dirk Kuyt challenge, which when you look back was a stonewall red.'

Later in the podcast, Clattenburg joked with host Carragher as he referenced the former Liverpool player's foul on Joleon Lescott: 'Look at what you did with Lescott,' Clattenburg says. 'You killed us! I wasn't allowed to referee Everton for seven years because of you. Everything went against Everton. You don't sometimes see it when you are in the game. I could have given the penalty and come out with less criticism and then refereed Everton over the next seven years, which I failed to do.'

Indeed, it was probably for the best that Mark Clattenburg didn't make an appearance at Goodison Park for so long, such was the animosity towards the Durham-born official. Almost 15 years later, there is little doubt that Mark Clattenburg, alongside Pierluigi Collina, retains the title of the most hated official among Evertonians, a fanbase who seldom forgive and forget.

Turning our attention back to Europe, Greek outfit Larissa travelled to Goodison Park just five days after the Merseyside derby, as boss David Moyes keenly expressed his belief that his side would not be distracted by the disappointing derby result, insisting that the injustice of the refereeing decisions could be used to his side's advantage: 'It will make us stronger as we had to play 12 against nine at one point at the weekend,' the Everton coach sarcastically stated. 'The players will benefit from the experience and become tougher mentally.' (*Daily Record*, 2007.)

The return of Tim Cahill to the starting line-up after suffering a broken metatarsal was an enormous boost, along with the return to the matchday squad of Thomas Gravesen, the Dane being one of the named substitutes.

The line-ups as Everton took on Larissa at Goodison Park on Thursday, 25 October were as follows:

Everton: Howard, Hibbert, Yobo, Lescott, Baines, Pienaar, Osman, Carsley, Cahill, Arteta, McFadden

Larissa: Kotsolis, Galitsios, Foerster, Dabizas, Venetidis, Cleyton, Fotakis, Kiriakidis, Sarmiento, Parra, Bakayoko

A little cagey in the opening period, Everton appeared nervous, though Cahill's energy in the midfield sparked the Blues into life, as the Australian international marked his return from injury and his 100th appearance for Everton with a goal, diving on to Leon Osman's cross on 14 minutes. Everton stepped into their stride and should have doubled their lead early in the second half, as James McFadden's wasteful effort was hit straight at Kotsolis's legs.

It wouldn't take long for Everton to put themselves firmly in charge, however, with Leon Osman's rocket finishing off what is perhaps my favourite team goal in the 24 years that I have been going to Goodison Park. After some smart work from the combative Cahill to find Leighton Baines bursting down the left flank, the Kirkby-born full-back played a first-time ball inside to Steven Pienaar, whose deft flick was weighted perfectly for the onrushing Osman to smash the ball past a motionless Larissa keeper.

Satisfying as it was to see Osman's superb strike hit the back of the net, the fluidity of the passing and movement of Moyes's side was most pleasing of all. The awareness demonstrated by Pienaar in particular, whose wonderfully weighted assist could not have been any more inviting, was a joy to watch. So too was witnessing the beginnings of what became one of the most formidable left sides in the Premier League, with Baines and Pienaar's telepathic interplay beginning to blossom.

David Moyes's Everton side were often described as little more than hard-working, a team possessing a stubborn refusal to roll over in the absence of finesse. However, by the 2007/0 8 campaign, Moyes had assembled a squad that were without doubt playing some of the most attractive football in the Premier League at the time. The 'workmanlike' stereotype associated with Moyes's Everton was at best lazy journalism, at worst a reluctance to acknowledge the rapid progression of a club that only a few years previously had been battling relegation.

Fighting off a late scare, Everton ended the evening with a 3-1 victory and as Group A leaders; with AZ earning a 1-1 draw in St Petersburg, and Nuremberg not scheduled to play their opener for another couple of weeks, Everton's victory over Larissa secured a two-point advantage at the top of the group.

'I thought the goals we scored were really good and getting Cahill back and Thomas Gravesen was a bonus,' Moyes stated at full time. 'Scoring is what Tim does for us and he has been doing it for years. He did it again and you see what it means to him. It is a big thing for our squad and thankfully he is back and came through it with no problems. It will benefit him in the coming weeks.' (Mercer, BBC Sport, 2007.)

A trip to Pride Park followed as Everton took on a struggling Derby County, who had only managed a solitary victory out of the opening ten fixtures of the season and had failed to find the net in over four hours of football prior to kick-off. A comfortable 2-0 victory for Everton condemned Derby to bottom place in the league, with Yakubu the standout player in blue for the afternoon. A clever dummy from the Nigerian international allowed Phil Jagielka's pass to find Mikel Arteta in space, the Spaniard taking advantage by firing Everton into a 26th-minute lead. As the Rams struggled to impose themselves on the game, Everton seized the initiative and added a second on 63 minutes, with Steven Pienaar grabbing an assist to top off his fine performance. This time, it was Tim Cahill's turn to play a subtle dummy, allowing Yakubu to fire past Stephen Bywater inside the six-yard box.

'What we know is when he [Yakubu] gets through on goal he doesn't miss,' said Moyes, pleased with the performance of his record signing. 'Today he delivered with an impressive goal that took the pressure off us and a great dummy. He showed intelligence and awareness. But in Britain what we enjoy is seeing players put in their graft. That's part of our culture and Yakubu did that and got a standing ovation for us.' (Chowdhury, BBC Sport, 2007.)

Back-to-back league victories and three consecutive wins in all competitions ensured that Everton travelled to Nuremberg for their second game of the UEFA Cup group stage in fine form. With Larissa hosting Zenit St Petersburg in the other Group A match of the evening, a win for the Blues in Bavaria would maintain their place firmly at the table's summit.

Nuremberg will have perhaps approached the game seeking a distraction from their dreadful league form, having won only two games all season, though David Moyes was cautious not to underestimate the Bundesliga opposition: 'It is their first game in the UEFA Cup this season and it could give them some respite from the league. They may be struggling but then again Germany were written off before the last World Cup. German teams can often pull out the stops when they need to.' (Hunter, *The Guardian*, 2007.)

The Blues travelled to Germany without youngster James Vaughan, who was suffering with a recurring thigh problem, as well as fellow striker Andy Johnson, as he recovered from ankle surgery. Unavailable though he was to face Nuremberg, the England forward had no hesitation in committing his long-term future to the club, joining Mikel Arteta and Tim Cahill in signing a five-year contract. The contract extension ended months of speculation that the striker was unhappy in the north of England. 'The rumours were starting to get stupid,' the 26-year-old centre-forward stated. 'They were coming out every two or three weeks and it was pathetic. Signing the new deal proves that I enjoy it here.' (North Wales Live, 2007.)

Moyes too was delighted with Johnson's commitment to the football club, stressing the importance of retaining the quality that he had brought into the squad: 'I think this football club has always had the capability to win a cup competition and this team certainly does. We have had some really tough draws in the Champions League and the FA Cup and there have been times when we have let ourselves down, but this is a squad that belongs in Europe, and it is important we keep them together. When I arrived at the club, I said I didn't mind not having a great deal of money providing my best players were not taken away from me. On one occasion that did happen [Wayne Rooney] but now we have done everything we can to keep the players we really want. We desperately want a good cup run. That has been missing from my time [with Everton].' (Hunter, *The Guardian*, 2007.)

Indeed, it was a feeling echoed throughout the fanbase. Despite Nuremberg's easyCredit Stadion holding a capacity of 47,000, Everton received an allocation of just over 2,500 tickets, though the club's head of communications Ian Ross insisted that an allocation of 10,000 would have failed to meet demand. 'We got the biggest allocation of tickets we possibly could, but we could have sold that five or six times over.' (Hunter, *The Guardian*, 2007.)

The limited supply prompted a large number of Evertonians to purchase tickets for the home sections of the ground online, directly from Nuremberg. However, upon advice from UEFA, the Bundesliga club cancelled the tickets the week before the game, offering a refund to the roughly 1,500 fans affected. As many of them were still expected to make the trip to Germany without a ticket, UEFA placed a 'high risk' classification on the game, prompting Moyes to urge restraint to avert the possibility of a UEFA sanction.

'I am very disappointed for those who bought tickets in good faith, paid for their flights and hotels, and then found out they couldn't go to the game. But we are only just back in Europe, and we don't want anything to put a dampener on it in any way. Our intention is to be in Europe for years to come and we don't want anything to put that in jeopardy. I hope the supporters do get to see the game, but the most important thing is that it all goes peacefully.' (Hunter, *The Guardian*, 2007.)

When asked if those fans who'd purchased tickets directly from Nuremberg deserved to be reimbursed for their travel and hotel expenses as well as their match tickets, Everton chairman Bill Kenwright commented, 'You would think so. [By] Nuremberg I would have thought. I would have thought these boys do have the right to some sort of compensation. The bad news began weeks ago when we were given our allocation, which is very small. Evertonians will do anything to see their team, especially in Europe. The fact that these lads, who work hard for their money, have invested money not only in the tickets but in flights and hotels – they are wondering whether they should go. Some of them will want to be there. They have waited a long time to be in Europe. I do feel for them, and I do feel they have been dealt a blow by UEFA. We can only ask our fans that wherever they watch the match, they continue to be the great ambassadors of this football club that they have always been.' (*Liverpool Echo*, 2007.)

As we arrived in Nuremberg, we got a shuttle bus to the city centre and joined up with the many thousands of Evertonians who had made the journey. This was my second European away trip in as many months, and I was getting a taste for it. A couple of days off school and a skinful of German beer with my dad, I loved every second. The local police had a clear presence in the city centre, though they were happy to pose with Everton flags and have a kick-about with fans. Indeed, just as Kharkiv fans had been misrepresented within the media just a few weeks earlier, it seemed now it was the turn of the travelling Evertonians.

As Lee Carsley recalled in the *Liverpool Echo* in 2014, 'I've been all over Europe with Everton and there's never been a whiff of trouble. Our fans just don't have that kind of mentality. I remember being in Nuremberg and looking out of my window to see scores of Evertonians enjoying themselves, hanging off trams and bus stops, but it is always good-natured fun and never nasty.'

We made our way to the easyCredit Stadion (now the Max Morlock Stadion), an impressive ground on the outskirts of the city. Originally built in 1928, the stadium had recently undergone extensive renovation in preparation for Germany's host status for the 2005 FIFA Confederations Cup and the 2006 FIFA World Cup. The stadium is surrounded by a large area of parkland resembling woodland from a Brothers Grimm fairy tale, lending an eerie atmosphere to a night game. A member of our group disappeared into the dense forest to have a burst behind a tree and didn't reappear until we were at the airport some hours later.

The line-ups as Nuremberg hosted Everton on Thursday, 8 November were as follows:

Nuremberg: Blazek, Schmidt, Glauber, Wolf, Reinhardt, Galasek, Kluge, Mnari, Mintal, Misimovic, Saenko

Everton: Howard, Neville, Yobo, Lescott, Valente, Arteta, Carsley, Cahill, Osman, Pienaar, Yakubu

The noise inside the stadium was charged, and it was clear that Everton's passionate following had left an impression on the squad. 'I didn't need to provide a motivational speech,' said Moyes. 'We only had to see the thousands greeting us on the way to the stadium to know how much Europe means to Everton. We are desperate for success.'

Indeed, the support was magnificent, and Everton put in a performance worthy of the outstanding backing, almost taking the lead after 24 seconds, with Mikel Arteta's fierce drive parried into the path of Tim Cahill by Jaromir Blazek, before the Nuremberg keeper deflected Cahill's rebounded effort on to the post and out for a corner.

In a thrilling encounter, both teams created a flurry of chances to open the scoring, as Blazek and Tim Howard each had to earn their crust to keep the score level. Peer Kluge fired a shot inches wide of the post for the hosts moments after Cahill was just a hair away from getting on the end of a whipped Leon Osman cross. The Blues almost gifted the Bundesliga side an opener as a misjudged Steven Pienaar dummy afforded Dominik Reinhardt an attempt on goal, but a full-stretch Howard was on hand to deny the German midfielder. A swing and a miss for Yakubu moments before the break spared Blazek's blushes, as the keeper's weak punch from a corner landed right at the feet of the Nigerian forward, only for the Blues' record signing to uncharacteristically squander the opportunity.

The gung-ho tempo continued after the break, with Howard again saving well from a left-footed effort from Marek Mintal, before a teasing Arteta cross was fumbled by a now nervous-looking Blazek, the Czech keeper recovering before

Everton could take advantage. By the 75th minute, Moyes decided it was time to replace the tiring Yakubu with the fresh legs of super-sub, Victor Anichebe, who had an almost instant impact. Picking the ball up deep in Nuremberg's half, the Nigerian forward powered his way into the penalty area, leaving defender Leandro Glauber little choice but to wrestle him to the ground. With 83 minutes on the clock, Arteta coolly dispatched the subsequent penalty, sending the voluminous away end into blue euphoria.

The formidable Anichebe's cameo was not quite over however, and with two minutes remaining, Big Vic bounced aside a dawdling Jaouhar Mnari before calmly finishing under Blazek to double Everton's lead. With important strikes against Metalist Kharkiv and Larissa, Victor Anichebe was proving to be quite the asset to David Moyes's European hopes, the young forward's brutal showing in Germany earning Everton a 2-0 victory and a place at the summit of Group A. A 3-2 win for Zenit St Petersburg away at Larissa ensured Everton retained a comfortable two-point cushion at the top of the group.

After two games, the Group A table of the 2007/08 UEFA Cup looked like this:

Team	Pld	W	D	L	GF	GA	GD	Pts
1. Everton	2	2	0	0	5	1	+4	6
2. Zenit	2	1	1	0	4	3	+1	4
3. AZ	1	0	1	0	1	1	0	1
4. Nuremberg	1	0	0	1	0	2	-2	0
5. Larissa	2	0	0	2	3	6	-3	0

16

The Best Little
Spaniard We Know

WITH FIVE consecutive victories in all competitions, including a composed away win in Europe, David Moyes's side were beginning to show signs of perfectly balancing the demands of European football with their ambitions in the Premier League, as illustrated by Mikel Arteta: 'We are a very British team, we know that, but we now have the players to change games around and who are learning quickly in Europe. Tim Cahill is a big influence on that, for example, and because of his qualities and the runs he makes from midfield he is the ideal player behind the striker.' (Hunter, *The Guardian*, 2007.)

David Moyes too was pleased with his side's clear progress, and with the individual performance of the young Victor Anichebe in particular. 'Victor made some impact, what a way to finish that was,' the Everton boss said. 'He has been struggling with a broken hand and I wasn't sure whether to put him on; just shows what I know. Overall, I thought it was a good performance, we did well enough. They had one or two chances early on as we did, but they are a good side too.' (Hunter, *The Guardian*, 2007.)

A trip to Stamford Bridge followed, three days after the smash and grab win over Nuremberg. Chelsea were also recovering from a midweek game in Germany after their 0-0 draw against Schalke 04, though the south London club had the luxury of 48 hours' additional rest, having played their

Champions League game in Gelsenkirchen on the Tuesday. Both teams went into the match in fine form, with Moyes's Everton having won five on the bounce in all competitions and Chelsea unbeaten in their last seven fixtures, including four consecutive Premier League victories.

A battling display from Everton earned a 1-1 draw at Stamford Bridge, with a late acrobatic finish from the talismanic Tim Cahill salvaging a deserved point. 'We made a brave decision,' Moyes stated, explaining why he subbed defensive midfielder and captain Phil Neville for James McFadden at half-time. 'I always thought we were in it.'

Indeed, it was refreshing to see Moyes manage with a boldness befitting the quality at his disposal. With Lee Carsley protecting the back four for the second half, Moyes altered his tactics from a 4-5-1 to a bold 4-4-2, with McFadden supporting the in-form Victor Anichebe, who came on in place of Yakubu. Tim Howard continued his excellent run of form, pulling off a string of outstanding saves throughout the match, though he could do little to prevent Didier Drogba's glancing header from opening the scoring with 20 minutes remaining.

However, Moyes's gallant half-time substitution paid dividends with a minute to go, as McFadden's attempt from the left bounced off a scrambling Juliano Belletti, only for Tim Cahill to produce a sublime overhead kick – seemingly out of nothing – to level the scoring, as his incredible acrobatic effort flew past Carlo Cudicini. A hard-earned point at Stamford Bridge only 36 hours after a tricky away tie in Europe: Moyes was full of praise for his side's dogged performance.

'In the first half they had one or two chances and we missed a good one too,' the Everton manager said. 'We had to change it to get a better grip of the game and I felt we did that. We were never out of the game; we were gritty and determined. We always felt if we could hang in there, we had people on the pitch who can score goals and that's what Cahill does for us. McFadden's been unfortunate not to be involved. He made a difference in the second half with Anichebe. We had to change it, we were brave and got our rewards for it.' (Soni, BBC Sport, 2007.)

With confidence running high throughout David Moyes's Everton side, the Blues produced an emphatic 7-1 demolition of Roy Keane's Sunderland at Goodison Park. You would have had to go back 11 years to see an Everton side score seven goals, with Joe Royle's side annihilating Southampton at Goodison Park on 16 November 1996. It was worth the wait, however, with Mikel Arteta's virtuoso performance the standout in what was a fantastic team display. A Yakubu opener on 12 minutes put the Blues in front, before a Tim Cahill header five minutes later put Everton firmly in control, after a tormenting Arteta run tore the Sunderland defence apart. A Steven Pienaar strike on 43 minutes added a third for the Blues, before Dwight Yorke pulled one back for the Black Cats moments before the interval.

Tim Cahill bagged his second and Everton's fourth goal of the game just after the hour mark, effectively putting the tie to bed, though there was no mercy for the opposition, as Yakubu added a fifth, his second of the afternoon, 11 minutes later. Andy Johnson, back in the matchday squad after recovering from ankle surgery, scored on his return to the team with virtually his first touch, having replaced Yakubu late in the game. Wave after wave of attack continued to tear through an exhausted Sunderland defence, as Leon Osman added a seventh Everton goal with five minutes remaining, running from his own half almost unchallenged before finishing past an over-worked Craig Gordon.

'That was probably the best performance in my time here,' a jubilant Moyes insisted to BBC Sport. 'Some of our football was fantastic and our passing and movement was just outstanding. It is how I have been hoping to get an Everton team playing and I hope we see Everton playing that way more often – hopefully it's the first of many. Mikel Arteta's first 45 minutes was nothing short of magical. The things he did on the ball and the opportunities he created for us were just something else.'

Moyes continued, 'Everton have to go back 11 years to the last time we scored so many in a match against Southampton. I had felt a big win would come along soon, so I was not really surprised today because I said a couple of weeks ago in training that we were looking good enough for some special performances. This is certainly the best performance I've been concerned with in my time here. It's been a great day and we had the bonus of Andrew Johnson back in action and scoring a goal. With a fully fit squad, we could have some exciting times ahead.' (Keeling, *The Guardian*, 2007.)

Exciting times indeed, as the Blues welcomed Dick Advocaat's Zenit St Petersburg to Goodison Park for the third game of the UEFA Cup group stage.

In front of 38,407 spectators at Goodison Park on Wednesday, 5 December 2007 the line-ups that night were as follows:

Everton: Howard, Neville, Jagielka, Lescott, Baines, Pienaar, Cahill, Carsley, Arteta, Johnson, McFadden

Zenit St Petersburg: Malafeev, Aniukov, Skrtel, Lombaerts, Kim, Tymoschuk, Zurianov, Shirl, Arshavin, Dominguez, Pogrebniak

Everton went into the game against Zenit with the knowledge that a victory over the Russian champions would all but guarantee qualification to the round of 32, and the Blues began brightly, with Mikel Arteta and James McFadden both creating chances within the opening ten minutes. The movement and vision of Andrei Arshavin was a constant threat, alongside strike partner Pavel Pogrebniak, who had bagged two goals in his last two European games, against Larissa and Nuremberg respectively. With the game relatively evenly matched as the first half progressed, Everton were handed a slice of good fortune, as Icelandic referee Kristinn Jakobsson deemed that Tim Cahill's goalbound effort had been handled on the line by Nicolas Lombaerts, resulting in the dismissal of the Belgian centre-half and the Blues being awarded a spot kick.

Zenit no doubt felt hard done by, with replays showing that the ball struck the defender on his thigh and chest, though there was little sympathy among the Goodison crowd. However, the injustice of the decision was soon evened out, as Arteta sent his penalty blazing over the bar – the third occasion on which Everton had missed a penalty in the 2007/08 UEFA Cup, following Andy Johnson's two missed spot kicks at home to Metalist Kharkiv.

Zenit soon began to fashion the clearer openings, with both Konstantin Zurianov and the in-form Pavel Pogrebniak failing to capitalise, and the game looked destined to end in stalemate. With time running out, Everton launched a ceaseless period of pressure, and with five minutes left on the clock, Zenit keeper Vyacheslav Malafeev denied a Joleon Lescott effort, but Tim Cahill scrambled home the rebound to score his fourth goal in as many games.

The hard-earned victory over Zenit St Petersburg made it three out of three in the UEFA Cup group stage for David Moyes's Everton, ensuring their passage to the next round with a game to spare. Perhaps more significantly, however, the qualification for the round of 32 also meant that Everton would be playing European football beyond Christmas for the first time since 1985, when the Blues had gone on to lift the European Cup Winners' Cup.

Notwithstanding the years during which English clubs were banned from competing in Europe following the Heysel Stadium disaster (1985–90), the fact that it had taken the club so long to progress this far in a European competition is one of the great failures in the modern history of Everton Football Club. However, with new ground broken, the Blues could start the New Year dreaming of emulating Howard Kendall's Rotterdam glory.

'It is a tremendous achievement for the whole club,' said Moyes at full time. 'Qualifying for the UEFA Cup last season was an achievement and so to qualify from a strong group, and to win the group – that's right, isn't it? – is fantastic for everyone involved. I'm delighted. Our performance tonight was better that Zenit's. We played well and we could have had more goals. Zenit have one or two great players and had a really good chance in the second half, but we created chances throughout the game. Our final pass and our finishing could improve, but we scored seven here last time out [against Sunderland] and tonight we created chances against the champions of Russia. We just couldn't convert many.' (Hunter, *The Guardian*, 2007.)

A Yakubu hat-trick secured a 3-0 win over Fulham at Goodison Park three days later, helping to maintain the feelgood factor in L4, with the victory over the Cottagers stretching Everton's unbeaten run to ten games, the best sequence in David Moyes's five and a half years in charge. Indeed, there was a confidence that had seeped into the bones of Everton during this time, and the Blues boss was again full of praise for his players.

'Yakubu did what he does best – scored goals,' said the Scot. 'He is getting better at the other things we want from him, but his strength is scoring goals and he's done it everywhere he has been. He scored three in the second half, and I think if we had scored six no one could have questioned it. Some of our football in the second half was as good as we have played.' (McNulty, BBC Sport, 2007.)

Fulham manager Lawrie Sanchez was equally keen to reference Everton's quality in his post-match comments, stating, 'It is difficult to cope with good quality players like Tim Cahill and Mikel Arteta, and Yakubu made the most of his chances. I know it sounds like whingeing again, but I thought the first goal was offside. It was another poor decision that went against us. It gave Everton a lift and formed the bedrock of their second half display. We had to go forward from then, and that meant we could be opened up by a good side – and that is what Everton are.' (BBC Sport, 2007.)

Continuing with a packed Christmas schedule, Everton prepared to face West Ham United at Upton Park twice in the space of three days, starting with a League Cup quarter-final on Wednesday, 12 December 2007. With both teams selecting what would be considered their strongest starting line-ups, no doubt both managers saw the competition as a sound opportunity to deliver silverware to their respective clubs.

A Carlton Cole opener gave the Hammers an early lead after 12 minutes, but an unaffected Everton scored a deserved equaliser five minutes before the break, thanks to a deflected Leon Osman strike. In a tense affair, there was little to separate the two sides, with a sense that only a mistake or a moment of brilliance would prevent a stalemate. A casual Mikel Arteta backheel afforded Freddie Ljungberg an opportunity late on, but his hesitation allowed the Blues to recover well. With two minutes left on the clock, a seemingly aimless ball upfield from Phil Jagielka appeared harmless, until a lack of communication between West Ham keeper Robert Green and defender Danny Gabbidon allowed the ball to roll kindly for Yakubu, who gratefully snatched a late victory.

Just 36 hours later, West Ham would have the opportunity to avenge their League Cup exit, as David Moyes's side made their second trip of the week to Upton Park. No doubt eager to make amends for their cup departure, the hosts created a string of chances throughout the first half, though it would be Everton's midweek hero Yakubu who opened the scoring on the stroke of half-time. Alan Curbishley's side continued with their attacking intent after the break, but Everton's defence remained resolute, and a deadly counter-attack in the 90th minute saw substitute Andy Johnson loop an effort over a retreating Robert Green to secure an Upton Park double.

'It probably shouldn't be a surprise to him that he's a leading goalscorer,' said David Moyes of Yakubu, who had found the net five times in his last three league games. 'He scores goals, he gets in the right position and his play has been really good – he's linking the team up and his work-rate is excellent. We think we've got good players, a great football club, and we're trying to make strides in the Premier League.' (BBC Sport, 2007.)

With a game every three to four days throughout the month of December 2007, the packed domestic and European schedule tested the depth and resolve of David Moyes's squad. Having already secured top spot in Group A and qualification to the round of 32, the Blues travelled to the Netherlands to take on an AZ side in possession of a formidable European record on their home turf. Unbeaten at their DSB Stadion home in 32 consecutive European games, surpassing Ipswich Town's record of 31 with a 1-0 victory over Larissa on 29 November, the Eredivisie side had never lost a European tie at home.

With AZ needing a victory to qualify from the group, the Dutch side will have no doubt felt confident prior to kick-off, especially as David Moyes had left a number of key players at home in preparation for the visit of Manchester United to Goodison Park three days later, including Tim Cahill, Mikel Arteta, Tim Howard, Leighton Baines, Phil Neville and Yakubu.

The line-ups at the DBS Stadion on 20 December were as follows:

AZ: Waterman, Jaliens, Opdam, Pocognoli, Mendes Da Silva, Cziommer, Dembele, De Zeeuw, Steinsson, Vormer, Pelle

Everton: Wessels, Hibbert, Jagielka, Lescott, Valente, Pienaar, Gravesen, Carsley, McFadden, Anichebe, Johnson

Alongside the unfamiliar line-up, Moyes sought to experiment with his formation, with James McFadden operating as a number ten, just behind the front two of Anichebe and Johnson, with Tony Hibbert protecting the back four in a diamond. Despite the unconventional shape, Everton made a perfect start, with Andy Johnson firing the Blues in front inside two minutes. Future Southampton forward Graziano Pelle netted 15 minutes later to level the tie, before Phil Jagielka made it 2-1 to Everton on the stroke of half-time, the defender's first goal for the club.

I'm sure if you ask anyone who was in attendance at the DBS Stadion that evening, they will tell you in no uncertain terms that it was the coldest game they have ever been to.

Half-time seemed to take an age to pass, as I began to lose all feeling in my hands and feet. To keep warm, the thousands of Evertonians stacked into the away end began to jump up and down in unison, singing, 'I've never felt more like singing the Blues, when Everton win and Liverpool lose. Oh Everton, you've got me singing the Blues.' Verse after verse of this song was sung, as Liverpool had indeed lost the previous evening, a 2-0 defeat to Chelsea in the fifth round of the League Cup. It was a fantastic atmosphere, and no doubt saved many of us from potentially losing a foot to frostbite.

Needing a win, AZ threw everything at Everton, and on 65 minutes Kew Jaliens rose at the far post to head home an inswinging corner from substitute Julian Jenner. At 2-2, AZ continued to push for the win that they required to qualify, but an Everton counter-attack on 79 minutes scuppered their hopes of progression, with youngster James Vaughan's effort trickling past keeper Boy Waterman and over the line. With ten minutes to go, a 16-year-old Jack Rodwell made his Everton debut, replacing Thomas Gravesen, to see out an impressive 3-2 victory in the Netherlands.

'I didn't want to mention it [AZ's impressive European home record] to the players,' Moyes told BBC Sport at full time. 'They all performed really well against a good AZ side. I think we're getting stronger as we go along. We've not won anything but that takes time. We've got players in good form, but they have to keep their form up because they've seen tonight there are players pushing to come into the team.'

Most satisfying perhaps was the apparent competition for places within the squad, a luxury Moyes often lacked at Everton. Indeed, academy graduates Victor Anichebe and James Vaughan began to offer competition to the first team options of Andy Johnson and Yakubu, with match-winner Vaughan stating, 'The performance from the lads was excellent as usual. Everyone gave 100 per cent. We've left a lot of quality players at home. You just want to take your chance when you get the opportunity and that's what I've tried to do.' (Gaunt, *The Guardian*, 2007.)

Maintaining a 100 per cent record in Group A, Everton became the first side to beat AZ at their DBS Stadion home in Europe and qualified for the UEFA Cup round of 32 alongside Nuremberg and Zenit St Petersburg.

The final Group A table looked like this:

Team	Pld	W	D	L	GF	GA	GD	Pts
1. Everton	4	4	0	0	9	3	+6	12
2. Nuremberg	4	2	1	1	7	6	+1	7
3. Zenit	4	1	2	1	6	6	0	5
4. AZ	4	1	1	2	5	6	-1	4
5. Larissa	4	0	0	4	4	10	-6	0

17

Dreams Never End

WITH A run of 13 consecutive games unbeaten in all competitions, Everton's impressive form came to an end on 23 December 2007, as David Moyes's side fell to a 2-1 defeat to Manchester United at Old Trafford, though it took a late Cristiano Ronaldo penalty to separate the two sides. The Portuguese superstar had opened the scoring with an unstoppable drive after 22 minutes, but it took Everton just five minutes to find a response, as Tim Cahill outjumped both Patrice Evra and Nemanja Vidic to score his seventh goal of the season.

Tim Howard, who had not conceded a goal in five and a half hours of football until Ronaldo's first-half strike, was putting in a superb performance on his return to his former club, with efforts from Anderson and Carlos Tevez bringing out the best in the American international. When the former United stopper was beaten, with Wayne Rooney's improvised lob looking set to restore the hosts' lead, Joleon Lescott was on hand to clear the danger. However, with two minutes remaining, Steven Pienaar inexplicably swung a leg out to bring down Ryan Giggs, with referee Howard Webb given little choice but to point to the spot. David Moyes could be seen on the touchline with his head in his hands as Ronaldo made no mistake from 12 yards.

'We're really disappointed at the decision Steven Pienaar's made,' said a despondent Moyes at full time. 'He's been outstanding of late and was very good again today, but it really was a moment of madness. But we played well today. You're never going to come here and have it all your own way or dominate possession, but we defended well when we had to and shut them out. I won't let the players be too down. This has been a good season for us so far, we're pushing forwards and people are realising we should be taken seriously, so we have a lot to be positive about.' (Lyon, BBC Sport, 2007.)

A 2-0 Boxing Day victory over Bolton Wanderers at Goodison Park ensured the Blues got back to winning ways, with second-half goals from Phil Neville and Tim Cahill, and despite a 4-1 humbling at home to Arsenal on 29 December, Everton started the New Year in sixth place in the Premier League, just four points off fourth spot. Meanwhile, David Moyes's side had a League Cup semi-final first leg at Stamford Bridge to prepare for, with the Blues looking to reach a domestic cup final for the first time in 13 years.

'A cup final appearance is long overdue,' admitted Everton legend Graeme Sharp. 'And the signs under David Moyes and this squad are that one might not be too far away, but there is still a lot of hard work to do. I think maybe people got carried away with the start of the season we've had.'

Sharp continued, '[The] Oldham [defeat in the FA Cup] was a blow to them but it might bring people back to reality. There is still a long way to go. People have drawn comparisons to the mid-80s side that I was involved in but there is still a long, long way to go before those comparisons are valid.' (*The Guardian*, 2008.)

Indeed, rapid progress had been made in the little over five years since David Moyes had taken charge at Everton, but a piece of silverware would redefine the club from one with potential, to one of genuine accomplishment. Without question, the squad had developed considerably and a now expectant fanbase could sense their club just might be on the cusp of something. As Moyes explained, Everton's demanding schedule, balancing domestic and European responsibilities, was generating a squad filled with confidence.

'Games – I think it's as straightforward as that. Players improve the more games they have, and the more demanding games the better. We have always had a pretty good record at Goodison Park but some important away wins and a good European run have given the players a lot more confidence. We have a bigger squad now and it is a challenge to get into this team, but the size of the squad is still one where everyone feels involved and has to be involved.' (*The Guardian*, 2008.)

The line-ups at Stamford Bridge for the League Cup semi-final first leg on Wednesday, 9 January 2008, were as follows:

Chelsea: Hilario, Belletti, Alex, Carvalho, Bridge, Wright-Phillips, Mikel, Ballack, Malouda, Cole, Pizarro

Everton: Howard, Hibbert, Yobo, Jagielka, Lescott, Cahill, Neville, Carsley, McFadden, Johnson, Yakubu

Sitting at the back of Chelsea's Shed End was a bit like watching a game through a letterbox, but an energised support had travelled with a cautious optimism, as belief permeated the fanbase that the club's first 21st-century trophy was just around the corner. However, despite the momentum of the crowd, Chelsea took a deserved lead courtesy of Shaun Wright-Phillips after 26 minutes, as Everton allowed the expensively assembled opposition far too much time and space on the ball.

A John Obi Mikel sending-off ten minutes after the restart afforded Everton a renewed impetus and they levelled soon after as Yakubu emphatically hammered home from a James McFadden free kick. Suddenly, David Moyes's side looked more likely to steal a winner, with McFadden involved once more, the Scot hitting the post from a tight angle. Dominating the last quarter of the game, Evertonians could have been forgiven for being disappointed at only walking away with a draw, but a disastrous Joleon Lescott own goal in the final moments ensured a deflated return to Merseyside. A second-half Joe Cole strike in the return fixture a fortnight later ended hopes of a cup final, as the gulf between Moyes's ambitious Everton and the modern elite was brought into sharp focus.

Recovering from the League Cup semi-final defeat was a real test of character for David Moyes's side, with such a disappointment no doubt having the potential to derail an otherwise promising campaign. However, after swiftly dispensing with the UEFA Cup round of 32 opposition, SK Brann of Norway, with Everton securing an aggregate victory of 8-1 (2-0 away, 6-1 at home), the Blues could start to dream of European glory.

'It was a professional job and we put out a strong team,' Moyes told BBC Sport after the 6-1 demolition. 'We couldn't take any chances. We didn't play particularly well [in the first half hour] so you have to give them credit. In the end the finishing quality got us the result. The first goal was crucial, no matter who got it.'

Indeed, the 6-1 drubbing of SK Brann was Everton's biggest European win, and the seventh consecutive UEFA Cup victory, with hat-trick hero Yakubu no doubt the man of the match. Next up for Moyes's side was a round of 16 tie against Italian outfit Fiorentina, who'd also beaten Norwegian opposition with a 3-1 aggregate victory over Rosenborg, and the Everton coach expressed his belief that his team were up for the task ahead of them in Italy.

'I'm really excited by the challenge and am confident in the way we are playing,' said the Blues boss. 'I am wary of how well Fiorentina have been playing. Like us they are an up-and-coming side. They play with a decent tempo that is demanded by their coach. But our defending has been very good this season and they will be put to the test by Fiorentina and hopefully they will come through fine. This is the sort of level we want to play at, against a team in Fiorentina with a great reputation, and in Europe as well, although they have had their ups and downs in recent years.' (Hunter, *The Guardian*, 2008.)

The Everton coach continued, 'This is a big test for us. I still think Zenit were the biggest test we have faced so far, and I wouldn't be surprised if they got to the final, but that was in the group game where there was a greater margin for error than there is now. We cannot afford any slip-ups now. I saw them play against Livorno and watched their [3-2] win over Juventus at the weekend, which was very impressive. The injury to [Adrian] Mutu doesn't seem to have affected them at all. They are very similar to us in many ways; a good, hard-working side who by all accounts should have qualified for the Champions League last season and are going very close this season.'

I couldn't wait to get to Florence. Growing up watching *Football Italia* on Channel 4, I spent so much of my childhood imitating the audacious goals scored by Serie A icons of the 1990s onwards, such as Francesco Totti, Alessandro Del Piero and, of course, Fiorentina legend Gabriel Batistuta. There was something almost mythical about Italian football when I was growing up. The world-class talent, the iconic kits, ultras holding up flares and tifos, Italy felt like the undisputed home of football. Unfortunately, it is also home to some of the most hostile policing I have ever witnessed at a football match, with a liberal use of rough handling and dangerous levels of kettling prior to kick-off.

The line-ups at the Stadio Artemio Franchi on Thursday, 6 March were as follows:

Fiorentina: Frey, Ujfalusi, Gamberini, Dainelli, Pasqual, Kuzmanovic, Donadel, Montolivo, Jorgensen, Vieri, Osvaldo

Everton: Howard, Hibbert, Yobo, Jagielka, Lescott, Osman, Neville, Carsley, Pienaar, Cahill, Yakubu

'I am worried,' said Fiorentina manager Cesare Prandelli in his pre-match comments. 'This is a real team who will make us suffer a lot. We will be against one of the best teams in Europe. I am very curious to see how we fare. This game is going to be very difficult.' (Widdicombe, *The Guardian*, 2008.)

The Italian coach needn't have worried, as a nervous-looking Everton arrived in Florence and struggled to threaten Sebastian Frey's goal with any kind of meaningful attack. Falling to two late second-half goals from Zdravko Kuzmanovic and Riccardo Montolivo, Everton's pedestrian attack lacked the cutting edge to find a response, succumbing to a 2-0 defeat. Failing to find the net for the first occasion on their 2007/08 European tour, Everton had left themselves with a mountain to climb in the second leg. However, the result notwithstanding, the abject performance was perhaps most disappointing of all, as the confidence and swagger that had been such a joy to watch throughout the campaign was left at home, in its place a feeling that a real chance of European silverware had just slipped from our grasp.

'Some of our players didn't play to their potential tonight,' Moyes said at full time. 'In fact, the majority didn't. The better team won, and the performance wasn't good. I didn't think we got to the pace of the game at any time. That was disappointing. We never reached the levels we have done in recent months, and we have a big job ahead of us now. It will be a very big job on tonight's performance.' (Hunter, *The Guardian*, 2008.)

Indeed, it would now take a gargantuan effort from the Blues to come back from two goals down, with history not on their side. In the club's past, Everton had overturned a first-leg deficit in a cup competition only once, against Rotherham United in the 1992/93 League Cup. Progression beyond the UEFA Cup round of 16 would require a truly special night under the Goodison lights.

18

A Florentine Tragedy

RARELY HAS a fixture at Goodison Park generated as much anticipation as the round of 16 second leg against Fiorentina. With a place in the quarter-final of the UEFA Cup up for grabs and a two-goal deficit to overturn, Everton would need to be at their best both on and off the pitch, with a fortress-like atmosphere a must. Indeed, it was a sentiment shared by Everton boss David Moyes.

'We know there will be lots of stoppages,' he said. 'That's what happens when you play in Europe. But we know that our crowd can make a really big difference. I felt last week that the Fiorentina fans had an influence on the result … we would hope that our supporters can do the same for us. It's important not to concede and that's why we've talked about patience. There has to be an air of patience. It can't be all trumpets blazing and we have to try to play a bit more cleverly – we play that way now anyway. We've also scored a lot of goals at Goodison and if we get flowing and moving the way we can do, there's no reason why we can't score two goals.'

Moyes added, 'We've got great momentum and we've had that all season. The longer we keep that going the better, and I hope we can get that tempo to the game, and it isn't stopped and started, which I've got a little bit of fear about. We are going to need a strong referee, a good referee and if we get that hopefully we can turn it around. I think we saw that in the first game; it was very difficult to make any contact whatsoever and also, I have got to say the Italians are extremely clever, so

119

we have to understand that it is part of their game. Many of the games we have played in Europe we have won late on, and after 70 minutes last week it looked as if we had weathered the storm, even though we had not played well. I can't deny that Fiorentina deserved to win but the tie is not lost by any means.' (Chase, *The Guardian*, 2008.)

Everton had a lot in common with their Florentine visitors. Having recovered from financial turmoil, both sides had exceeded expectations in recent years, as relegation battles gave way to European nights and opportunities to win silverware. Both sides had passionate and loyal backing, proud of their heritage though impatient for the return of the glory days as rejuvenated squads finally provided hope to the long-suffering match-goers. Indeed, David Moyes was eager to repay Everton's dedicated following, particularly in light of their mistreatment by the Italian authorities.

'Our fans have been terrific in all our games in Europe. In the main they have been treated very well but I was disappointed at what happened it Italy. They tend to put away supporters in a pen in the corner. It is hardly worth paying money if that is what you get. Maybe that is why there are so many empty stadiums in Italy. I thought our fans were treated quite shabbily and hopefully we can give them something to shout about. If we could overhaul a two-goal deficit, it would rate as one of my biggest achievements. This is the best team that I've had.'

Moyes continued, 'We are on a learning curve here and I think we have found we have improved in Europe, and we understand it more. We are getting closer to competing more regularly with the teams at the top. I know we still have to beat them more often, and this is a big test. We've had great momentum all season and the longer we can keep that momentum going the better – hopefully all the way through to May.'

The Everton boss was equally keen to stress the importance of Mikel Arteta's return to the fold, following a groin injury that had seen the Spanish midfielder sidelined. 'He is an influential player who can make a difference in games, and I think we need him,' Moyes stated. 'Hopefully, the 90 minutes he got at Sunderland [three days prior] will help him, and there's no reaction. We need goals, but there has to be an air of patience, too. We will have to play cleverly and not go in all guns blazing. In all the games I've watched, and I have seen Fiorentina a lot, they don't concede many goals or many chances. It's difficult to get sustained periods of pressure against them.' (Prentice, *Liverpool Echo*, 2008.)

In front of 38,026 spectators at Goodison Park on Wednesday, 12 March, the line-ups were as follows:

Everton: Howard, Neville, Yobo, Jagielka, Lescott, Pienaar, Arteta, Carsley, Osman, Johnson, Yakubu

Fiorentina: Frey, Ujfalusi, Dainelli, Gamberini, Pasqual, Kuzmanovic, Donadel, Montolivo, Jorgensen, Osvaldo, Vieri

Other than the notable absentee Tim Cahill, who was unavailable with a foot injury, David Moyes had his best XI available, and in complete contrast to the nervous display in Florence, Everton played with a vibrant urgency that suited the impassioned Goodison crowd. Incessant Everton pressure visibly unsettled the visitors and after 16 minutes the Blues found a deserved breakthrough, with Sebastian Frey misreading Steven Pienaar's superb cross, allowing Andy Johnson to bundle the ball home with his chin.

Goodison's noise levels went up a decibel, as belief that the two-goal deficit could be overturned began to seep into the very foundations of the grand old stadium. Moyes's players too believed that a goal to level the aggregate scoreline was imminent, and had Frey not redeemed himself for his earlier error, Everton could have had the game wrapped up before half-time. A string of top class saves from the Frenchman denied Arteta, Yakubu, Johnson and Osman, and though the first half failed to yield a second goal for Everton, the indefatigable performance ensured that confidence was high at the interval.

The Blues had little choice but to approach the second period in a similar manner, with 45 minutes on the clock to rescue the tie. With pressure on Frey's goal continuing immediately after the break, fortune favoured Fiorentina as Phil Jagielka's goalbound header struck an unwitting defender on the line, bouncing away to safety. Without doubt one of the most exciting albeit torturous Goodison Park performances that I have witnessed, the noise inside the stadium was so deafening it could be felt in your teeth.

On 67 minutes, the atmosphere reached a level the likes of which I had never seen, as a stunning Mikel Arteta drive finally breached Frey's defiant resolve. Picking the ball up in his own half, the influential midfielder surged forward and, as La Viola's defence retreated in unison, unleashed a 25-yard drive that nestled into the bottom corner of the Gwladys Street's goal.

Certain moments stay with us as football fans and can be recalled with such clarity, it is as if the events occurred yesterday. No doubt like many of those in attendance at Goodison Park that night, Arteta's low, angled drive into the bottom corner is one of those moments for me. I can remember urging the Spaniard to shoot, and that split second between the ball leaving his right boot, and Goodison's euphoric celebrations reaching fever pitch. It seemed that Arteta had recovered from his persistent ailments at just the right time, and with just over 20 minutes remaining, there was still time for the Blues to cap the comeback with a winning goal.

The introduction of Giampaolo Pazzini, the first player to score at the reconstructed Wembley Stadium, for the veteran Christian Vieri, introduced pace to the previously muted Fiorentina attack. Indeed, in the absence of former Chelsea forward Adrian Mutu, who would end the 2007/08 campaign with 24 goals, Cesare Prandelli's attacking options were limited, though a late Pazzini header almost earned La Viola an invaluable away goal, were it not for the fingertips of Tim Howard. A remarkable double save from Frey denied Yakubu the headlines, and though Everton's onslaught continued into extra time, the decisive third goal was not forthcoming. And so, to penalties.

Everton have a chequered history with penalty shoot-outs. Of the nine shoot-outs in which the club participated between 1970 and 2008, the Blues came out on top in just three of them, losing on six occasions. Furthermore, out of the four spot kicks Everton had been awarded thus far in the 2007/08 season, only one of them had been scored. With this in mind, it is fair to say that a nervous tension now enveloped Goodison, with the optimism expressed during regulation time quickly receding.

Substitute Thomas Gravesen immediately alleviated some of that tension by hammering home the first spot kick of the evening, but Pazzini kept a cool head to level. The Yak was next up for Everton, but the Nigerian forward could only watch on as his penalty hit the inside of the post and bounced out, before Riccardo Montolivo, goalscorer from the first leg, put the Italians 2-1 up. Mikel Arteta levelled with a confident chip, but Dani Osvaldo restored Fiorentina's lead with a professional effort from 12 yards. A Frey hand denied Phil Jagielka, the French keeper adding yet another save to his countless tally for the evening before Mario Santana stepped up to send Tim Howard the wrong way and Everton crashing out of Europe.

'We are deflated. We battered them,' said a gutted-looking Moyes. 'It came down to missed opportunities in the 90 minutes but that was some effort. We should have had a third in normal time, although their keeper made some excellent saves, and we missed a few. It is a travesty we haven't gone through on that performance, but you have to say they performed better than us in Florence.' (Hunter, *The Guardian*, 2008.)

Rarely in my match-going experience has ecstasy so swiftly descended into agony. The unbridled joy of Mikel Arteta's thunderous equaliser, to desolation in the wake of Mario Alberto Santana's match-winning penalty for Fiorentina. I don't think I have ever heard Goodison fall so despairingly silent and as I stood in the Lower Gwladys, I felt a reluctance to leave the stadium, almost overwhelmed by the first of the five stages of grief: denial.

The 2007/08 campaign is without question my personal favourite of the 24 years I have been following Everton. Between September 2007 and March 2008, I travelled to five different countries with my dad and had the time of my life as a teenager, and though the season ended in disappointment, Everton had a team that we were willing to get behind. Evertonians and optimism don't usually go hand in hand, with pessimism a much more common bedfellow amongst a fanbase accustomed to heartbreak. However, there was a real and fervent belief that the club was moving in the right direction, and that David Moyes had built a squad that would finally end the wait for silverware.

The defeat to Fiorentina no doubt knocked Everton's Premier League campaign off course, as Moyes's side would only win two of the last nine league games after the UEFA Cup exit. Indeed, the psychological impact of the tie cannot be underestimated, though a fifth-place finish guaranteed a return to Europe for the 2008/09 campaign, securing qualification for the UEFA Cup first round. Moreover, for the first time since Peter Beardsley scored 20 goals (in all competitions, 15 in the league) in 1991/92, Everton had a 20-plus goal-a-season striker in Yakubu, the Nigerian international finding the net on 21 occasions, falling one goal shy of his promised tally of 22. Indeed, it's the hope that kills you, as the saying goes.

The Premier League table at the end of the 2007/08 season

Team	Pld	W	D	L	GF	GA	GD	Pts
1. Man United	38	27	6	5	80	22	+58	87
2. Chelsea	38	25	10	3	65	26	+39	85
3. Arsenal	38	24	11	3	74	31	+43	83
4. Liverpool	38	21	13	4	67	28	+39	76
5. Everton	38	19	8	11	55	33	+22	65

19

The Never-Ending Derby

THE SUMMER of 2008 began with the surprise resignation of controversial chief executive Keith Wyness, the man behind the club's proposed move to a new 50,000-seater stadium in Kirkby. 'Everton wishes to announce that Keith Wyness has resigned his position as chief executive officer and director of the club,' confirmed a statement on Everton's official website. With protests from fan groups over Destination Kirkby, the club insisted that the departure of Wyness had nothing to do with the potential ground move and issued a further statement confirming their commitment to the development. Wyness was succeeded by deputy CEO Robert Elstone on an interim basis before his position was made permanent in January 2009.

Manager David Moyes, meanwhile, was keen to reiterate his commitment to the club, despite reports casting doubt over the Scot's desire to sign a proposed contract extension. However, the Blues boss was just as eager to stress the importance of summer recruitment. 'Hopefully in the next week or so I will get [the new contract] tied down and get it done. I want the best for Everton, and I do not want to let the players down. I have told them that there will be more players coming to help them along the way. I want to make sure that is done before anything else. That is more important to me just now, but it is very close.' (Bryant, *The Guardian*, 2008.)

Indeed, the Everton boss would deliver on his promise of squad investment just a few weeks later, breaking the club's record transfer fee for the third consecutive summer with the signing of 20-year-old Marouane Fellaini. Arriving at Goodison Park on a five-year deal for a reported £15 million, the highest amount paid for a Belgian footballer at the time, the midfielder, who joined from Standard Liege, admitted that Moyes's determination to secure his signature was a key factor in his decision to make the move to Goodison Park. 'When they told me the manager had come out to do the deal I couldn't believe it,' Fellaini said. 'It showed how keen Everton were to go ahead. There was interest from other clubs, but it was Everton who turned up, put their confidence in me and who decided to pay the money.'

Everton's new record signing continued, with some famous last words, 'One of the reasons I'm reasonably pleased to be leaving the Belgian league is because I had a reputation there of maybe getting stuck in a bit too much. Hopefully here, referees will let things go a little bit more.' (Hunter, *The Guardian*, 2008.)

You've got to admire Fellaini's optimism, but ten bookings in his first 17 appearances for Everton indicated that Premier League referees were not inclined to 'let things go a little bit more'. A hearing with England's chief referee Keith Hackett ensured a lengthy suspension was avoided, after the Belgian vowed to improve his behaviour. Fellaini would pick up a further three yellow cards throughout the season, ending the campaign as the Premier League's most booked player.

David Moyes would return to Belgium a matter of weeks after his trip to sign Fellaini, only this time he returned empty-handed as Everton crashed out of the UEFA Cup first round to Fellaini's former club, Standard Liege. A 2-2 draw at Goodison Park on 17 September meant the Blues had to get a result at the Stade Maurice Dufrasne a fortnight later, but a 2-1 defeat sent Everton crashing out of Europe, with a 4-3 aggregate scoreline for Liege. The European exit compounded what had been a disastrous week for Everton, having already been knocked out of the League Cup courtesy of a 1-0 defeat at Ewood Park, followed by a 2-0 loss in the Merseyside derby at Goodison three days later.

Out of the two cups that had offered such promise the previous year, alongside a pedestrian derby display, the opening seven weeks of the 2008/09 season could scarcely have gone worse for Moyes's side, and with just two league wins out of the opening nine games, optimism was an understandable absentee around Goodison Park. Despite the lacklustre start to the campaign, however, any uncertainty surrounding Moyes's future ended with the signing of a new five-year deal with the club, more than doubling his weekly salary from £30,000 to £65,000 in a package worth an overall £16.9 million.

With his previous contract set to expire in the summer of 2009, the Scot committed himself to Goodison Park until 2013, becoming the highest-paid employee in the club's history. 'There have been many different things for different reasons, but we are here now and the biggest thing for me is I'm at Everton, as far as I'm concerned, for another five years,' Moyes told *The Guardian*. 'The job is to make us better than we have been. I am really excited and really pleased, for everyone. I'm pleased for myself and my family, who were desperate to get it signed and secured. It's what I always wanted to do.'

The Everton boss continued, 'I have enjoyed my time here so far and I am looking forward to the next part as well. There is definitely a consistency at the club. Players know what they're doing, staff know what they're doing. It's a great football club and I am privileged to be the manager. Since I took over six years ago, I think there has been an improvement and the job now is to see more of it over the next five years or so. I want the ambition to be greater, I want the expectancy to be higher – that's on and off the field. I am determined to try and take it forward.'

Meanwhile, new signing Marouane Fellaini continued his notable impact since his summer arrival, his 90th-minute winner at Bolton's Reebok Stadium sparking an upturn in form as October drew to a close. Fellow new boy Louis Saha also got off the mark, with three goals in two games to seal wins over Fulham and West Ham, with all three strikes coming in the 85th minute or later. A 1-1 draw at home to Manchester

United on 25 October saw the Blues come from behind to rescue a point at Goodison Park, with Fellaini on hand to cancel out Darren Fletcher's opener. Phil Neville provided Fellaini with the all-important assist that afternoon, though it was a crunching tackle on Cristiano Ronaldo for which Neville's contribution is perhaps remembered most, and it was a moment that the Everton captain considered to be a turning point in his Goodison Park career.

Discussing his time at the club in a 2013 interview with *The Guardian*, Neville recalled, 'He [David Moyes] made me captain after a month ... I really didn't want the captaincy and for 18 months it was really difficult ... There was a lot of scepticism from the other players ... They had some brilliant characters in that team – [Alan] Stubbs, [Lee] Carsley, [Thomas] Gravesen, [Alessandro] Pistone and many others – and the boss had put all that faith in me. David Moyes, from day one, wanted me to lead that team every single day. He wanted me to set a level of professionalism and a standard that the rest would follow. And he would never let me fall beneath those standards. He challenged me every day. There would be days when I might think, "I feel a bit tired today," but the minute he came on the training field I knew he wanted me to be at the front of the running, to be the most intense, to lead the others.

'I was replacing a great guy in David Weir ... but it did take the others longer to accept me. The fans too, maybe ... Everyone knew I was a United fan. Liverpool supporters used to sing: "Your captain's a Manc" ... I don't think I was properly accepted until I made that tackle on [Cristiano] Ronaldo [in the match v Manchester United at Goodison Park in October 2008].'

Neville explained, 'It's a great club, Everton. You don't just go there to work; you have to be part of the family. And, until then, I wasn't part of the family. I was like a stepson. I made that tackle, and I became a son.

'I didn't win a trophy with Everton, but that time is just as special as my playing career at United.'

A youthful-looking David Moyes

Rhino gets the Moyes era off to a flying start

Remember the name…

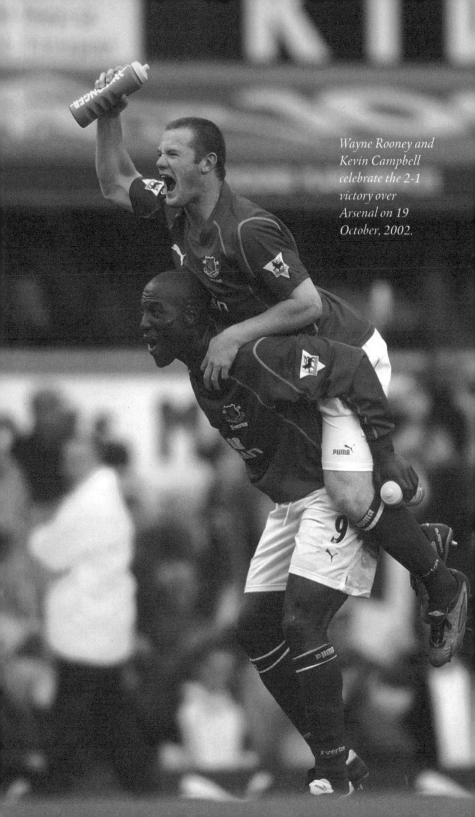

Wayne Rooney and Kevin Campbell celebrate the 2-1 victory over Arsenal on 19 October, 2002.

Wayne Rooney celebrates his emphatic Elland Road winner on 3 November 2002.

Duncan Ferguson throttles Leicester City's Steffen Freund on 20 March 2004.

Duncan Ferguson flattens Sami Hyypia in the Merseyside derby on 11 December 2004.

Everton players pile on Lee Carsley following his Merseyside derby goal at Goodison Park on 11 December 2004.

Duncan Ferguson's disallowed goal against Villarreal, 24 August 2005

Pierluigi Collina, the villain of Villarreal

Tim Cahill celebrating a goal against Aston Villa in March 2006 with his iconic celebration.

Andy Johnson celebrating Everton's 3-0 Merseyside derby victory at Goodison Park, 9 September 2006.

Mikel Arteta's rocket levels the aggregate scoreline against Fiorentina.

Penalty heartbreak against Fiorentina at Goodison Park.

Dan Gosling celebrates his late derby day winner.

Phil Jagielka's winning penalty sends Everton to the FA Cup Final

Everton players celebrate the FA Cup semi-final win over Manchester United

(Left) Louis Saha opens the scoring in the 2009 FA Cup Final at Wembley after 25 seconds.

(Right) Nikica Jelavic opens the scoring against Liverpool at Wembley, 14 April 2012

Tim Cahill and Leighton Baines. My two all-time favourite Everton players

End of an era

By the New Year, a run of improved results saw Everton climb to sixth in the league ahead of the Merseyside derby at Anfield, with the Blues unbeaten in six consecutive games in all competitions. Indeed, after such a poor start to the campaign, Everton were now just six points off a Champions League spot, with keeper Tim Howard crediting Moyes's instructions to play more directly as the reason for the side's progress. 'The key for me is that we have got back to the style of play that has made us so successful in recent times,' said Howard, who'd kept six clean sheets on the spin. 'I remember playing against Everton at Goodison Park [for Manchester United] and losing, and the abiding memory was the way they got the ball upfield double quick.' (Hunter, *The Guardian*, 2009.)

The American international continued, 'We went into the season trying to play a little bit more than we needed to. We were taking risks we wouldn't normally do. We had to get back to basics – smash people in the mouth, get the ball upfield and let the creative guys get it down and play. Liverpool are not easily ruffled, but we will play to our strengths and see if we can't at least put them to the test.'

Indeed, it would be a Merseyside derby double-header, with two trips to Anfield in less than a week for Moyes's Everton, as the two sides were set to meet in the FA Cup fourth round just six days after their Premier League showdown. It had all the hallmarks of a week from hell, though Everton were due a win across the park, as was manager David Moyes, who had yet to do so since his 2002 arrival. Liverpool went into the Premier League encounter as league leaders, though Everton had won five out of their last six in all competitions, as both sides had made a habit of winning over the festive period. There may be an old cliché that says form goes out of the window during the Merseyside derby, but a 1-1 draw was probably a fair reflection of the run each team was on, as Tim Cahill's late equaliser cancelled out a Steven Gerrard opener.

In the second 1-1 Merseyside derby draw in less than a week, it would be Liverpool's turn to come back from behind, with Gerrard on the scoresheet once more to cancel out Joleon Lescott's early strike. With nothing to separate the sides, a Goodison Park replay was scheduled, though Liverpool's failure to overcome Everton on two occasions at home provoked coach Rafael Benitez into reigniting the 'small club' jibe from a few years earlier. 'I am really pleased with my team. We deserved to win,' said an ungracious Benitez. 'To play like that against a team with ten players behind the ball is not easy but we worked hard, created chances and reacted very positively.' (Hunter, *The Guardian*, 2009.)

Everton had travelled to Anfield hamstrung by an absentee list which included Mikel Arteta, Marouane Fellaini, James Vaughan, Louis Saha and Yakubu, and so David Moyes's attacking options were somewhat limited, though Benitez's implicit critique of his supposedly negative tactics continued, the Spanish manager stating, '[I] never used those tactics at Valencia but sometimes I did with Extremadura.' (Hunter, *The Guardian*, 2009.)

Moyes's retort to the irreverent Benitez was equally loaded, as the Blues boss stated, 'This [Liverpool] is a great football club, but Everton do things with dignity and style. We have been here twice this week and drawn twice. I didn't come looking for a draw, although I would have taken one in the end. We look after our own business at Everton. We do things with a bit of dignity at Everton.'

No doubt Moyes enjoyed getting under the skin of his opposing manager ahead of a game so often mis-characterised as a 'friendly derby'. In the third meeting in as many weeks, the line-ups for the FA Cup replay at Goodison Park on Wednesday, 4 February were as follows:

Everton: Howard, Hibbert, Jagielka, Lescott, Baines, Osman, Fellaini, Neville, Arteta, Pienaar, Cahill

Liverpool: Reina, Dossena, Carragher, Skrtel, Arbeloa, Kuyt, Alonso, Gerrard, Lucas, Riera, Torres

Often referred to as the 'greatest ever derby', the 4-4 at Goodison Park in 1991 was a fifth round FA Cup replay after a less memorable 0-0 draw at Anfield. At the third attempt, the tie was eventually settled thanks to a Dave Watson header in a second replay giving Everton a 1-0 win. Now, with the clubs meeting in a Goodison Park FA Cup replay for the first time since, as omens go, it wasn't a bad one.

The opening exchanges gave little indication that this meeting would go on to be almost as highly regarded among Evertonians as the 1991 classic, however, as a scrappy and abrasive first half ended in stalemate. Everton had been the more positive of the two, particularly as the second half progressed, creating the first real opening of the game as Leon Osman's effort thrashed against the post. A sending-off for Liverpool's Lucas Leiva gave Everton a numerical advantage with 15 minutes remaining, but as the score remained at 0-0 after 90 minutes, the deadlock would have to be broken in a period of extra time to avoid the dreaded penalties.

Though not quite the goal-fest of 1991, the game built towards an equally tense and anxiety-inducing finale, as there was little doubt that whoever scored first would win the game. In a rare outing, the troublesome Andy van der Meyde made a substitute appearance for Everton and with just two minutes of extra time left on the clock, the Dutchman's cross landed at the feet of January signing Dan Gosling at the far post, the youngster's composed, curled effort finally settling the tie after more than 200 minutes of football.

While Goodison went into raptures celebrating Gosling's dramatic winner, those watching at home were left unaware of the scoreline, as ITV had cut for a scheduled advert break for Tic-Tacs, seconds earlier. It is understood that ITV's automated system for broadcasting adverts kicked in; a system designed for regularly scheduled programming, and incompatible with live events, particularly those with the potential for additional time. I imagine there will have been some contrasting reactions between the blue and red homes of Merseyside once the feed resumed.

'It is one of my proudest nights and there is more to come here,' David Moyes said, elated with his team's performance. 'It ranks right up there, but we will enjoy tonight and move on. To put two young boys into an FA Cup replay against Liverpool [Dan Gosling and Jack Rodwell] says a lot about them but also the team as well. We have played Liverpool three times now and done well against a very good team. That shows where the Everton players are. We have had so many injuries and we picked up more during the match. It meant we were looking around to see what we could change.'

The Everton boss continued, 'So, it was the young boys who had to come on and I did not have any worries putting the two lads on. They had the energy we needed, and it was not a worry for me to put them on. Gosling is a really good lad; he wants to learn and is a good trainer. He is a well-mannered boy who wants to improve and hopefully we can keep developing him. He can play in a few positions, and we paid £500,000 down with another £500,000 after a set number of games, that's all.' (Hunter, *The Guardian*, 2009.)

Indeed, looking back on this fixture, it is interesting that it was eventually settled by two players whose contributions during their time at Everton were minimal to say the least. Neither Andy van der Meyde nor Dan Gosling are well thought of among Evertonians, but a Merseyside derby assist or goal can make a hero out of even the most disliked player, even if only for a single night. A 3-1 victory over Aston Villa in the fifth round two weeks later, followed by a 2-1 quarter-final win over Middlesbrough meant a second domestic cup semi-final in as many years, as Everton marched with Moyes's army.

20

Jagielka's Redemption

'EVERTON WILL win a trophy soon, that is for sure,' David Moyes told *The Guardian*, confidently. 'The Champions League [qualification] would give you the higher revenue to try and add more players, which in turn would hopefully mean that you would get to more cup finals. But as a football man I feel the players at Everton will win a trophy soon and I'm looking forward to that happening.'

The Everton boss continued, 'The group we've built together is growing all of the time and as the team is growing, the performances are growing, too. I hope it is this time, but if it is not, it is going to be soon. We want to win a cup. Last season, we got to the semi-final of the League Cup, had a good run in the UEFA Cup, so we are getting better as a cup side. The pedigree is getting better. I've had to find other ways of playing this year because of the injuries and I've actually found that Everton need the football in Europe. We need it for the development of our players. We want to be doing it regularly. Manchester United have that experience. They'll be used to games like semi-finals. We are relatively new to it.'

There is little doubt that in 2009 it did indeed feel as though Everton were on the cusp of winning a trophy, and heading to London for the FA Cup semi-final, our thoughts turned to navigating our way past Manchester United. Of course, for many of those in my company as we meandered our way from pub to pub in the days before the game, seeing Everton at Wembley was not quite the novelty it was for me, and though some years may have elapsed since the national stadium was considered 'Goodison South', their recollections of a time when it was a home from home were as sharp as ever.

However, it was my first Wembley experience, and while a semi-final will never have the grandeur and occasion of a cup final, I was still overwhelmed by the prospect. Consequently, so much of the build-up is a blur to me, with sensory overload and countless bottles of Peroni inhibiting a clear recollection, though I do remember my mate accidentally setting fire to the leg of his jeans with a ciggie and taking an age to realise. As we continued our Wembley weekend, we encountered Everton everywhere, as London had seemingly become a sea of blue scarves and Fellaini wigs. Given United's southern following, I'd expected to see more of their fans, but blue was the colour and Everton the sound, as renditions of 'Tell me ma, me ma,' seemed to creep out of every pub doorway.

Though much of the media preamble was naturally United-centric, Everton boasted a passion for the occasion that our Mancunian counterparts simply couldn't match. Of course, as their success coincided with Everton's decline in the 1990s, the game no doubt meant more to Evertonians, with the first trip to Wembley since 1995 the latest marker of the club's rebirth under Moyes. Everton fans would be further buoyed by the news that Sir Alex Ferguson had decided to rest Cristiano Ronaldo, while Wayne Rooney would miss the game through injury.

The line-ups at Wembley for the FA Cup semi-final on Sunday, 19 April were as follows:

Manchester United: Foster, Rafael, Ferdinand, Vidic, Fabio, Welbeck, Gibson, Anderson, Park, Tevez, Macheda

Everton: Howard, Hibbert, Jagielka, Lescott, Baines, Osman, Neville, Fellaini, Pienaar, Cahill, Saha

There was deafening noise and expectation at kick-off and United's weakened starting XI no doubt gave us a psychological boost. However, there were few significant moments from the first half to speak of, though a rare sight of goal for Phil

Neville saw the Everton midfielder blaze his effort over the bar. Minutes after the restart, a 25-yard drive from Tim Cahill called Ben Foster into action, as Everton began to show real conviction.

United responded with efforts from Darron Gibson and Ji-Sung Park, before referee Mike Riley waved away a Danny Welbeck penalty shout as Ferguson frantically waved his arms in an appeal resembling a flightless bird attempting to take off. The introduction of Paul Scholes and Dimitar Berbatov late on added quality and experience to the United line-up, but Everton's attacking potency ensured the Blues maintained a threat up top, with Cahill forcing Foster into another save two minutes into extra time. Indeed, a miscued effort from substitute James Vaughan almost fell kindly for a persistent Cahill, but with neither side able to make a breakthrough, Everton would have to overcome their penalty shoot-out hoodoo to reach the FA Cup Final.

Tim Cahill blasting Everton's opening spot kick high over the bar didn't bode well, the Australian dropping to his knees in disbelief in front of the United end. However, a weak Berbatov effort was comfortably saved by Howard to restore Everton's hope before the ever-reliable Leighton Baines put the Blues in front. Howard's second save of the shoot-out from captain Rio Ferdinand denied United the opportunity to draw level, the ex-United stopper no doubt relishing his chance to get one over on his former club.

Another ex-red, Phil Neville, stepped up to accentuate Everton's advantage, sending Foster the wrong way. Nemanja Vidic calmly slotted past Howard before a mature spot kick and a kiss of the badge from teenager James Vaughan made it 3-1 to Everton. Anderson confidently pulled one back for United, but as long as Everton scored their next penalty, David Moyes's side would progress to the cup final.

'I don't think Phil [Jagielka] was entirely keen on taking one,' Moyes later stated. 'But he had scored in training this week and that stuck in my mind. I asked who wanted one and there were a few heads nodding. I looked at him and said, "You all right for one, Jags?" I think if he'd got his way, he might not have taken one, but I didn't have too many takers on the day.' (Hunter, *The Guardian*, 2009.)

Up stepped Jagielka, who had missed a penalty against Fiorentina in the round of 32 UEFA Cup shoot-out a little over a year earlier. Indeed, you have to respect Jags's bottle at taking his chance at redemption and with minimal fuss, the defender put his head down and his foot through the ball, sparking wild celebrations as Everton would indeed be going to Wembley, twice.

'James Vaughan went up and he's not played for four months,' Moyes said of the shoot-out. 'And Jags missed his last one against Fiorentina. There weren't many to pick from to be honest and then when Tim [Cahill] missed the first against United, who are probably the world's best at shoot-outs because they have done it so many times and won the European Cup on one, you fear the worst. But good on our goalkeeper, he made two excellent saves. It took great courage for James to go up – and Jags after what happened to him in the UEFA Cup last year. Jags has grown as a player and to take that pen shows how much he has come on in recent years.' (Hunter, *The Guardian*, 2009.)

21

Tell Me Ma

AFTER SO many years of ignominy, I couldn't stop dreaming about seeing Everton lift the FA Cup at Wembley. I, and presumably every other Evertonian, spent every waking second of the days leading up to the game picturing a winning goal, a climbing Cahill header in the dying seconds or a screaming Mikel Arteta drive. A jammy own goal would do, as long as we won. Unlike cup finals of years gone by, Everton forfeited the opportunity to venture into the music industry, deciding not to release a song to commemorate the occasion, as had been the tradition historically. Nevertheless, Evertonians only had to look to the club's 1995 collaboration with The Farm for a message that was just as relevant then as it was in 2009: 'All Together Now'.

While Everton had craved the now long-absent addition of silverware, our opposition Chelsea had been hoovering up cups, particularly in the years after Roman Abramovich's 2004 takeover. Indeed, between 1995 and 2009, Chelsea had added 11 trophies to their increasingly impressive honours list, attracting a wealth of world-class talent as they became a magnet for success. Just as in 1995, Everton would be underdogs at Wembley, a fact that Blues boss David Moyes was happy to play up to.

'It is refreshing that a club likes ours has done so well,' Moyes said in *The Guardian*. 'We are different, we might still get on EasyJet like the average man would do. We might just do that. We might just get on the bus. But in the same breath my job is to get up and feel that we can compete with the best. Our success won't be done on a chequebook, ours will be done by pretty hard graft.'

Whether or not Moyes's assertion that Everton were comparative minnows to Guus Hiddink's Chelsea was an attempt at mind games by the Scot, it is quite difficult to tell. No doubt, such a quote would play up to the 'plucky little Everton' media narrative, but I couldn't help feeling as though the club were being spoken about like a non-league side, one for whom success wouldn't be possible without Moyes's guidance. No doubt there was a clear disparity between the resources at Stamford Bridge and those at Goodison Park, but the idea that any success achieved by a Premier League side would be done so with hard work alone is quite ridiculous, as is the notion of a multi-millionaire footballer getting on a bus.

Meanwhile, when the FA finally released the ticket allocation for each side, the woefully inadequate 25,000 tickets apiece for the 90,000-seater Wembley was met with universal condemnation. 'We get 25,000, Chelsea get 25,000 and I think the FA get 40,000,' David Moyes stated. 'Something is not right when 40,000 tickets have gone to corporate people. I understand these people are the ones putting some money into it and probably helped build Wembley in the first place but it's not right for the average punter. It disappoints me when all through the season managers get questioned about not putting out their strongest team, leaving one or two players out, in FA Cup ties. The biggest disrespect has come from the FA in how many tickets they have given teams who get to the final.' (*The Guardian*, 2009.)

The Everton boss continued, 'It is a little bit hypocritical. They want us to support the competition, speak well about it, play everyone in it and then, when we get there, give the teams a limited number of tickets. There is nothing Everton can do but I feel really bad for the supporters. We could probably take three times the number of tickets we have got, and I'd love them to be there. I just hope they all get in somehow.'

Moyes was joined in his justified criticism of the measly allocation by Everton season ticket holder and the then secretary of state for culture, media and sport, Andy Burnham. 'Yes, I'm very disappointed,' Burnham said. 'At that level I don't think we are covering our season ticket holders and shareholders. I know the FA have a difficult job to do but the FA Cup Final is about the fans. It does trouble me – tickets were on the internet for £1,000 last week. If there is not a sufficient allocation, then ticket touts have a field day.' (*The Guardian*, 2009.)

As the build-up to the final continued, Jack Rodwell became the latest in a long line of injuries for the Blues, joining Mikel Arteta (knee), Yakubu (Achilles) and Victor Anichebe (knee). However, David Moyes believed that the biggest blow was losing centre-half Phil Jagielka, who ruptured an anterior knee ligament in the 2-1 defeat to Manchester City at Goodison Park. 'I think it really affected us all, we were so upset for the boy,' Moyes said in the *Liverpool Echo*. 'If anyone deserved to play in an FA Cup Final for Everton this season it was Phil Jagielka. He is going to miss out and we all feel for him. This one was slightly different from Mikel or Yak – whose injuries happened earlier on. Jags has played a big part and we are really disappointed. Football is not always fair but in this case it certainly isn't as he deserved the opportunity to play the game.'

Without doubt the biggest game of Moyes's managerial career, there was also no question of its significance to Everton Football Club. The club's first cup final of the 21st century, an opportunity to end a 14-year trophy drought and a potential catalyst for further success. 'If we are fortunate enough to win the FA Cup, it cannot stop here,' the Blues boss insisted to *The Guardian*. 'This is not the point where people say, "Thank goodness Everton have won a trophy and David Moyes has won one." The message I want to get through to everyone and the club as well is that we have to keep going.'

He continued, 'We have a definite momentum around Everton right now, a positivity that is going through the club and the team that we have to keep pushing forward. It is not easy to do ... But we are still climbing the mountain and we've not reached the top yet and I think there is more to come from the team, but we are going to have to show it at Wembley because we are facing a team of very good players.'

On his reluctance to celebrate Phil Jagielka's decisive spot kick at Wembley in the FA Cup semi-final against Manchester United, Moyes opined, 'We won on penalty kicks, and it is always difficult for the losers in that respect, so I wanted to be humble ... The congratulations took place in the dressing room ... If we beat Chelsea, then I hope you will see me in a different light.

'There is undoubtedly still a gap. Their team is [worth] something like £330 million, ours £90 million, but I think we have stepped up ... No one will be talking about the gulf between the two clubs when we cross the line, but it exists. That's why we go in as underdogs and that suits us. The pressure will be on Chelsea to perform. You cannot keep performing at the levels we have, with the consistency we have had, and not get rewarded somewhere in the end ... It would mean something very special to every Everton supporter if we could get a trophy.'

The line-ups at Wembley on Saturday, 30 May 2009, were as follows:

Chelsea: Cech, Bosingwa, Alex, Terry, Cole, Essien, Mikel, Lampard, Anelka, Drogba, Malouda

Everton: Howard, Hibbert, Yobo, Lescott, Baines, Osman, Neville, Pienaar, Cahill, Fellaini, Saha

As dream starts go, taking the lead after 25 seconds, with the fastest goal in FA Cup Final history, wasn't a bad one. So fast was the goal, no doubt many fans missed it, but Everton had waited 14 years to taste cup final glory, and clearly couldn't wait a moment longer to bring an end to the burdensome trophy drought which grew in significance with each passing year. With 89 minutes and 35 seconds left to play, a clean sheet would end that wait.

Despite the hype and excitement of the build-up, cup finals are often tense, cagey affairs with each side reluctant to show their hand in the early stages. Not so in 2009, with Moyes's side launching an attack straight from the off. A half-cleared Steven Pienaar cross fell kindly for Louis Saha to write his name into the history books with a superb strike. The Everton end lost itself in a frenzy of delirious celebrations to a chorus of 'We shall not be moved'. This wasn't just a great start; it was the best start in the history of the competition.

Indeed, Everton's early assault appeared to rattle Guus Hiddink's side in the opening minutes, though the complexion of the game soon changed as Chelsea settled, with Tony Hibbert earning himself a booking after just eight minutes for clipping Florent Malouda's heels. The Everton right-back continued to be left exposed and outpaced by Chelsea's width, as they quickly developed a rhythm. Taking advantage of space in behind, Frank Lampard's cross was met powerfully by Didier Drogba, the Ivorian outjumping an earthbound Joleon Lescott to level the tie after 21 minutes.

All square at the interval, David Moyes attempted to wrestle back the initiative in the second half, moving Tim Cahill higher up the pitch to support an isolated Saha, the Frenchman inches away from doubling his tally as his header from a Leighton Baines free kick came agonisingly close. The introduction of the industrious Michael Ballack on the hour mark exemplified the depth in Chelsea's squad, the German international taking a little over ten minutes to influence the game's outcome, his pass finding Frank Lampard whose rising effort got the better of Tim Howard, despite the American getting fingertips to the ball.

Chelsea scored a third soon after, though as Florent Malouda's drive bounced off the bar and over the line, those officiating the game failed to notice it, so Everton got away with one. Malouda's ghost goal bore little relevance to the eventual outcome, however, as Everton failed to capitalise on the moment of good fortune and the first opportunity of silverware in 14 years passed us by. It was a heart-breaking afternoon, paralleled only for me by the penalty shoot-out defeat to Fiorentina.

Naturally, we didn't stick around too long after the final whistle, and seemingly neither did all of Chelsea's following. Making our way to Wembley Park tube station, I overheard a conversation between two Chelsea fans regarding the 2008 financial crisis negatively affecting their investments. They weren't real fans, of course. It had been a day out to them, and their apparent lack of interest in seeing their team lift the cup infuriated me, so desperate was I to see mine do so. Maybe the FA Cup didn't retain its once glamorous prestige, or perhaps Chelsea were by now so accustomed to success that a cup final win no longer meant as much. Whatever it was, I couldn't begin to relate to their complacent attitude.

David Moyes too was left dejected after the final whistle, and when his post-match interview was interrupted by a mobile phone ringing in the audience, the cruel irony of the ringtone was not lost on him. Identifying the music instantly, 'Mission Impossible. Aye, that'll be right,' stated the Everton boss, as another opportunity to break modern football's glass ceiling passed him by.

'The team is still growing,' Moyes offered. 'The team is young and hungry enough to keep going but it will be hard because there's a lot of clubs wanting the best ... but we should all be hoping that somebody does break into that top four because that might alter the whole dynamic of football. If it's going to keep being money, money, money we all know something is going to go wrong in the future. But football goes in cycles. Teams are at the top at different times. I think Everton's cycle is a lot closer to coming around again. Everton had great teams in the 1980s and I think we're getting much closer to that.'

He continued, 'There's only two or three bigger clubs in England. Because we compete with someone who has more money, does that mean they're bigger? Not really. It might give you more scope, but it doesn't make you bigger. Everton are a great football club ... Last summer we didn't have the finances until late on. I'd like to get the money a bit earlier this time and do some deals earlier. It hurts me that we haven't won any silverware, but we'll keep going. After the game I felt as though we are not far away from them. We were beaten by the better team, but we weren't that far away. I have to take heart from that.' (Hunter, *The Guardian*, 2009.)

Captain Phil Neville was just as quick to take what positives he could from the game, stating that Moyes would have, 'learned more in defeat than he has all season, and we need to get better ... When I went up those steps, I felt empty. It was probably the worst feeling of my career. You feel as though you let everyone down, your family, friends, everyone. I saw my kids at the end, and I felt a failure. We have to use these feelings as a spur for next time.'

Indeed, Neville wasn't alone in feeling empty at full time. When Louis Saha scored so early in the game, even the most sedate fans lost themselves in a moment of unbridled joy, as belief momentarily enveloped an ignited Everton end only for it to be extinguished in predictably cruel fashion. Now, 14 years later, it is still the closest we have come to ending what is now the longest trophy drought in the club's history, underscoring the significance of the 2009 cup final defeat.

The Premier League table at the end of the 2008/09 season

Team	Pld	W	D	L	GF	GA	GD	Pts
1. Man United	38	28	6	4	68	24	+44	90
2. Liverpool	38	25	11	2	77	27	+50	86
3. Chelsea	38	25	8	5	68	24	+44	83
4. Arsenal	38	20	12	6	68	37	+31	72
5. Everton	38	17	12	9	55	37	+18	63

22

European Tour Part II

THOUGH THE 2008/09 season ultimately ended in cup final disappointment, a second fifth-place Premier League finish on the bounce guaranteed European football at Goodison Park once more, with Everton entering the Europa League (formerly known as the UEFA Cup). A comfortable 4-0 home win followed by a 1-1 draw away at Czech outfit Sigma Olomouc guaranteed qualification to the group stage, where Everton would be drawn with Greek side AEK Athens, BATE Borisov of Belarus and Portuguese giants Benfica. In an updated format since the club's last venture into the group stage of the competition, Everton would play each side twice, with the top two teams qualifying for the round of 32.

Meanwhile, with three defeats out of the opening four Premier League fixtures of the 2009/10 season, Everton looked to be suffering a post-cup-final hangover. Starting the campaign with a 6-1 humiliation to Arsenal, Everton suffered the worst opening day result in the club's history, and the heaviest home defeat since 1958, when Arsenal had inflicted an identical scoreline. Indeed, the mood around Goodison Park was sour from the off, as the announcement of Joleon Lescott's name by the club PA prior to kick-off was met with boos from sections of the crowd, as the wantaway defender had reportedly asked not to feature following interest from Manchester City. The England international would make the switch to Eastlands ten days later for a fee of £22 million.

Following the opening-day defeat, Moyes stated, 'I don't think there's much point in me shouting and bawling about that. I think they know all round that it just wasn't acceptable. There was a manager sacked for seven after one game so I'm not immune to that either. I'm the same. We've lost [by] six so it's no different for me than it is for any other manager. I'll need to pull my socks up and try and do better with the players that I have got. It's my responsibility to make sure those players do perform on the pitch, and they didn't perform so I take that responsibility.' (Hunter, *The Guardian*, 2009.)

The visit of AEK Athens to Goodison Park provided a much-needed distraction from Everton's Premier League woes, as Moyes's side opened their Europa League Group I account with a 4-0 dismantling of the Greek opposition. The victory saw Moyes equal Harry Catterick's record of 11 European wins, as goals from Joseph Yobo and Steven Pienaar, as well as new signing Sylvain Distin and Brazilian forward Jo, on loan from Manchester City, ensured the Blues started the campaign in convincing style.

Debutant Diniyar Bilyaletdinov, who signed in the summer from Lokomotiv Moscow for a fee believed to be in the region of £9 million, put in a display rich with promise, involved as he was with three out of the four Everton goals. Indeed, the quality of his left foot prompted Blues boss David Moyes to liken him, perhaps optimistically, to Goodison great Kevin Sheedy. 'He enjoyed it and I think the supporters enjoyed him as well,' the Scot said. 'There were encouraging signs that he is going to be a very good player. Evertonians know more about Kevin Sheedy than I do but he passes the ball nicely and passes it well. He is a modern-type player and keen to learn.' (Hunter, *The Guardian*, 2009.)

A Louis Saha sending-off blemished an otherwise therapeutic evening at Goodison, and with six referees present for UEFA's controversial Europa League experiment of increased match officials placed behind each goal, David Moyes criticised Polish referee Robert Malek, and his five colleagues, telling *The Guardian*, 'It is amazing they see the small arm but not the big kick with all the officials they've got now. They are there to help the referee and if he was helped in the Louis Saha incident, then they got it wrong.'

Despite being beset with injuries, Everton came from a goal down in Minsk to win 2-1 at BATE Borisov to make it two wins out of two in Group I, as Tim Cahill celebrated his second-half winner with a tribute to his Samoan heritage following the recent tsunami which had hit the Pacific islands. 'Me and my family are from Samoa,' Everton's match-winner said at full time. 'I've got a lot of family there that got caught in the tsunami, and it's just sad. [The celebration] was a little bit of a tribute, there are a lot of people going through a hard time at the moment, not just in Samoa but in Asia [Indonesia was hit with an earthquake in the same week]. I go every year to Samoa and it's hard to take, seeing family and other people where I'm from suffering like that. I just felt in my heart it was the right thing to do.' (*Daily Mirror*, 2009.)

Having travelled without the injured Phil Neville and Phil Jagielka, a thigh injury to Joseph Yobo forced Moyes to field an unorthodox back four in Belarus, with Tony Hibbert playing at centre-half and Dan Gosling filling in at right-back, though the Everton boss was full of praise for his makeshift backline. 'I thought Tony epitomised everything about Everton Football Club tonight,' he said. 'He never complained, though he was playing in a position unfamiliar to him. He did terrific and we came away with a great result. Dan Gosling, too, came in and did well at right-back. We were missing a few senior players and it's great credit to the ones who've got the result. It was probably coming from behind which pleased me as much as anything. Tim Cahill is always a threat in those kinds of situations but he has probably not scored as many goals as he should have done recently.' (Gaunt, *The Guardian*, 2009.)

Steven Pienaar was another notable absentee for Everton's trip to Minsk, the South African international picking up a knee injury in the 1-0 victory over Portsmouth a few days prior, as Moyes's injury worries deepened. 'There's no timescale at the moment but hopefully it will only be something short term,' said club physiotherapist Mick Rathbone. 'Steven took an almighty knock on the inside of the knee, so he's pretty sore. There's a lot of bruising and a lot of swelling around the area, so we've got him on crutches at the moment.' (*The Guardian*, 2009.)

By the end of November, Everton had won just four out of their opening 14 Premier League fixtures, as a 2-0 home defeat to Liverpool left the Blues in 16th place, with a precipitously steep climb up the table already required to better or equal the club's recent top-five finishes. Injuries had ravaged Moyes's squad, and a 5-0 hiding at Benfica ended the unbeaten Europa League run, as the club suffered its heaviest defeat in a European game.

'I would like to play Benfica with my best team,' Moyes remarked, wistfully, to *The Guardian*. 'I have only praise for the players who were out there because they all did their best in difficult circumstances. It is important to remember those lads who came in gave their all. There was no lack of enthusiasm or drive, but they were up against one or two serious players. I don't see why it should have a detrimental effect on any of them because it will give them an idea of what is required to play at the top level.'

With Everton having travelled to Lisbon without ten first-team players, with Leighton Baines the latest addition to the absentee list, Benfica's attack ran rampant, orchestrated by Angel Di Maria as the Argentine matched up against out-of-position debutant Seamus Coleman, who'd joined from Sligo Rovers in January 2009 for a fee of just £60,000. As the young Irishman filled in at left-back, Dan Gosling played at right-back with Tony Hibbert and Sylvain Distin the centre-back partnership in Moyes's makeshift backline. Despite the fact so many first-teamers were missing for the trip to the Portuguese capital, the Blues still took a 7,000-strong following to the Estadio da Luz.

Benfica legend Eusébio was present for his former club's Bonfire Night visit to Goodison Park in the second-leg fixture, making a return to the stadium in which he famously scored six goals at the 1966 FIFA World Cup. Of course, those who know their history will be aware that he should have had the opportunity to grace the Goodison turf on one further occasion, for the semi-final against England, before the FA switched the venue to Wembley at the last minute in a move typical of a London-centric Football Association.

A 2-0 victory for the visitors meant Everton were without a win in seven games in all competitions.

'We have tough games coming up and we knew the group was never going to be easy and it will prove that way, I'm sure. I think Benfica are a good side and it was a tough game, but it was tighter than the last one. We became a little open in the second half, maybe trying to score, and we got done on the counter for the first goal. We still had four defenders back though and the goals weren't like the goals in Benfica. One ricocheted off our player and fell to them, so I didn't think the goals were beautiful; they were poor defensive moments for us.' (Fletcher, BBC Sport, 2009.)

As Everton departed for Greece with only one established central defender on board the flight, David Moyes's side were hopeful that the Europa League tie against AEK Athens may provide them with an opportunity to regain some form, with Steven Pienaar stating in *The Guardian*, 'Europe can help our league form. If we win in Athens, it can lift our spirits in the Premier League as well. We didn't even consider we might get dragged into a relegation fight. You just don't think about it like that. Sometimes you can go on a bad run, and that's what is happening with us now. But there are still plenty of games to go, we have a few over Christmas, so if we can win two games in a row then we will be back up the table. It's nothing to panic about.'

Indeed, Everton travelled to the Greek capital on the back of three consecutive Premier League defeats, including a 2-0 loss to Liverpool at Goodison Park. Languishing in 16th place in the table, three points above the relegation zone having played one game more than third-from-bottom Bolton Wanderers, stand-in captain Tim Cahill admitted that the Blues' recent results were a cause for concern, but there were still positives to take from the Merseyside derby performance. 'I think that was the best we've played in a while,' said Cahill. 'Our passing was good, we made lots of space with our movement and had two disallowed goals. We were strong from corners too. It's hard to take, but at this stage it's not going to get any easier. We're in a lot of trouble, and the only way we can get out of it is by playing and working our way out of it.'

The Australian international continued, 'We couldn't hit a barn door at the minute but things like that change a season and I'm much happier with our approach. It's the overall attitude and mental toughness that counts. I'm gutted for the fans and gutted for the team. The attitude against Hull wasn't good enough but it was a lot better against Liverpool and we will keep fighting. We're too good to be in this position. It's just one of those things and nothing's going to fix it except our mental attitude as individuals and a team.' (Hunter, *The Guardian*, 2009.)

A much-improved performance in Greece earned Everton a 1-0 win over AEK Athens, making it three wins out of five games in Group I, securing a place in the knockout stage of the Europa League courtesy of a Diniyar Bilyaletdinov strike. Qualifying for the round of 32 with a game to spare was indeed an impressive achievement given Moyes's depleted options, and the Scot's name could be heard being chanted by those who'd made the journey from Merseyside. The victory, however, came at a price, as Jo, Distin and Gosling limped off as Everton's injury crisis worsened.

'I don't think Jo's injury is serious,' Moyes told the *Liverpool Echo*. 'I am concerned about Distin and Dan as both are hamstring strains. We will have them assessed tomorrow. I think the main reason for the injuries is down to overloading them. Sylvain has had to play just about every minute of every game. This showed there is a heartbeat in this football club. I feel as if there is blood pumping through the veins again. It was tough but it can be the start of something more for us.'

Indeed, it was the start of Everton's best run of form thus far in the campaign, as the Blues went unbeaten in the league throughout December 2009 and January 2010. An FA Cup defeat to Birmingham City on 23 January notwithstanding, Everton's only other loss during this period was a 1-0 defeat in the dead rubber tie at home to BATE Borisov in mid-December, with David Moyes obtaining UEFA permission to promote some untested youngsters from his European B-list into the first-team squad, including 16-year-old left-back Jake Bidwell, whose inclusion in the starting line-up would make him the club's youngest appearance-maker in a European tie.

Unable to catch Benfica in top spot of Group I and with qualification via second spot secured, Moyes decided to announce his starting XI ahead of the visit of BATE Borisov to avoid accusations of short-changing the Goodison crowd, with tickets for the game still valued at £25. The naming of such an inexperienced line-up even drew unfair comparisons to Wolverhampton Wanderers manager Mick McCarthy, who in December 2009 made ten changes to his usual line-up in a visit to Old Trafford, therefore saving key players for a relegation six-pointer against Burnley five days later, a decision which eventually earned the club and manager a £25,000 fine each.

'What Mick [McCarthy] did was totally understandable,' said Moyes, 'but what we are doing is totally different. We have treated the competition with respect by playing the strongest teams we had available in previous games and by winning away at AEK Athens and BATE we qualified. We have earned the right to make these changes and with the amount of injuries we've got, I have to protect my players for the Premier League. I think the Everton supporters would expect us to change the team for this game. I'm sure they would be questioning the wisdom of putting out a full team.' (Hunter, *The Guardian*, 2009.)

Despite the 1-0 defeat, reserve goalkeeper Carlo Nash expressed his delight at making his debut for Everton, having supported the club since boyhood, and was full of praise for his young team-mates. 'It was great, a bit like a reserve game to be honest,' the goalkeeper stated. 'I've played a few times with the reserves with these lads, and I thought they did tremendously despite the score. They go out fearless these days, the kids. They showed that tonight. The goal was slightly unlucky with a slight deflection, but we matched them across the pitch and thought the draw would have been a fair result.' (Gaunt, *The Guardian*, 2009.)

2009/10 Europa League Group I table

Team	Pld	W	D	L	GF	GA	GD	Pts
1. Benfica	6	5	0	1	13	3	+10	15
2. Everton	6	3	0	3	7	9	-2	9
3. BATE	6	2	1	3	7	9	-2	7
4. AEK Athens	6	1	1	4	5	11	-6	4

23

Destination Kirkby

MEANWHILE, EVERTON Football Club's long-proposed relocation from Goodison Park continued to divide opinion, at least among those running the club and those involved in local politics. Seemingly few match-going Evertonians were in support of the potential ground move to the Merseyside town of Kirkby, just outside the boundary of the city of Liverpool, exemplified by the formation of the 'Keep Everton in Our City' campaign, which launched in March 2007, shortly after the plans for the 50,401-seater stadium were announced.

Indeed, the wholly inadequate location notwithstanding, the design of the potential new ground also left a lot to be desired and did not befit a football club of Everton's stature. Reportedly loosely based on German side FC Köln's RheinEnergieStadion, the development would have included a retail park, a hotel and a Tesco supermarket, with the design of the stadium drawing criticism from government body, the Commission for Architecture and the Built Environment (CABE), who in March 2008 stated, 'This scheme does not meet the criteria in terms of design quality set out in PPS1 (Planning Policy Statement 1) and we do not think that it should receive planning permission.'

A thoroughly depressing thought no doubt, but while Everton awaited confirmation that they could proceed with Destination Kirkby, the then leader of Liverpool City Council, Warren Bradley, proposed an even more unthinkable idea on 7 June 2009. Bradley, whose primary concern was the potential inclusion of the city of Liverpool as a host city in England's bid to stage the 2018 FIFA World Cup, opined that the two Merseyside clubs should solve both of their ground troubles by entering into a joint project.

Bradley, who was head of the city's 2018 bid committee, insisted in *The Guardian*, 'We've got to do something if we are serious about being a bidding city for the World Cup. I don't want to see everything migrate down the M62 to Manchester where there are two fabulous stadiums. There is a need for a 60,000 fit-for-purpose, 21st-century stadium in Liverpool. It could cost around £300 million. Sure, we still have the tribalistic supporters in the city who would say, "I won't sit in it after a Liverpudlian or Evertonian has." But that's not the argument, is it? I don't see any reason why it can't work – it does so across the southern hemisphere, and in Germany, Italy, and America.'

He continued, 'What I've said is absolutely right and is now being amplified in the city in business, at the clubs privately, and with the supporters. When you speak privately to different people at the clubs – at director level – they tell you what they think but will never publicly go on record. There is a groundswell of support now that it is the only way forward for both football clubs.'

With the decision on Everton's controversial move to Kirkby expected by autumn 2009, club spokesperson Ian Ross responded vociferously to Bradley's comments, stating, 'Yes, the Everton directors have one view ... we should push ahead with the destination project ... We have spent nearly three years working on Destination Kirkby and are giving absolutely no consideration to any other scheme. Perhaps Councillor Bradley should have fought somewhat harder to keep Everton inside the Liverpool city boundary if he is that intent on a joint stadium.'

Ross continued, 'We would have welcomed more help from our city council. That never happened ... For Councillor Bradley to now claim there is a weight of opinion to suggest we should now have a joint stadium would appear to be opportunism of the first order.' (Jackson, *The Guardian*, 2009.)

On 25 November, Destination Kirkby was rejected by the UK government, after being the subject of a public inquiry. Indeed, with the neighbouring authorities of Liverpool, St Helens and Sefton all objecting to the redevelopment, it was decided that the negative impact on the surrounding areas outweighed the potential benefits to Kirkby and the Borough of Knowsley as a whole. The decision brought an end to a project once described by Warren Bradley as a 'glorified cow shed built in a small town outside Liverpool', but one that had stirred so much debate among football fans and politicians alike. Indeed, even the initial vote put to Evertonians by the club back in August 2007 failed to yield a conclusive consensus, with 15,230 out of a total 36,662 voting in favour, while 10,468 voted against and 10,901 chose to abstain.

While Councillor Bradley's 'glorified cow shed' comment may not have been too far from the truth, it was a statement seemingly at odds with Liverpool City Council's application to be considered as a host city for England's bid for the 2018 or 2022 FIFA World Cup, with Everton's Kirkby-based stadium part of that proposal. Everton's former chief executive, Keith Wyness, who stepped down from the club in 2008, said at the time of the 2007 vote that the move represented the 'deal of the century', owing to the club's financial limitations. Wyness stated that Everton would not be able to afford to build a new stadium without an enabling project, such as a retail development, and partnering with Tesco would leave the club with debt that 'could be as low as £10 million'. This calculation, based on assistance from Tesco, the sale of Goodison Park and the sale of naming rights for the new stadium, was subsequently discredited.

Regarding the outcome of the public inquiry, Everton boss David Moyes stated, 'I have nothing to say.' A spokesperson for Keep Everton In Our City (KEIOC) said, 'This was never a boundary issue; it was a location issue. This stadium would have been nine miles outside the city centre, further from the city centre than any other Premier League ground. While we are pleased the stadium has been rejected, and we have been saying for three years that it goes against planning policy, we are not pleased that Everton have been left in a hole. The club has needed a new ground for over ten years and has been badly advised by so-called experts who, we believe, have been paid over £4 million for this advice.' (Hunter, *The Guardian*, 2009.)

Twenty-four hours after the government rejected the Destination Kirkby project, Everton chief executive Robert Elstone stated that Everton would consider a ground-sharing arrangement with Liverpool if the move made financial sense. 'It's certainly one of the options that we will need to cover,' Elstone said. 'A shared stadium is perhaps an option if it's affordable. We have to look at where we can raise money, because potentially Liverpool will obviously have to contribute to that, and Liverpool City Council perhaps might need to find some money. Our history is one of creativity and innovation and if we are the first major English club to look at sharing then we're not scared of making those decisions.'

However, Liverpool deputy executive director Peter Shaw played down the possibility of the two clubs sharing a ground, indicating Liverpool were intent on building a new £350 million stadium on land at Stanley Park, despite numerous delays to the project. 'Liverpool are progressing forward with our own stadium. That is the position we are still in. The LFC stadium is quite far progressed and once the financial markets reopen for business [following the 2008 recession] the LFC stadium will progress further.' (Gibson, *The Guardian*, 2009.)

Of course, the LFC stadium never materialised, though thankfully neither did a shared one, which no doubt would have been a nightmare for all involved. The possibility of renovating Goodison Park to meet modern standards was briefly suggested as a solution to Everton's stadium issue but was ruled out by Elstone as such a project would not be financially viable. 'It's a very small site,' Elstone said. 'It's locked in by houses and businesses and a church and a pub and a school, so to redevelop would be incredibly challenging.

When something is challenging and perhaps ambitious, the other word that often goes with that is "expensive".'

Elstone continued, 'We believe the redevelopment of Goodison would be very expensive. Future stadium potential for Everton is probably not necessarily about land, it's more about cash, the money, the affordability and that was the beauty of the Kirkby scheme which did come with a substantial subsidy from Tesco. Any alternative is going to have to address affordability. I would say as well that Kirkby for a long, long time has divided the club and divided the fans, and who knows really the proportion of fans that were for or against it? We don't know that.' (*The Guardian*, 2009.)

The Destination Kirkby development would have been disastrous for Everton Football Club, leaving us in a soulless flat-pack stadium near the motorway for the next 100 years. It's frightening how close it came to being a reality for the match-going fans, whose opinions clearly carried little weight at the club, if Robert Elstone's comments are anything to go by. Thankfully, pressure groups such as Keep Everton In Our City won an unlikely battle, and while we are now only a couple of years away from moving to a world-class stadium on the banks of the Royal Blue Mersey, the Destination Kirkby project looks to be a real bullet dodged. Indeed, Everton's currently unnamed stadium, under construction on the city's northern waterfront, is one of the rare examples of the club living up to its motto in the modern era. Had we moved to Kirkby, it would have been less *'Nil Satis Nisi Optimum'* (Nothing but the Best is Good Enough) and more *'Quid Satis Est'* – Anything is Good Enough.

24

We're Forever Everton

THE AFTERMATH of the unresolved stadium situation saw the fertile rumour mill run amok with reports of an imminent departure for Everton boss David Moyes, as the club's failure to build a ground supposedly vital to its financial future meant the Scot would have to continue without the projected transfer kitty that Destination Kirkby would have allegedly provided. However, Moyes was quick to deny such claims, stating, 'That is complete nonsense. I've been here seven and a half years and worked really hard to get here ... We are in a bad moment just now, but I'll carry on trying to get through this. I've got great respect for the supporters. If the fans thought it wasn't David Moyes they wanted, I would have to think about that, but at the moment I need to keep working hard with the players.'

He continued, 'Why should I stay? Because it's the right thing to do ... Maybe now with Kirkby coming to an end it's the time for anyone who was interested in investing in the club to come forward ... I think if there are any suitors out there, this is their chance, even though the world is not in great shape financially.

'People know we're not going to Kirkby ... Liverpool City Council said they didn't want us to leave, so I am now looking forward to seeing the sites that they recommended we move to. Can we redevelop Goodison? I would love it to be Goodison, to see if we could find any way of redeveloping it, but I don't know if that's viable.' (Hunter, *The Guardian*, 2009.)

While the stadium saga dragged on, Moyes's side continued to struggle with injuries and languished in the bottom half of the table. The Everton boss was keen to stress that the buck stopped with him. 'I'm the man responsible for signing all the players here, so I take responsibility,' Moyes asserted in *The Guardian*. 'And they should all be shaking my hand and thanking me for giving them the chance to play for Everton, because it's such a great club and for some of them it might not get any better.'

Strong words from the Blues boss, and with the transfer window open for business in January 2010, one player who arrived certainly did embrace the opportunity of representing Everton Football Club, even if it was only for a few months. USA international Landon Donovan joined the club on 1 January on a ten-week loan from MLS side LA Galaxy. Donovan's impact was immediate and gave Moyes an outlet in attack that had been lacking throughout the campaign. Named as the club's Player of the Month for January 2010, the forward scored two goals in 13 appearances during his short stay at Goodison Park.

Indeed, an upturn in form over the Christmas period had David Moyes insisting that his side could still finish in a European place. Unbeaten in the Premier League throughout December and January, Everton moved up to ninth in the table as the boss looked to draw a line under the miserable start to the campaign. 'I'm ambitious and I want to be managing in European competitions,' said the Scot. 'I tell the players that. I want them to have the same drive as me. In the past few years, we have been closer to it but this year we are not. We are going to have to fight incredibly hard and somehow scrape in by the skin of our teeth. But we have to keep believing we can make it.' (Hunter, *The Guardian*, 2010.)

Having qualified for Europe in four out of the past five seasons, Moyes was eager to stress the importance of consistent European qualification for both the development of his squad, and his capacity to attract top talent to the club. 'European football has helped both me and the team develop,' Moyes said. 'It has been good for us and we want to make it last so we will try and push again; there is a long way to go but we will see if we can finish in the top half and see what happens. I would miss it, the players would, and so would the club. Good players want to play in Europe, and we want to be there to make us attractive to these players. Players want to see European football. They want the Champions League, and if not that, the Europa League is the next best thing. We have to show potential. We have to show people this is where we should be, and that we are making headway and moving in the right direction.'

Indeed, and with Everton's Europa League round of 32 opponents Sporting CP without a win in four games and 21 points behind Portuguese league leaders Benfica, it was no doubt an opportune time to face Carlos Carvalhal's team. However, the Lisbon club had history on their side, with Sporting having faced English competition on six occasions in European knockout games, progressing to the next round each time. Moyes, however, had something close to his best XI available, though the news that Marouane Fellaini would be sidelined for the remainder of the campaign was a blow. Still, the Everton boss was keen to stress that he anticipated a much different game than the last time Everton faced Portuguese opposition.

'They are similar to Benfica in that they have a big history as far as European football is concerned,' said Moyes. 'However, when we played Benfica, they were in a really good moment, and I am not sure that Sporting are. Knockout football is what everyone has enjoyed about the European game over the years, and we have developed our approach to it. When we lost to Villarreal a few years ago I thought it was important that we just went out and won, rather than stopping the opposition scoring an away goal and judging it over two legs. We missed the likes of Mikel Arteta and Steven Pienaar earlier in the competition when we had a very thin squad and struggled to retain possession. Having them back makes you not quite so fearful.' (Rich, *The Guardian*, 2010.)

The line-ups in this round of 32 Europa League tie at Goodison Park on 16 February were as follows:

Everton: Howard, Baines, Yobo, Distin, Neville, Donovan, Arteta, Cahill, Pienaar, Osman, Saha

Sporting Clube de Portugal: Rui Patricio, Carrico, Tonel, Grimi, Abel, Mendes, Izmailov, Fernandez, Veloso, Moutinho, Liedson

The reduced capacity due to the tea-time kick-off lent the game an air of a pre-season friendly rather than a European knockout, though Everton's approach to the tie did not lack competitiveness, with the Blues confident in possession and eager to pressure Sporting's backline early on. After a few half-chances, Moyes's side finally created an opening on 35 minutes as Steven Pienaar, making his 100th appearance for the club, marked the occasion with a rare right-footed finish to give Everton the lead.

A Leighton Baines corner four minutes into the second half eluded a static Sporting defence before striking Sylvain Distin on the arm and rolling over the line. Despite the presence of six officials, including an additional assistant referee behind the net, the goal stood, much to the surprise of everyone in the stadium. So clear was the handball, that the goal was not replayed on the big screens at either end of Goodison Park, much to the annoyance of Sporting coach Carvalhal: 'It was a clear handball,' said the Portuguese. 'It's funny, they showed the first goal three times on the TV screens, but they didn't show the second goal once.' (Hunter, *The Guardian*, 2010.)

At 2-0 up, Everton were cruising to a comfortable first-leg victory. However, with five minutes remaining, a moment of carelessness undermined an otherwise professional performance and gifted Sporting the away goal that Moyes was so eager to avoid. Everton's wounds are so often self-inflicted, and substitute Jack Rodwell's overhit pass to an unsuspecting Sylvain Distin was just such an example. As Distin's touch eluded him, allowing Liedson to claim possession of the ball, the Blues centre-half had little choice but to bring down the Brazilian-born forward inside the penalty box. Miguel Veloso obliged, halving Sporting's deficit by sending Tim Howard the wrong way.

Perhaps even more frustrating than the late goal was the dismissal of Distin for his foul on Liedson, meaning the French centre-half would miss the return leg. With Jonny Heitinga also ineligible, Moyes would once again have to travel to Portugal with a makeshift defence. 'The tie looks a lot different now,' said the visibly frustrated Everton boss in *The Guardian*. 'I thought we looked more likely to finish 3-0 than 2-1 but we didn't go for it enough late on. We've also lost Fellaini with an injury similar to [Robin] Van Persie's and think he'll be out for six months, although we won't know for sure until he's had an operation. We have missed him, but it was a seriously bad tackle.'

Moyes went on: 'We are disappointed we have not seen the job through, which we should have done. We gave Sporting an opportunity when it looked as though they might not have one. We did enough to be 2-0 in front and I did not see a goal coming. But it was not to be. It keeps the game alive.' (BBC Sport, 2010.)

David Moyes and his side had little time to dwell on their frustration, however, as they now had to prepare for the visit of Manchester United to Goodison Park. In resurgent league form with just one defeat in 11, and with European qualification still a possibility, there was no doubt an optimism around a packed and vibrant Goodison Park that the Blues' impressive run could continue. Though Marouane Fellaini and Tim Cahill were notable absentees, with both their aerial threat in front of goal and physical presence a huge loss, Everton produced a vintage display as Moyes's continued faith in the youthful contingent of his squad paid dividends.

At 1-1 inside the opening 20 minutes, as Diniyar Bilyaletdinov's emphatic strike cancelled out Dimitar Berbatov's opener, both sides were eager to trade blows in what was an entertaining encounter, with Leon Osman pulling the strings brilliantly in the heart of Everton's midfield. A point apiece began to look the likeliest outcome, then after the introduction of the youthful enthusiasm of Dan Gosling for the tiring legs of goalscorer Bilyaletdinov with 20 minutes remaining, the Blues began to apply the pressure, as the 19-year-old took just six minutes to give Everton a deserved lead.

A late cameo for Jack Rodwell afforded the youngster the opportunity to make up for his midweek faux pas, and the Southport-born teenager did just that in quite some style. Receiving the ball just beyond the halfway line from Mikel Arteta, the young midfielder's powerful run left the United defence incapable of keeping up with him, his precise finish past Van der Sar just the *coup de grace* Everton required to seal the points. 'I really wanted to have a go at United,' Moyes said. 'We keep saying we can beat anyone when everyone is fit – and we've not got everyone fit at the moment – but it just shows the sort of spirit we've got at the club.'

He continued, 'We grew into the game, getting stronger as it went on. I keep being told we don't beat the big boys often enough, and we don't, so the last couple of results have been terrific. When we have our whole squad together, we can be a match for anyone, but it's nice to know we can do it even with key players missing.' (Wilson, *The Guardian*, 2010.)

The victory over Manchester United, just Everton's second league win over the Red Devils out of the previous 30 meetings, lifted the Blues to eighth in the Premier League, just four points off a Europa League spot and seven points adrift of a place in the coveted top four. However, Moyes's side would have to swiftly turn their attention to the second leg of the round of 32 clash with Sporting, with just five days' rest until the Blues travelled to the Portuguese capital. A 2-1 victory for Everton in the first leg was a precarious lead to take to Lisbon, but it was a lead nonetheless, and manager David Moyes was confident his side were good enough to progress to the next round. 'We feel we are good enough to beat Sporting,' Moyes said. 'Playing there is going to be a different story and that's why it is unfortunate to give up a goal, but they still have to score.' (*The Guardian*, 2010.)

With a place in the last 16 of the Europa League at stake, Everton took their slender advantage to the Estadio Jose Alvalade looking to secure a passage to the next round of the competition, where the winners of Galatasaray and Atletico Madrid would provide the opposition. Indeed, David Moyes's side would hold the unique record of being the only English team to eliminate Sporting Clube de Portugal from a European competition should they avoid defeat in the Portuguese capital, travelling as they were with a 2-1 lead from the first leg. Of course, Everton's last visit to the city of Lisbon the previous October had been one to forget, and despite the vast improvement in the performances since then, the outcome was all too familiar for the travelling Evertonians.

Though it may not have been quite as humbling an experience as Benfica five months earlier, a 3-0 defeat on the night against Sporting, with an aggregate result of 4-2 to the Portuguese side, ensured another season without silverware, with the Europa League Everton's last opportunity to put a trophy on the table for the 2009/10 season. Indeed, as manager David Moyes suggested after the first leg, the concession of the late goal at Goodison Park proved costly, ensuring as it did that Carlos Carvalhal's side approached the game with a renewed optimism.

There was a vocal if far from capacity crowd in attendance, with just 17,609 spectators inside the Estadio Jose Alvalade, though Everton once again travelled in numbers. The Blues had the ball in the back of the net moments before the interval, as the on-loan Philippe Senderos converted a deep Leighton Baines free kick before the linesman flagged for offside. Louis Saha, who had been recalled to the French national squad, looked an isolated figure up top, but Everton appeared content to defend their first-leg advantage.

However, Sporting gradually grew into the game and when Miguel Veloso beat Tim Howard at his near post to level the aggregate scoreline, there was a sense that Everton were riding their luck, and so Moyes's side began to show an urgency that had previously been startlingly absent. It proved to be too little, too late, however, when former Spurs and Portsmouth midfielder Pedro Mendes gave Sporting the advantage, with a fortuitously deflected effort. Still, a goal from Moyes's side would take the tie to sudden death, and with Everton pushing late on, the Blues were caught on the counter-attack and Matias Fernandez quashed hopes of any last-gasp drama, as his 93rd-minute goal sealed the tie for Sporting.

'I feel sorry for everyone; we were too concerned with what they were doing,' Mikel Arteta reflected. 'We have not been positive enough, we tried to defend too deep, we never got a grip of the game and when we tried to attack it was too late. It was not just their late penalty at Goodison that has cost us, it was all the chances we missed in the last 20 minutes of that game.'

Everton boss David Moyes too conceded that his side were simply second best against Sporting: 'We didn't play well enough,' Moyes said. 'From the start Sporting got a grip of the game, put us under pressure. I thought we'd weathered it before half-time, but we never caused them enough problems.' (*The Guardian*, 2010.)

A 2-1 defeat at White Hart Lane three days later compounded a dispiriting week for Everton, though a 5-1 demolition of Hull City at Goodison Park a week later restored some optimism that a European place was once again achievable, though seventh-placed Aston Villa maintained a four-point advantage over the Blues. It was an invaluable three points, a convincing win and a sixth in succession at Goodison Park.

Indeed, the victory over Hull City on 7 March sparked an unbeaten run that Moyes's side maintained for the remainder of the campaign, a total of 11 consecutive games without defeat, including a 2-0 win at the City of Manchester Stadium, with goals courtesy of Tim Cahill and Mikel Arteta. In the rearranged fixture, originally scheduled for the second league game of the season but postponed due to Everton's Europa League play-off game at home to Sigma Olomouc, tensions flared in the closing stages between David Moyes and City boss Roberto Mancini, prompting referee Peter Walton to dismiss them both moments before the final whistle. With minutes remaining, City were awarded a throw-in near the dugout. With Mancini eager for his side to resume play, the Italian manager clattered into Moyes as he rushed to retrieve the ball, sparking a melee on the sidelines. However, any animosity between the two coaches did not extend beyond the final whistle, though Moyes was keen to stress that his sending-off was harsh, to say the least.

'I wasn't the one waving my hand for bookings,' Moyes said of the incident. 'I was very surprised; I didn't know what I had done wrong. I shouldn't have been sent off, simple as. I held the ball longer than I should have but I was trying to make a change. He [Mancini] showed his passion for his team and his club, and I can accept that.' (*Liverpool Echo*, 2010.)

Roberto Mancini stated, 'I've spoken now with David [Moyes] and if I made a mistake, I am sorry. I wanted to get the ball because there was another five minutes at the end. This can happen sometimes in a game, but it is finished now. I was frustrated for the players.' (*The Guardian*, 2010.)

A confidence-boosting win, no doubt, the victory over City put Moyes's Everton within three points of seventh-placed Aston Villa and sixth-placed Liverpool. Firmly in contention for a European spot going into the final months of the season, Everton's unbeaten run could not have come at a more opportune time, but three successive draws away at Wolverhampton Wanderers and fellow European hopefuls Aston Villa, and at home to West Ham United, put a dent in the Blues' ambitions. A dramatic 3-2 win at Ewood Park got them back to winning ways, with Yakubu coming off the bench to score and claim an assist for Tim Cahill's 90th-minute winner, closing the gap on Aston Villa to a single point, with two points separating Everton from rivals Liverpool.

In a closely contested fixture, Everton dominated the ball from the first minute, with the post-match report on BBC Sport stating, 'Rovers went into the match having kept three clean sheets in their last three games, but they were stunned by Everton's blistering opening which saw them keep possession in a manner akin to Barcelona.' Indeed, Everton's football at Ewood Park was sublime, and it was former La Masia prospect Mikel Arteta, who opened the scoring from the penalty spot after four minutes, pulling the strings in the middle of the park for the Blues. The Spanish midfielder was extremely fortunate to avoid a red card, however, when he responded angrily to a reckless Morten Gamst Pedersen challenge by poking the Norwegian in the cheek and then the eye, with both players receiving cautions.

'Our football today was up there with the best,' Moyes said at full time. 'Some of the stuff we played on a difficult pitch was excellent. They scored two pretty good goals from distance, but I was disappointed because I thought we'd created lots of chances but could not finish them off. I thought the team was terrific from the first minute and it was great that Yakubu came off the bench to score a goal and make another. I've had a word with Mikel Arteta about poking Morten Gamst Pedersen in the eye – he should not have done it and I've told him so. But we should talk about his football; he was head and shoulders above anybody on the field today.'

Arteta was once again at the heart of the action a week later as Everton welcomed Fulham to Goodison Park, with the Spaniard's 94th-minute penalty earning his side a late 2-1 victory. Fulham, who had lost on 16 consecutive visits to Goodison Park prior to kick-off, made nine changes for the Sunday afternoon tie, as they prepared for a Europa League semi-final second leg against Hamburg, scheduled for the following Wednesday. An Erik Nevland opener gave the Cottagers a first-half lead, however, before a Chris Smalling own goal restored parity just after the restart, setting it up for Arteta to steal the points from 12 yards after Chris Baird's rash challenge on Tim Cahill.

A five-point gap separated seventh-placed Liverpool and eighth-placed Everton going into the penultimate game of the season, with the Blues needing a win away at Stoke City on Saturday, 1 May, with Liverpool welcoming Chelsea to Anfield 24 hours later. A win for the Blues at the Britannia Stadium would have kept Everton's European ambitions alive, and with Tony Pulis's side going into the game on the back of a 7-0 drubbing against Chelsea at Stamford Bridge the previous week, the opportunity to catch the hard-to-beat side at a low ebb presented itself for the Toffees. However, in an uninspiring encounter, neither side looked likely to break the deadlock, with the home side threatening from Rory Delap's long throw-in speciality on a few occasions, though Everton's backline were hardly troubled.

Each side approached the second half with greater intensity, with chances at both ends of the pitch. A Victor Anichebe penalty appeal was waved away by Howard Webb, as the Nigerian forward was bundled over in the penalty area by Ryan Shawcross, though contact was deemed insufficient to award a spot kick. With time running out, it seemed Everton's chance to secure the three points required to remain in contention for a Europa League spot was slipping away, before Phil Jagielka's downward header from a Mikel Arteta corner late on provided the Blues with the elusive breakthrough. Celebrations were short-lived, however, as the linesman raised his flag, with Anichebe standing in an offside position.

Protestations fell on deaf ears and as the tie ended in a 0-0 draw, so too ended Everton's European ambitions for the 2009/10 season, with the Blues failing to qualify for the first time in three years. The result did extend Everton's unbeaten run to ten consecutive league games, the first time the club had reached double figures since the period between April and September 2006, though ultimately the impressive run of form during the second half of the campaign proved to be too little, too late. Frustratingly, Liverpool would fall to a 2-0 defeat at home to Chelsea 24 hours later meaning that, had Everton earned all three points against Stoke City, the opportunity to qualify for Europe would have gone down to the final game of the season.

On Phil Jagielka's disallowed goal at the Britannia Stadium, Everton assistant manager Steve Round stated, 'We thought it was a perfectly good goal. We cannot quite understand why it was disallowed. But the officials made the decision, and we have to respect that. He [Anichebe] is in an offside position but is he interfering? I don't know. We have taken a corner and it has been headed straight in the net. We are very disappointed as we wanted to win today to keep the pressure on. We felt after Stoke's defeat last week [against Chelsea] they would be in an aggressive mood and determined to show everyone it was a one-off. We were hoping to take control of the game in the last 30 minutes but unfortunately, we could not quite do it.' (*Daily Post*, 2010.)

The final game of the season saw already-relegated Portsmouth visit Goodison Park, and with neither team capable of affecting their final league position, and Pompey looking to cause an FA Cup Final upset against league champions Chelsea six days later, no doubt both managers were happy to see out the inconsequential fixture with no fresh injury concerns. With seconds remaining, and the score at 0-0, Diniyar Bilyaletdinov produced a 25-yard left-footed screamer to secure a late 1-0 win for Everton, a memorable moment in an otherwise unmemorable encounter.

'We came off the FA Cup Final [at the end of the 2008/09 season] feeling good and that we'd finished the season well, but we couldn't cope with the changes and injuries at the start of the season,' Everton boss David Moyes told BBC Sport at full time. 'Hopefully we'll be better prepared next season. I'm disappointed, I don't want to be eighth but that's where we are. You can make all the excuses you want but that's where we are. I hope [having fewer games by not being in Europe] works in our favour, but I'd still rather be in Europe.'

Perhaps it was simply a poor choice of words, but to hear David Moyes state that he and the team were 'feeling good' after the 2009 FA Cup Final is quite jarring. That season did not finish well, it ended in heartbreak and extended a trophyless run by at least one more year. No doubt it felt as though the club was moving in the right direction, but a cup final defeat and an end-of-season feelgood factor rarely go hand in hand.

The final Premier League table at the end of the 2009/10 season:

Team	Pld	W	D	L	GF	GA	GD	Pts
1. Chelsea	38	27	5	6	103	32	+71	86
2. Man United	38	27	4	7	86	28	+58	85
3. Arsenal	38	23	6	9	83	41	+42	75
4. Spurs	38	21	7	10	67	41	+26	70
5. Man City	38	18	13	7	73	45	+28	67
6. Aston Villa	38	17	13	8	52	39	+13	64
7. Liverpool	38	18	9	11	61	35	+26	63
8. Everton	38	16	13	9	60	49	+11	61

25

Everton v Everton

THERE ARE few occasions in football when two teams who share a name compete against each other, but on 4 August 2010, Everton Football Club welcomed their Chilean namesake Everton de Vina del Mar to Goodison Park to play a pre-season friendly known as the Brotherhood Cup, in a fixture arranged by supporters' club the Ruleteros Society. Formed in 1909 by David Foxley, whose grandparents had emigrated to Chile from Liverpool, Everton de Vina del Mar's humble beginnings were as an amateur side of Anglo-Chileans who were inspired to form a football club following Everton's tour of South America in 1909; a tour which also saw namesake clubs emerge in Uruguay, Paraguay and Argentina.

A little over a century later, and Everton de Vina del Mar would make the return journey, travelling approximately 7,000 miles to L4, making it the first time a Chilean football club had been invited to play in Europe. A group of 171 Vina del Mar fans made the arduous trek to Goodison Park for the fixture (nine more than the 162 brought by Fulham for a league game during the 2009/10 season) and rarely has an opposition side been afforded such hospitality, with players in the blue and gold of our Chilean counterparts cheered and applauded just as much as those in blue and white. Referee Mark Halsey also received a rousing reception from the Goodison crowd, with the Hertfordshire-born official taking charge of his first match following treatment for throat cancer, which thankfully went into remission.

This unique fixture saw Everton Football club secure a 2-0 victory over their Chilean namesake, with goals from new signing Jermaine Beckford, who made his home debut having signed a four-year deal with the club following his free transfer from Leeds United, and Diniyar Bilyaletdinov, who doubled the Blues' lead with 25 minutes remaining. David Moyes's £1 million signing Magaye Gueye, who arrived from Strasbourg on a five-year contract, provided both assists, though perhaps of more significance was the unexpected return of Marouane Fellaini, who made a second-half appearance following six months out with ankle ligament damage. No doubt, the Brotherhood Cup was an unequivocal success, and hopefully one day the two sides will meet again for a return fixture.

However, despite a successful pre-season, the 2010/11 campaign started poorly, with Everton taking three points out of a possible 18 in the opening six games, with three draws and three defeats. Indeed, the poor start to the new season mirrored the inconsistent form from the opening fixtures of the one before. By autumn, there was already a sense of déjà vu at Goodison Park, as there was little doubt that Moyes's side would have to play catch-up if our hopes of competing in Europe were to be fulfilled, just as we had done throughout the 2009/10 campaign. No doubt, a distinct lack of investment had left the Everton boss with a squad in desperate need of a shake-up, with Moyes operating on a shoestring budget, bringing in Beckford and Gueye in the summer transfer window. With no significant incomings to speak of, perhaps it is little surprise the club made such a stuttering start to the season.

Indeed, the squad may have lacked new faces as the 2010/11 season began, but it retained a characterful resilience so often associated with Moyes's Everton, particularly against the free-spending elite. As Everton welcomed Manchester United to Goodison Park on 11 September, the Blues found themselves 1-0 up on 39 minutes thanks to Steven Pienaar, only for Darren Fletcher to cancel out the South African international's strike four minutes later. United cruised into a second-half lead courtesy of Nemanja Vidic, before Dimitar Berbatov added a third on 66 minutes. But for the outstanding Tim Howard in goal for Everton, United could well have been out of sight with 15 minutes remaining, the value of his contribution underscored in what was a stunning finale.

At 3-1, Sir Alex Ferguson's side no doubt felt that they had done enough to return to Manchester with a win, but two Leighton Baines crosses inside two minutes ensured that the points were shared. A 91st-minute cross into the box from the Kirkby-born left-back found Tim Cahill, who finished with a trademark header, to give the Blues what appeared to be a consolation goal; but 60 seconds later, an almost carbon copy cross once again found Cahill, with the Australian this time nodding the ball back for Mikel Arteta to volley Everton level, via a slight Paul Scholes deflection. A rapturous Goodison Park once again urged Moyes's side forward, with Everton looking to steal the unlikeliest of victories, and with Phil Jagielka poised to take an effort on goal, referee Martin Atkinson blew the full-time whistle to spare United's blushes.

'I don't know precisely how much time was left, but neither does anyone,' argued Moyes, who confronted Atkinson at full time, remonstrating that he had blown his whistle too early. 'There were two goals in stoppage time to take account of and there may have only been ten seconds or less left, but we had just scored two goals in two minutes and gone straight upfield from a corner, and before the move can develop the referee has blown. I don't think anyone in the ground would have complained had he blown after the shot, wherever the ball had ended up. People don't pay their money to see referees, they come here for excitement.' (Wilson, *The Guardian*, 2010.)

With the worst start to a Premier League campaign in over a decade, the Blues were winless after six games and rooted to the foot of the table. Moyes's Everton also had the unwanted record of being the only side in the top four divisions of English football without a win; a run which finally came to an end on 2 October, courtesy of a 2-0 away victory at Birmingham City. The win at St Andrew's ensured that the Blues climbed out of the bottom three going into the international break, though there was little respite for Moyes, who would find himself with a selection headache for Everton's next game – the Merseyside derby at Goodison Park.

In a bitter blow, record signing Marouane Fellaini picked up a hamstring injury while on international duty with Belgium, ruling the midfielder out for approximately six weeks, meaning he would be unavailable to face Liverpool five days later. Moyes, who was in attendance in Brussels to see Belgium draw 4-4 with Austria in a Euro 2012 qualifying game, claimed that Fellaini was advised by coach Georges Leekens to keep playing despite sustaining the injury, with the Blues midfielder eventually withdrawn in the 81st minute.

'It is a really big blow for us,' Moyes said. 'He [Fellaini] got a hamstring injury and was made to play on longer than he should have and that has made the injury worse. He could have been out for just a couple of weeks, not six, if he had come off straight away and I will be writing a letter to the Belgian FA to express my disappointment at what happened.' (Hunter, *The Guardian*, 2010.)

One win in seven games and a key player unavailable, no doubt a less than ideal set of circumstances to prepare for a Merseyside derby, though Liverpool had also had a troublesome start to their campaign. In a startlingly similar run of form, both sides had one victory, three draws and three defeats prior to derby day, with Liverpool in 18th place in the league table, and Everton just one place above, thanks to a superior goal difference.

Indeed, with Everton and Liverpool languishing at the lower end of the division, Blues attacker Tim Cahill acknowledged in an interview with *Guardian* journalist Andy Hunter how both sides would be eager to compound the other's troubled start to the campaign by inflicting a derby day defeat. 'It's definitely a game neither team can afford to lose,' admitted Cahill. 'We are both in a false position but there is a greater emphasis on this game because of our positions and because of that it is one of the most vital games we will have all season.'

Cahill continued, 'I believe in this squad ... It's just been the mistakes we have made in the seven games that have cost us ... It's so frustrating for us because we demand so much from each other ... There is so much spirit in this team. We might not get the result, but we will fight for it.

'What it means to us and to the fans makes this the most exciting part of my career. It's a chance to make yourself something special, to look back when you're older and say: "I remember that derby because I helped make a change." The feeling of beating Liverpool is up there with the best of my career...

'Whoever sets the tone and puts their stamp on things can have a big effect on the game ... I expect someone to try to rough me up. It's a compliment in football ... As long as it's done in the right manner, I'm all for it.

'They have high expectations because they've spent a lot of money ... Our manager has worked within a good budget and brought in players who love playing for the club. We don't have the chance to go and spend £40 million a season ... The pressure's been brought on by themselves, by what they've spent. Their fans expect results and when they don't get them, there will always be pressure.'

On Sunday, 17 October, in front of 39,673 fans at Goodison Park, the line-ups for the 214th Merseyside derby were as follows:

Everton: Howard, Baines, Heitinga, Jagielka, Distin, Neville, Coleman, Arteta, Cahill, Osman, Yakubu

Liverpool: Reina, Konchesky, Kyrgiakos, Carragher, Skrtel, Meireles, Gerrard, Cole, Maxi, Lucas, Torres

Having suffered derby-day defeats both home and away during the 2009/10 season, Moyes's Everton were no doubt eager to ensure that the three points stayed at Goodison Park, with the Blues showing the greater enterprise in the opening exchanges of a typically feisty match. Liverpool's new owners, Fenway Sports Group, were in attendance, though their presence in the stands did little to inspire Roy Hodgson's side, who struggled to emerge from a subdued start. Indeed, Everton looked by far the better team, and it wasn't long before Tim Cahill, so eager as he was to put his stamp on the fixture, as stated in his pre-match comments, opened the scoring for the Blues.

Seamus Coleman's industrious run down the right flank left Paul Konchesky for dust, the 22-year-old Irishman's cutback converted in deadly fashion by Cahill on 34 minutes. Notably, the goal took Cahill's career total against Liverpool to five, a haul unmatched by an Everton player since the great Dixie Dean, putting the Australian attacker in the company of a true club legend. After the interval, Everton picked up where they left off, with Mikel Arteta doubling the Blues' lead five minutes after the restart. A Leighton Baines corner, cleared by Sotirios Kyrgiakos, dropped invitingly for Arteta, who fired the ball emphatically past a helpless Pepe Reina to put Everton two goals to the good.

Having cruised to a 2-0 victory, Everton jumped to 11th in the table, condemning Liverpool to 19th, prompting a chorus of 'Going down, going down' at full time. David Moyes, delighted with his players, stated: 'Their attitude was spot on, and they got their reward. I thought we have played better in the majority of the games than we did today, but it was a derby and a different kind of game. Some of our performances [earlier in the season] were good but we did not get the result, but today we did enough. We are getting away from the wrong end of the table. We are a good enough team to be at the top end.' (North Wales Live, 2010.)

A 1-1 draw at White Hart Lane followed by a 1-0 win over Stoke City at Goodison Park, with Yakubu scoring the winner and ending his six-month goal drought, saw Everton go unbeaten in the month of October, earning Moyes the Manager of the Month award. A visit to Bloomfield Road a week later saw the Blues twice come from behind to earn a 2-2 draw, with Tim Cahill scoring his 50th league goal for the club, and Seamus Coleman scoring his first. The welcome news that Marouane Fellaini would be available two weeks ahead of schedule for the visit of Bolton Wanderers bolstered

Moyes's options, as the Belgian international earned an immediate recall into his starting XI.

Everton dominated possession, though a profligate display in front of goal saw the game heading for a stalemate, until Ivan Klasnic converted a rare Bolton chance with 11 minutes remaining to give Owen Coyle's side a late lead. The Blues were down to ten men five minutes later, when the fit-again Fellaini earned himself a straight red card for kicking out at full-back Paul Robinson, in a mindless act of retaliation following a foul from the Bolton defender. With seconds remaining, Bolton looked set to secure their first victory on Merseyside in five years, and end Everton's six-game unbeaten run in doing so, until Jermaine Beckford's fine finish salvaged a late point for the Blues.

'My idea was always to bring him off the bench in games where we needed a goal,' said Moyes of Beckford, who had made the jump from League One to the Premier League. 'I shouldn't have started him so early on in the season. That was a mistake of mine. Anybody who has watched Leeds will tell you he can score an array of goals. It was a fantastic finish, it really was. That is what Jermaine has got. There's a lot he will have to learn in being a Premier League player but the one thing we can't teach him and what he came with was the ability to score goals.' (*Liverpool Echo*, 2010.)

A 2-1 defeat to Arsenal at Goodison Park ended Everton's unbeaten run, on 14 November, then came a 2-2 draw at the Stadium of Light, with a late Mikel Arteta goal rescuing a point on the road. A 4-1 capitulation at home to West Brom, Albion's first league win at Goodison Park since 1979, left Everton 16th in the table, two points above the relegation zone. Cahill scored his eighth goal of the season, assisted for the sixth time by Leighton Baines, their fine individual form the only positive from an otherwise torrid performance. A straight red card for midfield metronome Mikel Arteta compounded Moyes's misery on an embarrassing afternoon for the Toffees. Typically, Arteta's suspension coincided with Fellaini's return, with the Belgian available for the Blues' next game away at Chelsea, though Moyes would once again be without a full-strength ensemble for a tough away tie.

A much-improved performance the following week earned Everton a 1-1 draw at Stamford Bridge, the fifth consecutive league draw at Chelsea, thanks to an 86th-minute equaliser from Jermaine Beckford. With five draws and two defeats, Everton were without a league win in seven games before they recorded an unexpected 2-1 victory at the City of Manchester Stadium on 20 December to deny Roberto Mancini's side the chance to top the league table at Christmas for the first time since 1929. Tim Cahill scored his third goal at Eastlands in as many years to put the Blues in front, before assisting Leighton Baines, who doubled Everton's lead inside 20 minutes. Yaya Toure pulled one back for City with 18 minutes remaining, but Moyes's side held on to secure a valuable three points, though Everton's poor disciplinary record continued, as Victor Anichebe became the third player in seven games to see red for the Blues, following two yellow cards.

Moyes's squad faced further disruption as the January transfer window approached, with key player Steven Pienaar linked with a move away, with both Chelsea and Spurs interested. With the possibility of losing the South African international on a free transfer at the end of the season, Moyes insisted a departure in January was likely, though warned that any funds raised from the sale would be minimal due to the short length of time remaining on the winger's contract.

'It may well come to it in the January transfer window that we have to consider selling Pienaar to raise money, because he is out of contract in the summer,' Moyes admitted. 'We know we need a striker, and realistically, the sort of money we will raise through [selling Pienaar], what type of player is it going to buy for us in the January market? The sort of money I'd raise, I don't think it will attract the type of player we need, the type of player we are looking for to provide the goals. The sort of money it will cost, I don't think selling a player will solve that particular problem, and it is probably a reality that we will have to look at bringing in a loan player, that it will be the loan market we will need to look at to provide some sort of solution.' (Metro, 2010.)

Meanwhile, frozen pipes at Goodison Park meant the Boxing Day visit of Birmingham City was postponed, earning Moyes's side some additional preparation time for a trip to Upton Park on 28 December, where the points were shared in a 1-1 draw. A 2-0 defeat at Stoke City on 1 January 2011 was a less than ideal start to the new calendar year, but it was Everton's first league defeat on the road since the previous August, ending a run of eight games unbeaten away from home, though seven of those fixtures ended in a draw. A 2-1 win over Spurs at Goodison Park ensured Everton got back to winning ways, a victory recorded despite the absence of top scorer Tim Cahill, who was on international duty with Australia competing in the Asia Cup.

Next up for the Blues was a visit to Anfield in the 215th Merseyside derby, with both sides level on points going into the game, 11th-placed Everton one place above Liverpool thanks to a superior goal difference. Inconsistent form had hampered progress for each side throughout the campaign, with only four points separating both of them from the relegation zone. Everton's 2-0 victory back in October afforded the Blues the opportunity to secure a league double over Liverpool, though doing so would require Moyes to record his first win at Anfield since taking over as Everton boss in 2002. With four league draws, four league defeats, plus one draw in the FA Cup, his record at Anfield was underwhelming, though the Scot was eager to point out that it was a reflection of the financial gulf between the two clubs.

'If people question my record with Everton at the big clubs, and also perhaps in Europe, then I am relaxed about it, because you can't ignore the big differences between the clubs,' said Moyes, whose winless run at Anfield, Old Trafford, Stamford Bridge and the Emirates/Highbury stretched back 35 Premier League games. 'When you don't win at places like Anfield then you are questioned on it, and no one considers the financial gap, and that's the bit that gnaws away at me. I'd need to come back at that and say, "yeah, we maybe haven't done as well at the top clubs as we should have done and, yeah, maybe we've lost the odd game in Europe we shouldn't have done", but with what we've done here – how many years have we been in Europe and competed in the top half of the league? Maybe that's as good as Everton can do on the financial resources Everton have got.' (Hunter, *The Guardian*, 2010.)

No doubt Everton's financial limitations hampered Moyes's efforts when visiting the likes of Anfield and Old Trafford, operating as he so often was with one hand tied behind his back. It is, of course, a valid argument that those with deeper pockets are likely to prevail over those with fewer resources, more often than not. However, without a single league victory at Liverpool, Manchester United, Chelsea and Arsenal, at what point does a valid argument become a convenient excuse?

Moyes continued, 'It's not as if we have been to Anfield and done badly. We would like to win more but you can't talk about that without talking about the whole situation. There is more in it. Maybe you should be turning around and saying the draws Everton got at Anfield were unbelievable, rather than we haven't won there. To have drawn so many games at Anfield over that period is incredible when you look at the difference in spending. People always look at it and say we've not won, but maybe they should approach it from a different angle because there's been a lot more to it.' (Hunter, *The Guardian*, 2010.)

With Tim Cahill still on international duty for Australia, Everton would be without their top scorer for the Merseyside derby, as well as Steven Pienaar, left out of the squad by Moyes, having been heavily linked with a move to either Chelsea or Spurs in the January transfer window. Meanwhile, Kenny Dalglish, who had replaced Roy Hodgson as Liverpool manager eight days previously, was without the suspended Steven Gerrard and the injured Jamie Carragher.

The line-ups for the 215th Merseyside derby at Anfield were as follows:

Liverpool: Reina, Johnson, Agger, Kelly, Skrtel, Meireles, Maxi, Lucas, Spearing, Torres, Kuyt

Everton: Howard, Baines, Heitinga, Distin, Neville, Coleman, Arteta, Osman, Fellaini, Beckford, Anichebe

Liverpool began the game the brighter of the two sides, with Tim Howard called into action throughout the opening period before the American international was eventually beaten by a Raul Meireles effort on 29 minutes. In contrast, Everton rarely threatened Pepe Reina's goal in the first half but had turned the game on its head within seven minutes of the restart. Drawing level just 38 seconds into the second half thanks to Sylvain Distin's header from a Mikel Arteta corner, the Blues were 2-1 up by the 52nd minute, with Jermaine Beckford firing Everton into the lead.

With renewed impetus, Moyes's side appeared to be in control of the game, a now anxious-looking Liverpool seemingly bamboozled by Everton's quickfire double. However, with a little over 20 minutes remaining, Dalglish's side were gifted a route back into the game, when Maxi Rodriguez tumbled over Tim Howard in the penalty box and referee Phil Dowd instantly pointed to the spot. Dirk Kuyt stepped up to level the scoring. In a tense finale, both sides, inseparable in terms of league points, threw players forward to secure the bragging rights, though there was nothing to separate the two after 90 minutes.

A point at Anfield in the absence of Tim Cahill and Steven Pienaar, and four points out of a possible six over our local rivals during the 2010/11 season, is perhaps not the worst record. However, I can't help but feel that Liverpool were there for the taking and an opportunity to earn an away win in the derby for the first time since 1999 had passed us by. With four defeats out of their last five league games, a managerial departure and the noteworthy absence of both Steven Gerrard and Jamie Carragher from the matchday squad, it was a fantastic opportunity for Moyes to end his winless run at Anfield, though one he failed to take.

Two days after the 2-2 draw at Anfield, Steven Pienaar's inevitable departure was confirmed, the South African making the switch to White Hart Lane for a reported fee of around £3 million. Everton's Player of the Season for the 2009/10 campaign, the loss of such an influential player was a blow to a squad that Moyes had steadily developed, his almost telepathic relationship with left-back Leighton Baines perhaps the best left-sided partnership since the days of Pat Van Den Hauwe and Kevin Sheedy. Indeed, Moyes's assertion that any funds generated from Pienaar's sale would be insufficient to bring in the type of quality forward required was proven to be correct, with Greek attacker Apostolos Vellios arriving at the club for an undisclosed fee on the final day of the window.

Our next league victory came on 5 February, which also happened to be my 19th birthday, and no doubt I was in a celebratory mood at full time as Everton earned all three points in an entertaining 5-3 win over Blackpool at Goodison Park. With four goals from the enigmatic Louis Saha, the Frenchman's superb individual display was too much for the Seasiders, the forward matching his tally for the whole of 2010 in a single match. Indeed, with seven goals in his last six appearances, the in-form Saha would have ended the game with five goals had it not been for a hasty whistle from referee Kevin Friend, who failed to play the advantage, instead pulling Everton's move back for a free kick, disallowing a smart near-post header late in the second half.

With just one defeat in the next eight league fixtures, and 17 points out of a possible 24, the second half of Everton's 2010/11 season told a similar story to that of the year before. After a slow start, the Blues were pushing for a European spot, with a solitary point separating Everton from sixth-placed Liverpool midway through April. An extensive injury list that included Arteta (hamstring), Cahill (foot injury), Fellaini (ankle surgery) and Neville (hamstring), not to mention the recent departure of Pienaar, meant that Everton's unbeaten run throughout spring 2011 papered over the cracks for a squad that was running on fumes.

By the end of April, the gap had stretched to four points, with Liverpool having a game in hand to boot, and for the second consecutive season, the Blues looked set to miss out on European qualification at the final hurdle. With such a depleted squad, to remain in contention for a European place going into the final weeks of the season was a testament to the character within Moyes's camp, but without significant investment in the summer, there was little doubt that Everton would struggle to build on any progress made in recent seasons.

Furthermore, high-profile departures such as Joleon Lescott and Steven Pienaar to fellow Premier League clubs saw the Blues fall further down the food chain, so it begged the question, for how long could Everton expect to retain the quality within the squad without consistent European football or winning some silverware? Indeed, Everton's domestic cup displays during the 2010/11 season were ripe with familiarity. They made a third-round exit from the League Cup at the hands of League One Brentford, with the West London club progressing thanks to a 4-3 penalty shoot-out win after a 1-1 draw at full time. In the FA Cup, the Blues made light work of a trip to Scunthorpe United, before a 1-1 draw with Chelsea at Goodison Park. A second 1-1 draw in a Stamford Bridge replay took the tie to penalties, with Everton progressing as Phil Neville's decisive kick earned a 4-3 shoot-out win. The Blues' first triumph at Stamford Bridge since 1994, and the first away victory over a fellow top-flight side in the FA Cup since 1990 earned Everton a fifth-round home tie against Championship side Reading. Reading won 1-0.

The final month of the Premier League campaign saw Everton in equally frustrating form, a 1-0 defeat at West Brom sandwiched between impressive home victories over Manchester City and Chelsea. The victory over Chelsea saw Jermaine Beckford reach double figures for goals in all competitions for the season (eight in the league, one in the League Cup and one in the FA Cup), with a superb solo effort that emphasised the forward's progression since taking the step up from League One. Ultimately, Everton had to settle for a seventh-place finish in the league, four points adrift of sixth-placed Liverpool. However, neither Merseyside club would secure a European spot, with Europa League qualification going to Spurs (fifth in the league), Fulham (fair play), Stoke City (FA Cup runners-up) and Birmingham City (League Cup winners).

The final 2010/11 Premier League table looked like this:

Team	Pld	W	D	L	GF	GA	GD	Pts
1. Man United	38	23	11	4	78	37	+41	80
2. Chelsea	38	21	8	9	69	33	+36	71
3. Man City	38	21	8	9	60	33	+27	71
4. Arsenal	38	19	11	8	72	43	+29	68
5. Spurs	38	16	14	8	55	46	+9	62
6. Liverpool	38	17	7	14	59	44	+15	58
7. Everton	38	13	15	10	51	45	+6	54

26

The Arteta Money

THE SUMMER of 2011 was a worrying time for Everton Football Club. A fruitless search for fresh investment had left the club stretched to its financial limit, promising few incomings in the summer transfer window, with an exodus of talented individuals a very real possibility. A £10 million bid from Arsenal for Phil Jagielka was rejected on 21 July, though reports suggested an offer closer to the £20 million valuation was likely to be accepted. Jags was one of two Everton players that had caught Arsene Wenger's eye, the second being Mikel Arteta, as the Arsenal boss looked to replace the departing Samir Nasri and Cesc Fabregas.

Of course, while losing such key players would be less than ideal, provided Moyes received the funds to reinvest within his squad, his keen eye for a player would have left few Evertonians in any doubt that replacements would have been of a high standard. However, with reports that Barclays Bank had demanded that Everton repay outstanding debt, while also reducing the club's £25 million overdraft, a more likely outcome was that any funds raised via sales would simply balance the books, leaving Moyes without a transfer fund for the second consecutive summer.

In a meeting with the Blue Union, a coalition of Evertonians alarmed by the lack of investment in the club, Everton chairman Bill Kenwright admitted that proceeds from recent player sales, as well as the £9 million generated from the sale of the Bellefield training ground, had been paid to Barclays to reduce debts of £45 million. Kenwright laid bare the constraints on Moyes's ability to operate within the transfer market, stating: 'What do you think our squad is valued at for insurance purposes? It's about £180 million but the banks won't take that as security. You have to battle with your bank, daily for me. When David [Moyes] started I told him: "I'll make you a promise, I've got no money, but we'll move heaven and earth to give you £5 million a year." On average we give him £5.6 million every year. Nine years, that's £45 million we haven't got. Add to that the overdraft [and] you can see the trouble we're in.'

The Everton chairman continued, 'Look, we have just done a document to the bank which says you can't stop the football club from trading. Do you not think the bank doesn't ask me every week how we're doing with the sale [of Arteta]? They're desperate. So, what I've told them is: "Don't kill us this season." No, I will not sell Jagielka, just as last year I was hung, drawn and quartered for not selling Arteta. You know the four players we don't dare sell? Baines, Jagielka, Fellaini, and Tim Howard. In simple arithmetic if you want me to show you, £5 million a year for nine years is £45 million. The Pienaar money [£3 million] has gone to the bank.' (Hunter, *The Guardian*, 2011.)

Much to the embarrassment of the football club, it was revealed that football financier Keith Harris introduced Kenwright to two potential investors: one claiming to be head of ICI in the Far East, the other an inventor. Harris believed the pair controlled a hedge fund and set up the meeting with a view to the duo purchasing Everton. However, after due diligence was completed, it transpired that the so-called head of ICI lived in a one-bedroom flat and the alleged inventor was based in Manchester, with Everton falling victim to an elaborate hoax.

Despite the perilous financial situation, the meeting with the Blue Union also revealed that the club were still on the lookout for sites for a new ground, including the possibility of a shared stadium with Liverpool. 'There are six sites we're looking at,' Kenwright confirmed in the *Liverpool Echo*. 'Three of which we're really keen on: Edge Lane, Speke and the one on the East Lancs [Stonebridge Cross]. I'm led to believe John Henry is willing to discuss it [a shared stadium]. I don't know; the last lot weren't interested [Liverpool's previous owners]. To be fair, neither were we.'

However, while the meeting between Kenwright and the Blue Union provided fans with an insight into the alarming financial situation of the club, Everton responded angrily to the transcript of the meeting being made public, stating that the conversation was taped without Kenwright's knowledge or consent. A statement on the club's official website read, 'It must be pointed out that, after agreeing at the start of the meeting that there would be no note-taking, the members of the Blue Union secretly taped the entire conversation. Bill Kenwright spent three and a half hours of his day with them, but they saw fit to treat both him and the football club with a total lack of respect. We accept that they neither speak for nor are representative of the vast majority of Everton supporters.'

Indeed, an incensed Everton even consulted their solicitors, such was their outrage at the taped revelations, though decided against pursuing legal action. Ultimately, covertly taping a conversation with the club's chairman was the act of a fanbase desperate for transparency in extremely uncertain times. Football clubs will never be able to share every detail of the running of their business with their fans, such is the nature of the sport, but communication is key. With supporters kept in the dark for so many years, disenfranchised by an apparent lack of progress off the pitch and stagnation on it, it was a matter of time until fans took matters into their own hands. Covertly taped or otherwise, this short transcript provided Evertonians with a real insight into the state of the football club for the first time in many years.

After such explosive revelations, few expected anything other than a high-profile player departure before the end of the summer, and in the final hours of the transfer window, on 31 August 2011, Everton sold Mikel Arteta to Arsenal for a reported fee of £10 million. With an initial bid of £5 million abruptly rejected, the Gunners doubled their offer and, though the Spaniard's value was determined to be in the region of £20 million, the bid was accepted following Arteta's request to leave, reportedly accepting a wage cut in order to force the move. 'Mikel indicated to me that he wished to join Arsenal,' said Moyes in the *Liverpool Echo*. 'I am very disappointed to lose him, but the prospect of Champions League football was something I wasn't able to offer him.'

With Arsene Wenger's side receiving £35 million for Cesc Fabregas on 15 August and £24 million for Samir Nasri on 24 August, Everton had every right to feel aggrieved at receiving such a small fee for Arteta, as well as the lateness of the bid. No doubt, Arsenal intentionally waited until the final hours of the window to make their move, taking advantage of Everton's financial limbo to secure a cut-price deal. However, it was no secret that the money generated from any sale would be headed straight to the bankers at Barclays, so the fact that Moyes had no time to find a replacement was actually of little consequence, as he was never going to see any of the money for reinvestment anyway. The Arteta money was used to balance the books.

Further deadline-day departures included Yakubu's switch to Blackburn Rovers, for a reported £2 million, and Jermaine Beckford's £3 million move to Leicester City. As anticipated, incomings were scarce, with Moyes turning to the loan market to fill the gaps in his squad. Dutch winger Royston Drenthe arrived from Real Madrid and forward Denis Stracqualursi joined from Argentinian side Tigre, both on season-long loan deals.

Meanwhile, the 2011/12 season had already started in earnest, though Everton's opener at White Hart Lane had to be postponed due to riots in London, sparked by the deadly shooting of Mark Duggan by a police officer. Consequently, Everton's opening game of the season was a 1-0 defeat to QPR at Goodison Park, with the Blues recording their first win of the season a week later, 1-0 at Ewood Park, courtesy of a

Mikel Arteta penalty – the midfielder's final appearance in an Everton shirt, four days prior to his deadline-day move.

Everton welcomed Aston Villa to Goodison on 10 September, and with the transfer window finally closed, David Moyes could now look to get the Blues' season started without the prospect of player departures detracting from the fixtures at hand. A peaceful protest orchestrated by the Blue Union was arranged prior to kick-off, amid frustration at the continued lack of investment in the squad, with a clown bearing a cake marching down Goodison Road to mark the two-year anniversary since Everton made a significant signing.

A statement confirming the protest read, 'The aim of the Blue Union is simple, it's not to get Bill Kenwright out, it's certainly not some mindless attempt to sack the board. Its aim is to promote the concept of allowing the CEO to be left to concentrate on reducing costs, developing our revenue streams, and repairing the relationship with the fanbase whilst leaving the board to appoint a fully autonomous group of professional individuals who can effectively develop and implement a strategy that will identify and sell the club to a buyer who can demonstrate an ability and a genuine desire to take the club forward on both a commercial and a football level.' (Hunter, *The Guardian*, 2011.)

As if to emphasise the point made by the protests, Everton started the game without a recognised forward, with Victor Anichebe suffering a groin injury while on international duty with Nigeria, compounding the club's issues up top. With the deadline-day departures of Yakubu and Jermaine Beckford, and Louis Saha short on fitness, the Blues once again relied on Tim Cahill to provide a focal point in attack. Loan signing Denis Stracqualursi and 19-year-old Apostolos Vellios were on the bench.

Everton were dominant in possession, and went 1-0 up through Leon Osman 19 minutes in, though a plethora of squandered opportunities ensured Villa remained in the game. Boos greeted the appearance of Bill Kenwright on the big screen midway through the first half but were drowned out by scattered applause in a moment that exemplified the fractured state of the fanbase. With Moyes's side leading 2-1 with seven minutes remaining, Gabriel Agbonlahor headed home an undeserved equaliser for the visitors, Everton's lack of cutting edge costing two merited points, as was so frequently the case. A late Royston Drenthe cameo provided hope, but the Blues had to settle for a 2-2 draw.

'The crowd was terrific,' said Moyes at full time. 'It is not for me to say [about the protest] and I don't know how many people were involved but what I saw was a unity within the ground, certainly on the field from the players, and I thought that fed back into the stand, or vice versa from the stands down.' (*The Guardian*, 2011.)

It was clear Everton missed the influential presence of Mikel Arteta and though comfortable in possession for large parts of the game, creativity was often in short supply. With so few options available, no doubt that aforementioned unity would have to do a lot of heavy lifting as the season progressed. 'Mikel is one of my closest friends and he texted the other night to wish all the boys good luck for the game,' said Tim Cahill. 'Mikel has been a great servant to the club, but it was good business for everyone. This is a great football club that means as much to the players as the fans and we have to pull together. Hats off to the fans. When Royston came on, they nearly took the roof off and that gave all the players goosebumps. We didn't get the win, but this is a good, strong squad.' (*Liverpool Echo*, 2011.)

Indeed, Everton did retain some quality individuals throughout the squad, though with Pienaar's January switch to Spurs, followed by Arteta's summer departure, a dangerous precedent was being set that could jeopardise attempts to tie down key players to long-term contracts. 'It could do,' Moyes confirmed to *The Guardian*. 'It could set a precedent, I accept that, but on this occasion [Arteta] I thought it was the right one to do.'

With negotiations ongoing with Marouane Fellaini regarding a three-year contract extension, with two years remaining on his existing deal, the club could ill afford to repeat the mistake they had made allowing Pienaar to reach the final six months of his contract, before being forced to sell. 'I think an agreement is close,' Moyes said. 'I might be wrong in the end, but I think that one is close. We will probably have to act if it's not. I don't know if January is the exact timescale, but we do have to keep the player's value.'

When asked whether he would have funds made available to him in January, Moyes stated, 'I don't know yet. We had hoped we would lose players a little earlier [in the summer] and that would have allowed me to do something.' (Hunter, *The Guardian*, 2011.) It seemed that the club was beginning to embrace, forcibly or otherwise, its position as a selling club, hoping for the player to depart at the most opportune time, or making do with what's left. Protests are by their very nature divisive, especially within the world of football, but if this was not the time to protest at the stagnant nature of the football club, then when would be? Everton had a manager in Moyes who had done very well with little resources, but for how long could that be maintained?

By Bonfire Night 2011, Everton were slumped in 16th place in the league, four points above the relegation zone after a predictably slow start to the season. Three wins and one draw out of the opening ten league games painted a bleak picture, though Moyes's side had visited Manchester City and Chelsea, as well as welcoming Liverpool and Manchester United to Goodison Park during this period, in a testing run of fixtures. A 2-0 defeat in the Merseyside derby on 1 October left Evertonians reeling at the injustice of a Jack Rodwell sending-off in a contest sharply divided by money.

'It would be difficult because Liverpool have got a great brand,' said Moyes, when asked if the two sides could one day compete on an equal financial footing. 'On the pitch, we have not been that far apart in recent years. But the amounts Liverpool have had to spend have been considerable. Maybe they have not spent as much as Manchester City or Chelsea, but I bet it is as much as anybody else. They can't argue they've not had it.' (Rich, *The Guardian*, 2011.)

Indeed, in the nine and a half years since David Moyes took over at Goodison Park, he had spent approximately £25.8 million more than he had received in transfer fees, £84.9 million less than Kenny Dalglish's expenditure in the eight months he had been in the Anfield dugout, with Liverpool's net outlay during this period a whopping £110.7 million. Of course, Everton had been at fault over the years for squandering opportunities to close the financial gulf, most recently following the Champions League qualification in 2005. 'Would making it into the Champions League [group stages] have cracked it?' pondered Moyes. 'Possibly, but I think all the clubs who have really made it have had real financial backing as well, but it would certainly have helped.'

Uneven as the contest may have been in terms of financial backing, the 216th Merseyside derby was a finely balanced affair, before Martin Atkinson's intervention tilted it irrevocably in Liverpool's favour. A straight red card for Jack Rodwell on 23 minutes baffled the Goodison crowd, the 21-year-old's clean, one-footed challenge on Luis Suarez prompting Atkinson to draw red, no doubt influenced by the Uruguayan's theatrics. Goodison Park needs little inspiration to identify a villain, and Martin Atkinson had a history still fresh in the mind of Evertonians, blowing for full time as Phil Jagielka was poised to shoot in a 3-3 draw against Manchester United the previous September. The decision to allow him to officiate the Merseyside derby at Goodison Park a little over 12 months after such as incident was always going to end in controversy, and if such an outcome was desired, then no doubt the decision-makers will have been very pleased by what must have been an entertaining TV spectacle.

Down to ten men, Everton struggled to rediscover a foothold in the game after the interval, with Liverpool running out eventual 2-0 winners, thanks to second-half goals from Andy Carroll and Suarez. Dirk Kuyt saw his penalty attempt saved superbly by Tim Howard, after Suarez once again found himself on the floor thanks to a Phil Jagielka challenge. Ultimately, Rodwell's dismissal shaped the outcome of the match, as David Moyes concurred in his blunt appraisal of Atkinson's performance.

'It ruined the game,' Moyes told *The Guardian*. 'There are a lot of questions that people ask about derbies, about tackles, about sending-offs, and about players but that wasn't down to a bad tackle by a player. I would have been disappointed if it had been a free kick and if he had given a yellow card, you would have said: "What is that for?" You [the media] want managers to come out and say things, but it also needs people who watch and play the game and understand it and write about it to see it because it is easy for me to say it. Too often people talk about the players not doing it right, but it wasn't the players today. I don't think anyone in this world thought it was a sending-off, but it is one of those things that we just have to take that it was wrong and move on.'

Back-to-back victories over Wolves and Bolton in mid-November ensured Everton would win two league games on the bounce for the first time during the 2010/11 season, and with the welcome news that Marouane Fellaini had signed a new contract, committing himself to the club until the summer of 2016, Everton's prospects began to look a little brighter. Also committing himself to a four-and-a-half-year deal with the club was 18-year-old Ross Barkley, with Everton fending off interest from Manchester United and Chelsea for the youngster's signature. With a run of four unbeaten games, two wins and two draws, from December into early January, Everton started to put together a consistent run of results, hard-fought as they were, with Moyes stating on BBC Sport, after a 1-1 Boxing Day draw at the Stadium of Light, 'This has been the toughest season since I've joined the club.'

Indeed, it was a telling statement by Moyes, witnessing as he was the squad he had built being slowly dismantled, though there were still members of it eager to stick around. Heavily linked with a move to Arsenal the previous summer, Jagielka expressed his unwillingness to hand in a transfer request in an interview with *The Guardian*'s Andy Hunter, instead displaying a renewed commitment with a contract extension and a run of form that underlined the reason behind Arsene Wenger's interest. 'I think that is down to how I am and how I feel at Everton ... you know, the grass isn't always greener.

'I've seen a lot of players who have handed in requests and gone to other places, and two or three years down the line ... they are either not playing or not enjoying themselves ... Everton has been a fantastic club for me and hopefully it will be that way for a few more years yet. Obviously, we are going through a time when we are selling more players than we are bringing in but there is nothing I can do about that.'

The England international went on to stress the recent departures of Mikel Arteta and Steven Pienaar had affected Everton's creative output. 'It was difficult to see Mikey [Arteta] go ... Sometimes you don't know what you've got until it's gone,' Jagielka said. 'It was the same with Steven Pienaar. Maybe not a lot of people appreciated how good he was for us until he went ... I wish he was still here, but he's gone on to play Champions League football and I think most of the fans at Everton would wish him good luck as well.'

With the January transfer window set to open, Jagielka expressed his desire to see Moyes provided with the funds needed to strengthen his options. 'We sold two strikers [Yakubu and Jermaine Beckford] and Mikey [Arteta] in the summer ... We have missed a creative spark ... The whole squad hopes there are going to be more people brought in in January.'

Jags pointed out that a number of Everton players were aged 30 to 31, while there were also quite a lot of 19- to 24-year-olds, with fewer in the prime 25–28 years. 'It's not a case of starting all over again but four or five years down the line about four or five members of this squad won't be playing football anymore.'

Few could argue with Jagielka's reasoning, though perhaps more pressing was the question, would Moyes remain in charge long enough to oversee the rebuilding of the squad?

In a fixture rearranged from the opening day of the 2011/12 season, Moyes's side travelled to White Hart Lane to face a Spurs team heavily linked with making an approach for the Scot, should the FA see fit to replace the out-going Fabio Capello with Spurs boss Harry Redknapp as manager of England. The Everton boss lamented the widening gulf between the resources at his disposal and those of fellow European contenders Tottenham Hotspur. 'It is a little bit sad they are starting to pull away from us a little bit more than I would like,' Moyes said. 'It is frustrating because all managers will tell you when you are close and competing with teams, you never like to see them go away from you, but we are looking at them going away from us at this present time. They have continued to kick on and over the years they have got in some really good players. Rafael van der Vaart is one and Scott Parker is another recently.' (Hunter, *The Guardian*, 2012.)

By contrast to Spurs' continued recruitment, David Moyes had had no fresh investment in his squad for consecutive transfer windows, a situation compounded by the departure of Mikel Arteta in the summer of 2011. With Everton demanding an apology from the *Liverpool Echo* in August 2011 for reporting that Moyes would not be given the £10 million generated from the sale of Arteta to strengthen his squad, the Blues boss confirmed that he would not be given the proceeds after all. 'I think everybody knows that the bank wanted the money,' Moyes said. 'I think you all knew that.' (Hunter, *The Guardian*, 2012.)

Interestingly, the match was to be refereed by Martin Atkinson – his first involvement in an Everton fixture since he controversially dismissed Jack Rodwell in the Merseyside derby three months earlier, a decision that was eventually overturned by the FA, but one that remained a source of frustration for the Scot. 'It would have been interesting to see if they'd have given him the job at Goodison instead of away from home,' the Everton boss said in *The Guardian*, though Moyes could have few qualms about the result at White Hart Lane, as an in-form Spurs ran out 2-0 winners, though Everton did have a late penalty appeal turned down. Despite the gulf in investment between the two sides, it was only the second time Spurs had beaten Everton out of their last nine meetings.

With a run of seven unbeaten in the league, starting on 14 January 2012, it was no coincidence that Everton's New Year form was much improved after the return of Landon Donovan to the club, arriving on a two-month loan from LA Galaxy on 15 December, with the USA international eligible to play for the Blues from 4 January onwards. Returning for his second short-term spell with the club in two years, Donovan said, 'The opportunity to return to Everton and play for such a well-respected club and a manager that I hold in such high regard was something that was simply too good to pass up. I thoroughly enjoyed my time at Everton in 2010 and I'm hopeful that we can experience similar success this time around.' (Prentice, *Liverpool Echo*, 2012.)

A 1-0 Goodison Park win over Manchester City on 31 January saw Donovan provide an assist for new signing Darron Gibson, on a day which also saw Everton bring in Croatian forward Nikica Jelavic on a £5.5 million deal from Glasgow Rangers, as well as a return for fan favourite Steven Pienaar, who re-signed for the club on a six-month loan deal. 'When I came back in this morning the lads welcomed me with open arms,' said Pienaar upon his return to Everton. 'It's a good feeling, like coming back home. I understand if the fans are angry. It's part of football. One moment you're playing for a club, and everyone supports you and the next you just walk out. It's like walking out of your child's life. To get the acceptance back you have to work and show that you deserve to be forgiven. Hopefully if I can score a goal in the derby [in six weeks' time] then the guys will forgive me.' (Hunter, *The Guardian*, 2012.)

A man-of-the-match performance from Pienaar on his second Goodison Park debut in a 2-0 win over Chelsea will have no doubt earned him some clemency, with the South African international opening the scoring after five minutes.

In a successful afternoon for Everton's recent recruits, an emotional Denis Stracqualursi's first league goal for the club on 71 minutes sealed the points for the Blues, with Landon Donovan assisting in his final match before returning to Los Angeles – his seventh assist in nine appearances since arriving on loan, proving the old theory that you shouldn't return to former clubs does not apply to every player. 'Of course, I'll miss it,' Donovan admitted. 'How could you not want to be a part of this?'

The USA international continued, 'I think I came with a fresh perspective. The team had struggled a bit in the first part of the season. Even when I was watching the games back home, the energy seemed a bit down. It was almost like: "We're going to dominate possession, create chances, and then let a goal in." It was almost as though people were waiting for that to happen. But Steven Pienaar came with a fresh perspective, so did Gibbo [Darron Gibson], and that kind of changed the way the team functioned.' (Hunter, *The Guardian*, 2012.)

Indeed, while Everton's league form was much improved, there was progress too in the FA Cup with a comfortable 2-0 win over Tamworth, in a game which saw chairman Bill Kenwright confronted by protestors prior to kick-off. In a two-minute-six-second video posted online, Kenwright can be seen arriving at Goodison Park, with protestors asking, 'Where's the Arteta money?' and 'How much are you selling for, Bill?' Kenwright declines to respond, with further questions such as, 'Who's next Bill, Rodwell? Barkley?' followed by, 'You used to talk to the Everton fans, Bill, can we have some answers?' At this point, Kenwright approaches the protestors and states, 'I really did speak to all the Everton fans, all my life, until your Blue Union really betrayed this club.'

As Kenwright walks away, a protestor responds, 'Betrayed the club? How dare you? You've riddled it with debt. You've betrayed the club, Bill.' The demonstrators go on to list the failed stadium moves under Kenwright's stewardship, such as the Kings Dock and Kirkby, and the threat of Goodison Park losing its safety certificate should it fail to meet Premier

League standards. The Everton chairman then exits the frame to a chorus of, 'Let go if you love the club'. The video has been watched on YouTube over 65,000 times.

27

A Decade at Everton

EXTENDING THE unbeaten run to ten games in all competitions, Nikica Jelavic's winning goal on his Goodison Park debut saw Everton secure victory over Spurs, with the Croatian striker already delivering on his promise to bring 'Goals, goals, goals' to Everton, following his move from Rangers. Louis Saha was named on the bench for Spurs, having made the January deadline-day switch to White Hart Lane on a free transfer, leaving Goodison Park after four years and 35 goals in 115 appearances. Despite an alleged gentlemen's agreement between David Moyes and Spurs coach Harry Redknapp not to play Saha, the French striker made a late substitute appearance for his new club, hitting the post from close range in the dying minutes.

The victory over Spurs on 10 March 2012 got Moyes's ten-year anniversary celebrations off to a flying start, with the Scot just days away from marking a decade in charge of Everton Football Club. In an interview with Andy Hunter of *The Guardian*, the league's third-longest-serving manager stated that his ambition remained as fierce as ever.

'I have never been able to get my hands fully around the top teams and grab them and grasp them and pull them back into us, but there have been times when I have touched them,' Moyes said. 'There have been signs over the years that we are getting closer.'

He continued, 'When I took the job, I knew there wasn't going to be great money. The only thing I asked for was that we didn't sell any of the players unless I wanted them to go … I can't go now [to the chairman] and say I need loads of cash, but Everton's actual progression is needing to be stepped up.'

With rumours of a departure circulating for some time, with Spurs heavily linked with snapping up the Everton coach, Moyes was non-committal when questioned about his future, stating, 'I have a year to go on my contract and will speak with Bill [Kenwright] at the end of the season and then decide where we go from there.'

The Everton boss went on to insist that he remained appreciative that the club turned to the Championship when in search of a replacement for Walter Smith back in 2002. He recalled, 'The phone rang, and it was Bill asking would I come to meet him … I went to Bill's house in London. Jenny [Seagrove] his partner made us something to eat, we sat talking for a couple of hours, then I got back in the car … I got in at 5am. Bill says that I kept on talking about winning. He also says that Jenny liked me. Jenny was a good judge and she picked me.'

Recalling his early days at the club, Moyes says, 'The reception I got on my first day against Fulham made the hairs on the back of my neck stand up. The thought of it still does …

'I am quite embarrassed about the whole ten years thing. I am not coming in here with a couple of trophies to show people … but in its own way maybe being in charge of a club like Everton for ten years takes some doing.'

On 13 March, 24 hours away from celebrating a decade as manager of Everton, Moyes and his team travelled across the park to Anfield for the Merseyside derby, to face a Liverpool side who had lost three on the bounce. Everton were looking to extend their unbeaten run to ten games in all competitions, with the opportunity to leapfrog Liverpool in the league should the Blues earn all three points. Indeed, football can be a romantic game, and without a victory at Anfield during his tenure, the Everton boss had the opportunity to celebrate his tenth anniversary in style, but with an FA Cup quarter-final against Sunderland in four days' time, Moyes rested key figures Nikica Jelavic, Tim Cahill, Leon Osman, Johnny Heitinga and captain Phil Neville. Liverpool won 3-0 courtesy of a Steven Gerrard hat-trick.

Moyes's knife to a gunfight approach in the midweek derby defeat did little good in ensuring safe passage into the FA Cup quarter-finals, as the Black Cats pounced on a slow start from the Blues, with Tim Cahill's first-half header cancelling out Phil Bardsley's early opener. A Stadium of Light replay ten days later, however, saw a dominant Everton side dismiss Sunderland on their own turf, with Nikica Jelavic opening the scoring with aplomb. A second-half own goal from David Vaughan doubled Everton's lead, as the Sunderland defender played the ball off his standing leg and into his own net, sending a sizeable away following into rapturous celebrations. Victory meant a third trip to Wembley in as many years, and it would be a first 21st-century meeting of the two Merseyside clubs at the national stadium, as Liverpool would provide the opposition for the FA Cup semi-final.

Of course, Everton and Liverpool had already met five times at the original Wembley Stadium prior to its demolition in 2000, the most recent of which was the 1989 FA Cup Final. Of the five previous Merseyside derbies to take place at Wembley, Everton had won only once, with Liverpool on the winning side twice and both teams sharing the spoils on two occasions.

Milk Cup (League Cup) Final, 25 March 1984 – Liverpool 0-0 Everton

For the first Merseyside derby at Wembley, there were more than 100,000 spectators in attendance, though neither the blue nor the red half of Merseyside saw their team score a goal. However, Evertonians could justifiably feel aggrieved at Graeme Sharp's goalbound effort being handled on the line by Alan Hansen, only for the Scottish defender's clear infringement to go unpunished. Liverpool won a Maine Road replay 1-0.

Charity Shield, 18 August 1984 – Everton 1-0 Liverpool

With Liverpool league champions and Everton FA Cup winners at the end of the 1983/84 season, the two sides met at Wembley for the second time in five months to compete for the Charity Shield. Remarkably, the first ever goal at Wembley in a Merseyside derby was scored by a goalkeeper. It was, of course, Bruce Grobbelaar's own goal, after Graeme Sharp's shot pinballed off Alan Hansen on to the Liverpool keeper's leg and into his own net.

FA Cup Final, 10 May 1986 – Liverpool 3-1 Everton

A first-half Gary Lineker strike opened the scoring for Everton, but a second-half goal by Craig Johnston sandwiched between an Ian Rush double sealed the victory for Liverpool. The less said the better about this one.

Charity Shield, 16 August 1986 – Liverpool 1-1 Everton

By now a home from home for both Merseyside clubs, the 1986 Charity Shield was the fourth time this fixture was played at Wembley in little over two years. An Adrian Heath goal in the 80th minute was cancelled out by an Ian Rush equaliser seven minutes later, and the shield was subsequently shared.

FA Cup Final, 20 May 1989 – Everton 2-3 Liverpool

In an emotional fixture taking place only five weeks after the Hillsborough disaster, in which the lives of 97 Liverpool fans had been lost, both sides wore black armbands and held a minute's silence before kick-off, in memory of those who'd perished. A 90th-minute goal from substitute Stuart McCall cancelled out an early John Aldridge opener, sending the game to extra time. Ian Rush once again gave Liverpool the lead five minutes into extra time, before Stuart McCall levelled again, becoming the first substitute player to score twice in an FA Cup Final. A second goal from Ian Rush on 104 minutes won the tie for Liverpool.

Of course, English football had changed considerably since the two sides last met at Wembley, with the 1980s having been a period of footballing domination for Merseyside. With a combined eight league titles, 16 domestic cups (including Charity Shields), and three European trophies, the 1980s had seen the city of Liverpool hoover up silverware. In 2012, neither side retained the pedigree from those glory years. Arguably, the pedigree of the FA Cup had also diminished in the modern era, at least in the eyes of those at St George's Park, with Wembley providing the setting for FA Cup semi-finals since 2008.

However, while the Football Association appeared keen to maximise revenues wherever possible, the FA Cup retained its significance in the eyes of fans, and for Everton it was a golden opportunity to end a trophy drought stretching back to 1995, the Blues' last success in the competition. Moreover, with European qualification via league position unlikely, the FA Cup paved a potential pathway into Europe, with a spot in the Europa League up for grabs. Indeed, even as losing finalists, Everton would qualify for the Europa League, should the cup winners qualify for the Champions League, and with fellow semi-finalists Spurs and Chelsea battling it out for fourth spot in the league, such an outcome was possible.

'It is a great incentive for us to know we could get back into Europe,' Moyes admitted. 'We've always said Everton is a club that has been there many times and it would be great for us all to get back there. We have to try and push on in the league games, but it's going to be tough for us to get into Europe through league position. But I wouldn't completely rule it out. I said when we reached 40 points that we'd look to see where we could go, but we need to be on a really good run between now and the end of the season to catch the top six.'

Moyes continued, 'For us to be close to Liverpool after the difficult year we have had was something that maybe we wouldn't have expected. Who knows, maybe we might not be close to them come the end. But, if someone had said that with eight games to go, we'd only be two points behind Liverpool,

I'd have taken that, knowing how difficult our year was going to be.' (Hunter, *The Guardian*, 2012.)

Indeed, in the weeks leading up to the highly anticipated fixture at Wembley, Everton were very much the in-form side, with only two defeats out of the last 17 games in all competitions, and while Liverpool had progressed well in the cup during this period, their inconsistent league form had seen them record just three victories since the turn of the year. Despite the financial disparity between the two clubs, Everton were a point and a place above Liverpool in the league and Blues boss David Moyes was of the belief that his side would have the support of the neutral during the Merseyside derby at Wembley.

'The neutral would want Everton to win,' said Moyes in *The Guardian*. 'The neutrals look at Everton and see the way we have tried to build the club, tried to develop the team. It gives hope to many other clubs. I'm not saying it is the right way, but it is our way. It has been done with real hard graft. It has taken a lengthy period – that's why we have not been in enough semi-finals and finals.'

Moyes was also quick to state that Everton would have been the preferred opposition for the other three competing semi-finalists, stating, 'If they had the choice, any of the other three teams would have said they wanted to play Everton. That's fine. I'm a football man. I understand that. They know they will get a hard game, against a tough side. We will have to go and play as well if not better than we are playing if we are going to reach the final.'

Regarding the prospect of cup success assisting the club in attracting fresh investment, Moyes stated, 'Globally it can certainly help Everton, the more we can show we are competing with the big clubs in the Premier League, although I thought that in the last cup final [against Chelsea in 2009] and nothing came from that day. I have always been keen to take Everton back to the days when they were a great football club and were one of the biggest clubs. I keep changing. One year I think we are getting close, the next we drop away. At the start of this year, we looked as if we were making little progress – if anything we were fading away. But it's great credit to the players, they dug in. When you find a way of winning, you come out the other end, get a bit of form, consistency, then your style improves – and when your style improves, everyone talks about your team. We are moving in that direction at the moment.' (Hunter, *The Guardian*, 2012.)

With 87,231 fans in attendance, the line-ups for the FA Cup semi-final at Wembley, on Saturday, 14 April were as follows:

Liverpool: Jones, Johnson, Carragher, Skrtel, Agger, Henderson, Gerrard, Spearing, Downing, Suarez, Carroll

Everton: Howard, Neville, Heitinga, Distin, Baines, Osman, Gibson, Fellaini, Gueye, Cahill, Jelavic

At 20 years old, I'd never experienced a Merseyside derby at Wembley before. Of course, they were a regular occurrence at one time, but the last time the two sides met in the capital was three years before I was born. This game may not have been a final, but there was still an intensity that a generation of fans were unaccustomed to, with more than bragging rights on the line. Everton's £5.5 million January signing Nikica Jelavic was in fine form going into the game, with four goals in his last nine appearances for the Blues, and with Liverpool's third-choice keeper Brad Jones starting in goal, with Pepe Reina and Alex Doni both suspended, I was dangerously close to feeling optimistic prior to kick-off.

A 24th-minute opener from the Croatian forward further emphasised what was in retrospect misplaced optimism, as Everton seized the initiative after a tense start to proceedings. Taking advantage of a hesitant Liverpool defence, Jelavic's composure inside the penalty box contrasted with the rash defending from the experienced partnership of Daniel Agger and Jamie Carragher, with the latter's rushed clearance deflecting off Tim Cahill into the path of the in-form forward, who finished with aplomb. The blue half of Wembley erupted, a cacophony of noise and jubilation that only a derby-day goal can create, settling any Everton nerves, as the Blues coasted to half-time, untroubled by an unimaginative-looking Liverpool.

Just 45 minutes away from a derby win at Wembley and a place in the FA Cup Final, there was little doubt Moyes's side would drop deep in the second half, inviting the opposition to break down the congested and well-drilled midfield. An unmarked Andy Carroll headed wide moments after the interval, a warning shot that Everton could ill afford to ignore, though the Blues quickly regained their composure, limiting Liverpool to half-chances and efforts from range. With one foot in the final, Everton seemed content to sit back and soak up any pressure that Liverpool may apply, though Moyes's unwillingness to build on the strong start made by his side would cost him dearly.

The defensive pairing of Johnny Heitinga and Sylvain Distin appeared to be in complete control, with the two forming a formidable partnership in the absence of Phil Jagielka, who remained unavailable due to a knee injury. Heitinga, who would go on to win Everton's 2011/12 Player of the Season award, and Distin, who himself picked up Players' Player of the Season, had commanded Everton's backline to their most consistent run of form throughout the entire campaign, losing just three games since Jags's injury on 4 January. Consequently, it would no doubt take a moment of brilliance from Liverpool, or an uncharacteristic error from Everton's defence to restore parity, with Distin the unfortunate perpetrator of such an error just after the hour mark.

A painfully short back-pass from the French defender afforded Luis Suarez his first clear-cut sight of goal of the afternoon, with the Uruguayan forward taking advantage of the defensive lapse to level the tie. The concession of such a cheap goal deflated an Everton side that had seemed to be in command, and Liverpool were quick to seize the initiative, forcing Moyes's side deeper and deeper into their own half. I couldn't keep still as the half progressed, my left leg involuntarily jittering, an anxiety-induced muscle tremor that would have allowed a body language expert to read me like a book.

With the game seemingly destined for extra time, a challenge on Steven Gerrard from substitute Seamus Coleman prompted referee Howard Webb to award Liverpool a free kick. Andy Carroll, Liverpool's £35 million signing, out-jumped Marouane Fellaini to latch on to substitute Craig Bellamy's delivery, his header ghosting past a motionless Tim Howard with three minutes remaining. It was the inevitability of it, that's what hurt the most. I make a point of never leaving the ground before the final whistle, no matter the score, but after Carroll's sucker punch, I couldn't bear to stick around.

'It didn't seem as though they caused us many problems. We pretty much handed the game over,' claimed Tim Cahill, in a chilling post-mortem. 'They scored the two goals, and they have to do that to beat us, but they are going to find it difficult to win the final. But they seem to have luck on their side when they play Everton. They get the rub of the green and a few decisions didn't go our way.' (Hunter, *The Guardian*, 2012.)

David Moyes provided a similar appraisal of his side's performance, stating, 'It was our own fault today because we gave them the opportunities. I thought we were always going to have to deal with Liverpool in the second half. They were 1-0 down in the semi-final of the cup – if it was the other way around, we'd be the same. Liverpool started brightly. I thought we'd weathered it and hoped we might get a second. As it was, we just got ourselves in a wee bit of trouble.' (*The Guardian*, 2012.)

A wee bit of trouble indeed. Everton's third defeat to Liverpool in 2011/12 ended the Blues' hopes of silverware for another season, simultaneously paving the way for Liverpool to compete in their second domestic cup final of the year, having beaten Cardiff City in the League Cup Final in February. The financial disparity between the two sides notwithstanding, it was David Moyes's lack of ambition that cost his side a place in the FA Cup Final, his proclivity to show Liverpool far too much respect. At 1-0, Everton were too cautious, too fearful to push for a second goal and it cost us dearly. Had Everton progressed, it would have set them up for a rematch of the 2009 FA Cup Final against Chelsea, who went on to win their third FA Cup in four years with a 2-1 victory over Liverpool.

A return to Premier League action following the FA Cup heartbreak saw Everton snatch a dramatic point at Old Trafford, with two goals in the final seven minutes earning the Blues a 4-4 draw. A 4-0 win over Fulham the following week saw Nikica Jelavic score his third brace since his January arrival, earning the striker the Premier League Player of the Month award for April 2012. A further goal from Jelavic in the final game of the season helped Everton beat Newcastle United 3-1 at Goodison Park to close the campaign on the back of a nine-game unbeaten run in the league, finishing above Liverpool for the first time in seven years, with Leighton Baines rewarded for a superb campaign by being named in the PFA Premier League Team of the Year.

Everton's consistent league form in the second half of the season wasn't enough to secure a place in the Europa League, however, meaning European football would be absent from Goodison Park. Nikica Jelavic, who arrived halfway through the season, finished the campaign as Everton's top scorer with nine league goals, and 11 in all competitions, exemplifying the lack of fire power throughout the rest of the squad, which ultimately cost Moyes's side a European spot. Moreover, it gave further credence to Moyes's continued pleas for investment, alongside those of the Blue Union. Had there been the necessary investment in the squad during the previous transfer windows, Everton's prospects could have looked brighter, but ultimately, the club's make-do-and-mend approach ensured Moyes had to work with one hand tied behind his back.

The Premier League table at the end of the 2011/12 season

Team	Pld	W	D	L	GF	GA	GD	Pts
1. Man City	38	28	5	5	93	29	+64	89
2. Man United	38	28	5	5	89	33	+56	89
3. Arsenal	38	21	7	10	74	49	+25	70
4. Spurs	38	20	9	9	66	41	+25	69
5. Newcastle	38	19	8	11	56	51	+5	65
6. Chelsea	38	18	10	10	65	46	+19	64
7. Everton	38	15	11	12	50	40	+10	56
8. Liverpool	38	14	10	14	47	40	+7	52

28

Hibbo Scores, We Riot

AS THE 2011/12 season concluded in frustrating fashion, and David Moyes entered the final year of his contract with Everton Football Club, the Blues boss was eager to state that he was to meet with chairman Bill Kenwright to discuss his future, but stressed his belief that he only required modest investment in his squad. 'I speak with Bill every day, but I plan to go down and see him in the next week or two to discuss things,' Moyes said. 'I've got a year to go anyway so it's not as though it's absolutely desperate. We will talk about it in the next week or so. I'll just have the conversation with the chairman. We didn't need a great deal of money to change things around in January. With £5 million we got Darron Gibson and Jelavic, and we also got Pienaar and Landon [Donovan] in on loan. Without an awful lot we gave ourselves a fighting chance and got Everton back on the rails again. We'd fallen off in the first half of the season. We don't need an awful lot. I just need to know there is a chink of light.'

He continued, 'I don't need reassurances about managing Everton. A lot of people would love the opportunity that I'm in and for me to have been here ten years is incredible. But I want to be able to compete and I want to be ambitious. I want to give the people something more to shout about than we have done. We have tended to pick up from January and have been more optimistic and then it has drained away during the summer because we have not been able to keep the fire in everyone's belly. I think that has affected the players as well.

We learned we had to get things done early six or seven years ago but if you don't have the money to get things done, what can you do?' (Hunter, *The Guardian*, 2012.)

With an air of resignation in David Moyes's tone, an acceptance that there would be limited funds available to him once more, there was little surprise that a contract extension was not forthcoming. Having been linked with a move to White Hart Lane throughout the 2011/12 season, speculation of Moyes's departure went into overdrive with Spurs' surprise sacking of Harry Redknapp on 13 June 2012, prompting the Everton boss to distance himself from such rumours, insisting that he had not been contacted about the vacant position.

'I hope to meet all my ambitions at Everton, but you never know in this game,' Moyes said. 'I've had no contact. I'm ambitious and I want to try and win things and ideally, I want to do that with Everton. We brought in two or three players in January, and you could see the difference it made to the club, so we want to try and do that again. I told my chairman four weeks ago [that investment was needed] so for me my concentration is on getting Everton ready for the start of the season, and hopefully getting off to a better one than we've had in recent years. I've always been loyal, and I will continue to be loyal to Everton – as long as they want me, I'm happy there.' (*Daily Mail*, 2012.)

There is little doubt that had Spurs made a serious approach for Moyes, he would have made the switch to White Hart Lane. With a year remaining on his contract at Everton, and a slim chance of significant investment, few would argue against the thought that the project had gone a little stale. By contrast, Spurs had European football, a top squad of players and financial backing, which will have been a tempting prospect for a manager accustomed to a much more modest budget. A distinct lack of movement regarding extending Moyes's existing contract with Everton was a clear indicator that if Spurs made a proposal, it would likely be accepted. However, on 3 July Spurs appointed ex-Chelsea boss Andre Villas-Boas, putting to bed any queries regarding David

Moyes's immediate future at Everton, though with contract talks ongoing beyond the summer, question marks remained regarding the Scot's long-term plans.

On 4 July Everton made their first acquisition of the summer transfer window, with Scottish international Steven Naismith arriving from Glasgow Rangers, and he was joined at the end of the month by Steven Pienaar, making his permanent return to the club in a £4.5 million deal, beginning his fourth separate stint at Everton (two previous loans and one previous permanent contract). Moyes's attacking options were further bolstered by the August signing of Belgian international Kevin Mirallas, who joined from Olympiacos for £6 million.

Meanwhile, Everton bid farewell to a player synonymous with the David Moyes era, and a personal all-time favourite, Tim Cahill, who made the switch to MLS side New York Red Bulls for a fee of £1 million after eight years at Goodison Park. 'I want to thank everyone at Everton,' Cahill said to the *Liverpool Echo* upon his departure from Goodison Park, 'from the club to the tremendous supporters. It has been a privilege to be an Everton player for the past eight years and it was a very difficult decision to leave. I will always support Everton and I wish the club the best of luck in the future.'

As one of the club's longest-serving players departed for pastures new, another celebrated a decade of service, with academy graduate Tony Hibbert awarded a testimonial against Greek side AEK Athens, the team against whom Hibbert made his 18th appearance in a European competition for Everton, equalling a club record. Wayne Rooney asked to play for Everton for Hibbo's testimonial, only for the game to clash with United's pre-season fixture against Barcelona in Gothenburg. 'It was great that he asked me,' Hibbert said of his former team-mate, 'but it just worked out that Manchester United also have a game and he was quite upset when he realised. It says everything about Wayne that he was willing to do that. He probably would have got a bad reception, but he is not fazed about that. He loves Everton. Deep down he is still an Evertonian.'

Hibbert continued, 'I know for a fact he still goes to games. He will do anything for Everton. It was a great honour for me that he wanted to play in the game. I was surprised when he asked whether he could play and if I would like him to. I jumped at the chance but obviously he has other commitments.' (Hunter, *The Guardian*, 2012.)

Hibbert, who held the unwanted record of having never scored a goal in his 309 appearances for Everton, stated he had no plans to take a penalty against AEK Athens, should one be awarded. 'Everyone has been asking me that. The manager hasn't said anything, nobody has. I would rather us win 1-0 than us get beaten 2-1 and I score the goal. I just want to win. I don't know why everyone is saying I should take a penalty either. It's an easy way of scoring, isn't it? If I'm going to do it, I want it to be a 30-yarder.'

With Everton 3-1 up against the Greek opposition, the Blues were awarded a 20-yard free kick in front of the Gwladys Street in the 53rd minute, and a purposeful Tony Hibbert stood over the ball. Teed up by team-mate Steven Pienaar, the Everton defender rifled a shot through the wall and past keeper Dimitris Konstantopoulous, prompting a pitch invasion in a good-natured and long-promised celebration of a goal from the full-back. Tony Hibbert scored, and Goodison rioted.

'Maybe I've been picking the wrong man for ten years to take the free kicks,' joked Moyes afterwards. 'I'll need to re-look at it. You couldn't write the script. It wasn't as if we set it up, it wasn't a penalty kick. I'd love to say it was a free kick we've worked on, but it wasn't. It was a terrific night and for him to get the goal and us to cap it off with a decent team performance, overall, we're pleased with that. I hope he did have a good night because he deserves it. Anyone who spends ten years at a club is a rarity, so he deserves that opportunity. He needed that game because he's been carrying a hamstring problem, so he needed it. It was just to get him off and the chance of an ovation. He's probably seen it before with goalscorers and that, so it was good to give it to him.' (*Liverpool Echo*, 2012.)

Meanwhile, as one academy graduate capped off a decade of service with a testimonial, another departed, as Jack Rodwell was sold to Manchester City for an initial fee of £12 million, a move foreshadowed by Blue Union demonstrators eight months prior during a confrontation with chairman Bill Kenwright, when one protestor asked, 'Who's next, Bill? Barkley? Rodwell?' Indeed, Rodwell's departure came as a disappointment, and though he failed to live up to expectations throughout his career, it would have been interesting to see how he could have progressed had he not been hampered by injuries and limited playing time at City.

On 20 August, Everton began their season with a home fixture against the previous year's runner-up, Manchester United. A 1-0 win for the Blues resulted, courtesy of a thumping Marouane Fellaini header just before the hour mark – the Belgian's arborescent frame rising high above Nemanja Vidic to give Everton a deserved lead. The goal earned Moyes's side their first opening-day victory in five years, with Everton's match-winner producing a rampant individual performance. A 3-1 win at Villa Park followed, and with the 2011/12 season having concluded with a nine-game unbeaten run in the league, Everton began the 2012/13 season by extending that overall run to 11. Avoiding defeat against West Brom a week later would see the Blues record their longest spell without losing a league game since the title-winning year of 1984/85. Everton lost 2-0 at the Hawthorns.

Sitting second in the table by the end of September, with 13 points out of a possible 18, David Moyes was awarded the Premier League Manager of the Month award, despite an early League Cup exit to Championship side Leeds United following a 2-1 defeat at Elland Road. On 19 October, Everton signed free agent Thomas Hitzlsperger on a short-term contract until January 2013, following the German international's release from VfL Wolfsburg.

A Julio Cesar own goal in a 1-1 draw at QPR ensured that Everton recorded their best scoring start to a Premier League season, with 15 goals in the opening eight league games, though a frustrating afternoon at Loftus Road saw Moyes's side fail to capitalise on a plethora of chances, compounded by Steven Pienaar's sending-off for two bookable offences, meaning the South African would be unavailable for Everton's next game: the Merseyside derby at Goodison Park. Everton had made their best start to a campaign since 2004/05 and looked to make amends for a 2-0 defeat in the corresponding fixture from the previous campaign, though Blues boss David Moyes expressed his concern that the game's outcome could be affected by the theatrics of Liverpool's Luis Suarez, just as it had been in 2011/12.

'People talk about the sending-offs in these derbies without talking about the decisions. Last year's one was a dive and a really poor decision by the referee. It ruined the game,' said Moyes, in reference to Jack Rodwell's dismissal for an alleged foul on Suarez in October 2011. When asked if he feared a repeat of such an incident, the Everton boss told *The Guardian*, 'I do because I think he [Suarez] has got history. But I'm not the referee. What it will do is turn the supporters away from football because they [players who dive] are very good at it.'

Moyes continued, 'It's a hard job for the referees, it really is, but it will turn supporters away from it if they think players are conning their way to results. People like to see things done correctly ... You're going to take every decision that you get going for you, but I don't think supporters like it when players are out to manufacture it. I don't think there are many players out there who really do it ... But I would hope if I got one who did I would be big enough to say: "Would you please stay on your feet and stop going down easy." Supporters just don't like the thought of people going down easily. Everybody who has played football at any level would hate that in their game. People who play the game find it very hard to go along with.'

It was a sentiment shared by Jim Boyce, vice-president of FIFA, who voiced his concerns over simulation following a controversial penalty appeal involving Suarez during Stoke City's visit to Anfield on 7 October 2012. Boyce stated, 'I watched the latest Suarez incident two or three times and to me it is nothing less than a form of cheating. It is becoming a little bit of a cancer within the game, and I believe if it is clear to everyone that it is simulation then that person is trying to cheat, and they should be severely punished for that.' (*Metro*, 2012.)

Stoke City boss Tony Pulis was equally forthright in his condemnation of Suarez's attempts to con officials, stating, 'Retrospective decisions are made on a Monday and Luis Suarez should be punished. The one in the penalty box was an embarrassment and how he wasn't booked [for diving] I don't know.' (*The Independent*, 2012.)

Pulis's request for retrospective punishment echoed similar calls made by David Moyes back in 2006 and reiterated in 2012. The Everton boss said, 'I'm of the view that retrospective viewing of diving should be more important than some of the technology they are already talking about bringing in. I think it would make the referee's job an awful lot easier if that was there. If you do it and you get banned for it, it wouldn't take long before you cut it out. It wouldn't take much – four or five people on a panel: referees, players and managers. It could be easily done.' (Hunter, *The Guardian*, 2012.)

In a January 2013 interview with the *Liverpool Echo*, Luis Suarez would admit to deliberately going to ground, with the Uruguayan forward making reference to the incident against Stoke City, stating, 'Football is like that. Sometimes you do things on the field and later you think, "Why the hell did I do that?" I was accused of falling inside the box in a match and it's true I did it that time, because we were drawing against Stoke at home and we needed anything to win. But after that everybody jumped out to talk – the Stoke coach and the Everton coach … I understand that the Suarez name sells [papers].'

Prior to the visit of Liverpool to Goodison Park on 28 October, the two sides had undergone contrasting starts to the new campaign, with Everton recording four wins, three draws and one defeat from the opening eight league games, while Liverpool had won just two games out of their opening eight, alongside three draws and three defeats. However, form matters little in the Merseyside derby, as Everton had to fight back from two goals down to earn a 2-2 draw in a game that predictably saw Luis Suarez fulfil his role as pantomime villain.

The line-ups for the 219th Merseyside derby in front of 39,613 fans at Goodison Park were as follows:

Everton: Howard, Coleman, Jagielka, Distin, Baines, Neville, Osman, Fellaini, Mirallas, Naismith, Jelavic

Liverpool: Jones, Enrique, Agger, Skrtel, Wisdom, Sahin, Gerrard, Allen, Sterling, Suarez, Suso

In an uncharacteristically open half for a Merseyside derby, Liverpool's inexperienced side started brightly, with Luis Suarez inevitably punishing a lethargic-looking Everton, following Moyes's criticism of the forward in the pre-match build-up. Unmarked at the back post, Suarez thrashed an effort across goal, with Leighton Baines's attempted block inadvertently deflecting the ball past Tim Howard to give Liverpool a 1-0 lead on 14 minutes. The Uruguayan international celebrated by running over to the Everton dugout and throwing himself to the ground in front of David Moyes, his mock-theatrics prompting referee Andre Marriner to have a word with the Liverpool forward.

A second from Suarez doubled Liverpool's lead six minutes later: completely unmarked for a second time, he scored with a glancing header from a Steven Gerrard free kick. Everton needed an immediate response, and got one inside two minutes, as Leon Osman's drive found its way through a packed goalmouth and into Brad Jones's bottom-right corner to halve the deficit. The Blues quickly grew into the game, with new signing Kevin Mirallas influential down the left flank, the Belgian combining with international team-mate Marouane Fellaini, who drove a ball across Liverpool's goal for Steven Naismith to prod home a deserved equaliser ten minutes before the break.

An injured Mirallas didn't reappear for the second half, no doubt to the relief of the tormented Andre Wisdom at right-back for Liverpool, though Everton retained the overall edge for the second half as the visitors relied on the counter-attack. As full time approached, Brendan Rodgers's side looked to have snatched the points as Suarez converted from close range after Sebastian Coates flicked on a Gerrard free kick, prompting the Liverpool captain to run half the length of the pitch and celebrate on his knees in front of the travelling fans. Gerrard, oblivious to the fact that the goal had been ruled out for offside, continued to celebrate as play continued behind him, as Everton launched a late counter-attack before Marriner blew for full time.

'I thought there were bits of it when we were unlucky not to go on and win it,' Moyes said after the 2-2 draw. 'Even in the first half when we got it back to two each, I thought we had a couple of good chances to make it 3-2, but when you go 2-0 down you think it's a long way back, so great credit to the players for keeping at it, sticking in there and eventually getting their reward for that.'

Moyes continued, 'I don't know if we actually deserved to be 2-0 down at the time. I didn't think we started that bad but we lost a goal, a little bit of a counter-attack and we lose a goal from it and it carries a little bit of luck as well because the shot's not going on target and it hits off Bainesy and goes in, but then it was unlike us to lose the goal the way we did from the free kick. We wouldn't normally be as poor as that. So, you find yourself 2-0 down, but the players stuck at it, done some really good things after that, were a little bit unlucky not to get more than the two goals we scored.'

On Luis Suarez's theatrical celebration, Moyes said, 'I really don't mind because if it had been me, I might have done it to him as well, but he might have to dive in front of a few managers now because I think there's more than me who said what I did.' (BBC Sport, 2012.)

Liverpool captain Steven Gerrard was quick to criticise Everton's style of play in the wake of the 2-2 draw, comparing the Blues' approach to that of Tony Pulis's notoriously physical Stoke City. Gerrard later withdrew the comments, explaining they were said in frustration at Suarez's stoppage-time goal being disallowed, though it was the second occasion in the opening months of the season that the Blues boss had to defend his team. Following Everton's opening-day victory over Manchester United, Sir Alex Ferguson accused Moyes of 'just lumping the ball forward' to Fellaini.

'I know, absolutely, that when Fergie has a dig at you it means it's a compliment in a way,' Moyes said in response to his critics. 'Maybe we have been competing better against United in recent seasons, and we are beginning to compete better against most top clubs now, so that's why these things are being said. I'd sooner get that, them having a dig, than people being nice about us because we've lost. When you're easy to beat then it's easy to be nice, but the things is, we are definitely not easy to beat these days.' (Hunter, *The Guardian*, 2012.)

Indeed, there is little doubt that Everton were playing some tremendous football at this time, and with just two league defeats prior to Christmas 2012 (against West Brom away and Reading at home), Everton's consistent form had Moyes's side in fourth spot by December, leapfrogging fellow Champions League hopefuls Spurs with a 2-1 win at Goodison Park. After going a goal down courtesy of a 76th-minute Clint Dempsey strike, the points looked to be heading back to north London, until Steven Pienaar latched on to Seamus Coleman's cross in the 90th minute to equalise with Everton's 1,000th Premier League goal. Goal 1,001 arrived exactly 88 seconds later when Nikica Jelavic converted from close range to conjure a dramatic win.

Everton would find themselves without the talismanic Marouane Fellaini for the final three games of the calendar year, however, as the Belgian received a retrospective three-match ban for a headbutt on Stoke City's Ryan Shawcross in a 1-1 draw at the Britannia Stadium on 15 December. A win away at West Ham followed by a Boxing Day victory over Wigan Athletic at Goodison Park stretched the Blues' unbeaten run to seven league games, before a 2-1 home defeat to Chelsea on 30 December disrupted Everton's streak, with

Moyes's side losing at Goodison Park for the first time since March 2012.

Meanwhile, with David Moyes's contract set to expire at the end of the season, the Everton boss declared in *The Guardian* that he would be unwilling to discuss the possibility of an extension until after the January transfer window, with the Scot suggesting that the club's immediate and long-term plans would likely influence his decision. 'I will probably wait until we have got over January and see how things go,' said the Scot. 'I want to see what we're going to do and where the club are looking to move to in the future. And that's what I'm really looking for as well. It's probably going to be after the New Year before we speak. I think most people would say the Everton job looks as though it is a good job and we've got a good team. It has taken a long time to get to this point but what we're looking to do at Everton is get to the point where it's easy to keep all our good players. That obviously means getting to the summit or getting around the summit.'

29

He's Not the Moyesiah, He's a Very Naughty Boy

EVERTON HAD a quiet transfer window in January 2013, acquiring 18-year-old defender John Stones from Barnsley in a deadline-day deal reported to be in the region of £3 million, and extending Thomas Hitzlsperger's short-term deal until the end of the 2012/13 season. Sylvain Distin also signed a one-year contract extension, keeping him at the club until the summer of 2014.

By the end of February, Everton's Champions League ambitions had taken a blow, with just two league wins out of the opening eight fixtures of the calendar year, plus three draws and two losses. Indeed, back-to-back defeats at Old Trafford and Carrow Road at the end of February 2013 saw Moyes's side lose two consecutive league games for the first time since March 2012. However, on 2 February, Everton recorded their 12th draw of the season, already one more than the whole of the previous campaign, as a lack of cutting edge looked likely to inhibit European qualification.

It appeared that David Moyes was poised to wait until the end of the campaign before deciding on his immediate future, having previously stated that he would wait until the end of the January transfer window. With just four months until his existing deal expired, 'Dithering Dave' had yet to make a decision, with fans and players alike kept in the dark over what plans the Scot had. 'I'll give as much as I can, but I've said – and I've spoken with the chairman – that I want to see how the team do,' Moyes said in *The Scotsman*, ahead of an FA Cup fifth round tie at League One Oldham Athletic. 'I want to see how we do in the cups; I want to see how we do in the league, and it's more than likely I won't make a decision until the end of the season. So, you can ask me every week, but I'll probably give you the same answer.'

Having progressed against Oldham, via a replay, Everton earned a home FA Cup quarter-final tie against relegation-threatened Wigan Athletic, presenting the Blues with the opportunity to return to Wembley for the second consecutive season, but three quickfire goals in three minutes and 23 seconds saw the visitors stun a shell-shocked Goodison Park, leaving Moyes to lament another missed opportunity to end the now 18-year trophy drought. Given the uncertainty surrounding his future, Moyes was adamant that his contract situation was not a source of distraction for his players.

'People will always draw conclusions about my contract situation,' the Everton boss said. 'Or the fact that I have been here for more than a decade, but that game today had nothing to do with those issues. I couldn't say if this was a defining moment.' (Lovejoy, *The Guardian*, 2013.)

Although Moyes dismissed suggestions that the uncertainty surrounding his future contributed to a dip in form from his players, his confused and contradictory comments indicate that indeed there may be problems behind the scenes, as the Everton boss admitted that he'd been concerned about aspects of his team's performances, most recently in the 3-1 victory over Reading on 2 March. 'I thought there were bits against Reading last week I wasn't so sure about,' Moyes told the *Liverpool Echo*. 'Obviously, I'm not going to publicise them and say what they are, and I'm not saying they're all of the things which came to fruition against Wigan.'

Indeed, as Moyes procrastinated over his contract, it became clear that his departure at the end of the campaign was increasingly likely. If he had hoped to crown off his 11-

year tenure with an FA Cup win, ending a trophy drought stretching back almost two decades, then he'd blown it. After the abject elimination, which saw Everton booed off at full time, Moyes welcomed league champions Manchester City to Goodison Park on the 11th anniversary of his appointment, as the Blues looked to bounce back in pursuit of Europe.

Though Roberto Mancini's side travelled to L4 without Vincent Kompany, Sergio Aguero and Yaya Toure, who'd fallen ill overnight, City still possessed enough top-class talent to put out an enviable XI, but returned to Manchester empty-handed nonetheless, as a ten-man Everton ran out 2-0 winners with a first-half Leon Osman strike and a late Nikica Jelavic effort sealing the points. Such a Jekyll and Hyde transformation from the wretched performance against Wigan eight days earlier no doubt left many Evertonians frustrated at the contrasting displays, though Moyes insisted that he expected a response from his players. 'I'd have been surprised and disappointed if I hadn't got that reaction after last week,' the Everton boss said in *The Guardian*. 'If you watched us regularly, you'd have to say what you saw today is what Everton do. We were resilient and hard to beat, putting bodies on the line to stop them scoring. We were rubbish last week, but that performance doesn't happen very often at Everton.'

Despite the FA Cup elimination, David Moyes was awarded the Premier League Manager of the Month award for March, his second of the 2012/13 season and his tenth in total during his time as Everton boss. A superb solo goal from Kevin Mirallas earned Everton a 1-0 win over Stoke City on 30 March, before the Blues recorded their 13th draw of the campaign at White Hart Lane. A further draw at fellow Champions League hopefuls Arsenal, followed by a 1-0 defeat at Sunderland, left Everton six points adrift of fourth-placed Chelsea, who also had a game in hand. With four games remaining of the campaign, Moyes admitted that Champions League qualification was no longer within reach.

'We won't get a top-four position,' said Moyes. 'Every game was becoming a must-win and that will be difficult now. It was an important game for us, and we could not take anything from it. We did not play well. We had an awful lot of pressure in the second half, but we maybe didn't have the quality to get the goal.' (BBC Sport, 2013.)

With fourth looking unlikely, Everton would need a fifth-place finish in the league to secure European football, with the other two Europa League spots going to Swansea City as League Cup winners, and eventual FA Cup winners Wigan Athletic, who were guaranteed European football regardless of the outcome of the cup final, due to fellow finalists Manchester City's Champions League qualification. A 1-0 win over Fulham at Goodison Park ensured Moyes's side remained in Europa League contention, with just three points separating sixth-placed Everton and fifth-placed Spurs, though the Blues had played one game more than Andre Villas-Boas's side.

A 1-0 victory for Spurs over Southampton on 4 May put the north London club six points clear of Everton, putting additional pressure on their 5 May visit to Anfield for the Merseyside derby. Everton took the trip across the park with a five-point advantage over Liverpool, who were sat in seventh place in the league. A win would not only keep the Blues in contention for Europe, but with only two games still to play, it would at least consolidate sixth place, ensuring Everton finished above Liverpool. Having finished higher in the table in the 2011/12 campaign, to do so in the 2012/13 season would mean successive top-flight finishes above Liverpool for the first time since 1936/37.

The line-ups in the 220th Merseyside derby at Anfield were as follows:

Liverpool: Reina, Johnson, Agger, Carragher, Enrique, Downing, Gerrard, Lucas, Henderson, Coutinho, Sturridge

Everton: Howard, Coleman, Jagielka, Distin, Baines, Osman, Pienaar, Gibson, Fellaini, Mirallas, Anichebe

Both sides were in strong form prior to kick-off, with Everton having lost just one out of the last eight league games, and Liverpool losing just one out of their last nine, though the home side were notably without Luis Suarez, who was serving a suspension following the infamous incident a fortnight earlier, when the Liverpool forward bit the shoulder of Chelsea defender Branislav Ivanovic in a 2-2 draw at Anfield. Indeed, without their most influential player, Liverpool were there for the taking, especially as a win would keep Everton in contention for European qualification going into the penultimate game of the season.

However, as Merseyside derbies go, this was a relatively low-key encounter, with neither keeper troubled all that much and the first booking not arriving until the 56th minute. In stark contrast to the 2-2 draw at Goodison Park in October 2012, this was a tame affair that had the appearance of an end-of-season fixture between two teams with little to play for. If this was to be David Moyes's final trip to Anfield as Everton manager, it was a game that mirrored his cautious approach on previous visits – there would be no gung-ho finale.

Everton had the better of the first half, while Liverpool grew into the game after the interval, but 11 minutes into the second period, Everton took the lead, or so they thought. As Sylvain Distin climbed above Jamie Carragher to head home a Leighton Baines corner, the Blues looked to have finally broken the deadlock, until referee Michael Oliver ruled it out, claiming that Victor Anichebe had blocked Liverpool keeper Pepe Reina. Anichebe's protestations fell on deaf ears and did little more than earn the Nigerian forward a yellow card as Moyes cut a frustrated figure on the touchline.

An immense performance from Phil Jagielka, captain for the day in the absence of the injured Phil Neville, illustrated why the England international was to be given the responsibility permanently, with Neville set to retire at the end of the campaign, though there was little else to shout about in the stalemate at Anfield. Bill Kenwright responded to the final whistle with a clenched fist raised in the air. Despite being denied all three points thanks to a dubious refereeing decision, leaving European qualification less likely, the Everton chairman embarrassingly celebrated the 0-0 draw at Anfield as if it were a win.

'It won't comfort me to finish above Liverpool,' Moyes said after the 0-0 draw. 'The comfort for me would be if we could qualify for Europe. We have very nearly got the best points total we have ever had [in the Premier League]. We got 61 a few years ago when we qualified for the Champions League. We are on 60 now so we've had a pretty good season and I will be disappointed if we don't get rewarded for it.' (Hunter, *The Guardian*, 2013.)

The draw at Liverpool left Everton five points adrift of fifth-placed Spurs, but a midweek draw at Stamford Bridge for Andre Villas-Boas's side put them six points clear in the race for Europe. Spurs also held a marginal advantage with their plus-18 goal difference, compared to Everton's plus-14, so Everton's chances of leapfrogging the north London club looked slim.

Meanwhile, on 8 May, Manchester United manager Sir Alex Ferguson announced his retirement from football, having guided United to their 20th league title with four games to spare. Just 24 hours later, three days ahead of West Ham United's visit to Goodison Park, David Moyes announced that he would be taking over in the Old Trafford dugout from 1 July, signing a six-year contract.

'The manager met chairman Bill Kenwright early yesterday evening and confirmed his desire to join Manchester United,' Everton said in a statement via the club's website. 'The chairman, on behalf of the club, would like to place on record his thanks to David for the massive contribution he has made to Everton since his arrival in March 2002. He has been an outstanding manager.'

Upon being offered the job at United, Moyes said, 'It's a great honour to be asked to be the next manager of Manchester United. I am delighted that Sir Alex saw fit to recommend me for the job. I have great respect for everything he has done and for the football club. I know how hard it will be to follow the best manager ever, but the opportunity to manage Manchester United isn't something that comes around very often and I'm really looking forward to taking up the post next season.'

He continued, 'I have had a terrific job at Everton, with a tremendous chairman and board of directors and a great set of players. I will do everything in my power to make sure we finish as high as possible in the table. Everton's fantastic fans have played a big part in making my years at Goodison so enjoyable and I thank them wholeheartedly for the support they have given me and the players. Everton will be close to me for the rest of my life.' (Jackson, *The Guardian*, 2013.)

Consequently, Everton's final home game of the 2012/13 season against West Ham United on 12 May 2013, proved to be David Moyes's Goodison Park farewell, and the ground rose to its feet prior to kick-off to give a round of applause to the man that the stadium announcer emphasised was 'still the Everton manager'. A wave to all four stands typified Moyes's no frills or fuss attitude, as did the routine 2-0 victory over Sam Allardyce's West Ham, with two goals from Kevin Mirallas either side of half-time – his eighth and ninth league goals of the season.

The teams for Moyes's final match in charge at Goodison Park were as follows:

Everton: Howard, Coleman, Jagielka, Distin, Baines, Mirallas, Gibson, Osman, Pienaar, Fellaini, Anichebe

West Ham United: Jaaskelainen, Demel, Collins, Reid, O'Brien, Diame, O'Neil, Collison, Nolan, Jarvis, Carroll

The last-minute introduction of substitute Tony Hibbert, the only player remaining from Moyes's first game in charge back in March 2002, indicated there was perhaps still a little room for sentiment. Indeed, it was an emotional day at Goodison Park, and the final home game of a season that deserved more. A win for Spurs at Stoke City meant that Everton would miss out on Europe, but with just one home league defeat, Everton's best home record since the title-winning 1986/87 season, and with Champions League qualification secured in 2004/05 with fewer points, 2012/13 was a campaign that promised much but ultimately delivered little.

Rousing renditions of 'Who the fuck are Man United?' rang around Goodison throughout Moyes's final home game in charge, though Everton's soon-to-be-ex-manager was given a send-off that brought tears to the eyes of the stoic Glaswegian. 'It was really emotional from the moment I came in to find all the stewards clapping me,' Moyes told *The Guardian*. 'I didn't really know what to do.

'It was the same on my first day here when I went on the pitch and the crowd probably didn't know who I was. I am fortunate I had the reception I had today. I am humbled. More important, was how well Everton played. They played like a top team, and they would have been a match for any side that came here.'

Moyes continued, 'What I will miss is what you saw in the second half. The supporters weren't cheering David Moyes, they were cheering their football club. That was the toughest part for me today. The crowd showed how big Everton are and what it means to them. Theirs is a club that has had some difficult times. I don't want to labour the point, but we don't have what a lot of people have got but we don't half make it up in other ways.'

Denied a farewell contribution by injury, Phil Neville, who was also leaving the club after eight years, joined his team-mates in forming a guard of honour for David Moyes after the game. Joining them was ex-player Tim Cahill, who had flown in from New York, having been denied a proper farewell himself following his 2012 departure. Walking out to 'Z-Cars' as Everton manager one final time, David Moyes completed a lap of appreciation around the pitch, as banners displayed messages such as, 'Goodbye and good luck' and 'Thanks for the memories'. As Moyes reached the Gwladys Street, he looked overwhelmed as his eyes glistened and his players embraced him.

David Moyes's Goodison Park Premier League record was as follows:

Pld	Won	Lost	Pts
213	113	47	392

David Moyes's final game in charge of Everton Football Club was a 2-1 defeat at Stamford Bridge, against a Chelsea side managed by old foe Rafael Benitez. The outcome of the game would have little impact on Everton's season, with the Blues having already secured a sixth-place finish in the Premier League. A win for Moyes's side would have seen Everton achieve their highest points total since the 1987/88 season, a measure of the progress made during the 11-year tenure, though perhaps also a microcosm of Moyes's overall time at the club.

The teams for Moyes's final match as manager of Everton Football Club, on 19 May 2013, were as follows:

Chelsea: Cech, Ivanovic, Cahill, Luiz, Cole, Lampard, Ake, Torres, Mata, Oscar, Ba

Everton: Howard, Coleman, Jagielka, Distin, Baines, Mirallas, Gibson, Fellaini, Pienaar, Naismith, Anichebe

An early Juan Mata opener was cancelled out with a smart Steven Naismith finish in a first half which saw chances at both ends of the pitch. Everton were playing with the coolness and cohesion of a well-oiled David Moyes team, but for the home side, the prospect of an unprecedented play-off for Champions League qualification loomed over Stamford Bridge, as a Chelsea draw and an Arsenal win at Newcastle United would see the two London clubs end the season with the exact same points total, goal difference and number of goals scored. However, with just under 15 minutes remaining, ex-Liverpool forward Fernando Torres scored his first league goal in 1,179 minutes to seal a 2-1 victory for Chelsea.

'Our players could have turned off and said that it didn't matter but we really gave Chelsea a good game,' Moyes said at full time. 'We played well, we were unlucky not to get more than nothing out of the game. It's been a great effort from the players. I've just said to them they've had a brilliant season. You can see the way they've played against the best in the country. Whoever takes the job will have a lot of pleasure working with them because they're honest, whole-hearted, have great energy and are a really good team as well. It's emotional because it's the last time I walk away from the players, but part of the job is you move on. It's rare to stay in a job for 11 years so I'm thankful for getting that opportunity and hopeful they're in a strong position to push on.' (BBC Sport, 2013.)

David Moyes's final campaign as manager of Everton Football Club saw him guide his team to a sixth-place finish in the Premier League, narrowly missing out on a European spot by nine points.

The Premier League table at the end of the 2012/13 season looked like this:

Team	Pld	W	D	L	GF	GA	GD	Pts
1. Man United	38	28	5	5	86	43	+43	89
2. Man City	38	23	9	6	66	34	+32	78
3. Chelsea	38	22	9	7	75	39	+36	75
4. Arsenal	38	21	10	7	72	37	+35	73
5. Spurs	38	21	9	8	66	46	+20	72
6. Everton	38	16	15	7	55	40	+15	63
7. Liverpool	38	16	13	9	71	43	+28	61

During Moyes's 11-year tenure at Goodison Park, Everton's league positions were as follows:

2001/02 (Moyes took over in March 2002): 15th

2002/03: 7th (David Moyes wins LMA Manager of the Year award)

2003/04: 17th

2004/05: 4th (David Moyes wins LMA Manager of the Year award)

2005/06: 11th

2006/07: 6th

2007/08: 5th

2008/09: 5th (David Moyes wins LMA Manager of the Year award)

2009/10: 8th

2010/11: 7th

2011/12: 7th

2012/13: 6th

30

End of an Era

AFTER 11 years, three months and 14 days in charge, David Moyes departed Everton as the club's second-longest-serving manager. His points percentage during his tenure was 51 and his win percentage 42.1, but his time at Goodison Park was about much more than numbers and statistics. It was a period of rebuilding. Indeed, not only was Moyes tasked with the reconstruction of an ageing squad inherited in 2002, but it was also his responsibility to rebuild Everton's status in English football. At one time considered to be amongst the elite, Everton had forfeited their position at the head table in the early-to-mid-1990s, and by the millennium had been regular relegation candidates.

'Before he arrived, life as a Blue had become a miserable thing. Imagine reliving the Benitez season on repeat and you come close,' Jim Keoghan recalls, a fellow Blue and Pitch Publishing author, whose fantastic 2016 work *Highs, Lows and Bakayokos: Everton in the 90s* dissects the decade before Moyes's arrival at Goodison Park. 'The gravitational pull of the relegation zone seemed to have an inescapable hold on the club. Two near-death experiences, a few near misses and season after season with an eye on mathematical safety, it felt like our luck would eventually run out, consigning the club to the second tier. It was particularly hard to bear when you consider that just a few years earlier we had been champions and part of the elite that had pushed for the creation of the Premier League. But where our peers had embraced life in the newly created division, Everton had collapsed, morphing from potential champions into potential Championship fodder.'

Of course, Moyes did not restore Everton to the summit of the footballing pyramid, though he did restore some pride in a club that had lost its way. The Blues became the best of the rest under the Glaswegian coach, meaning David Moyes's legacy at Everton remains under the glass ceiling of the Premier League, his accomplishments always operating just outside the parameters of genuine success. 'Perhaps not since Kendall did an Everton manager manufacture such a reversal in fortunes,' Keoghan summarises. 'Over the course of his 11 years with the club he managed to shift our perspectives, banishing the fear and likelihood of relegation and turning our attention instead to the European places. It's not hyperbole to say that Moyes resurrected Everton.'

Perhaps the very idea of what a successful football club looked like at Everton was redefined under Moyes's stewardship, or indeed had to be redefined, given the club's financial constraints. Paul McParlan, another fellow Evertonian and author of Pitch Publishing's phenomenal 2021 work *The Forgotten Champions – 1986/87: Everton's Last Title* says: 'Did he [Moyes] redefine the notion of a successful Everton side? I think Sky Sports and the Premier League redefined the notion of a successful side. Prior to Moyes taking over, Everton had nearly been relegated twice, in '94 and '98. Most fans craved stability more than anything. For most Premier League clubs, apart from the big six, achieving a European place combined with a cup run is considered a success. Everton along with clubs such as Aston Villa and Leeds have had to redefine what success was to them.'

Resurrecting a club on the brink of collapse and turning it into one competing for European football is an achievement that can't be overstated, and to do so with such a disadvantageous budget compared to some of his cash-rich contemporaries, emphasises how noteworthy this accomplishment was. 'He did it all on a shoestring. That cannot be forgotten,' remarks Keoghan. 'Financially, the Everton of Moyes was no different to the Everton of Walter Smith. We remained, pretty much, a tight outfit. There was no sudden influx of income, no boost to the transfer kitty. But Moyes showed that with the right approach, that didn't matter. Cut-price gems arrived, like Cahill, Baines, Jagielka, Coleman, Howard, Arteta and Pienaar. And they were joined by hard-working pros, like Distin, Neville and Naismith. Collectively, they forged sides greater than the sum of their parts. They were sides forged in Moyes's image; hard-working, tough and filled with character.'

I remember at the time, many fans and pundits alike would often ask the question, what could a manager like Moyes have done with greater resources? Indeed, it is a fair question, but one that can at least in part be answered by his doomed spell at Manchester United, a club with practically unlimited resources. The other side of the coin is, could a braver, more accomplished manager have achieved more with the squad of players Moyes had at the height of his time at Everton?

However, David Moyes built an excellent squad at Goodison Park, of this there is little doubt. By the time Everton were competing in the 2009 FA Cup Final against Chelsea, they had the strongest XI they'd had in a generation. A team that could play attractive football, and one difficult to break down, Moyes's Everton balanced the creativity of players like Pienaar and Arteta, with the workmanlike qualities of Neville and Jagielka. It was a pleasure to watch the squad develop over time, with players like Leighton Baines and Marouane Fellaini blossoming into some of the most consistent performers in the Premier League.

However, Moyes was guilty of being far too cautious tactically, his conservative approach no doubt a necessity in the aftermath of the Walter Smith era, but could he have been braver once he had developed his squad? Or could the appointment of a more tactically adventurous manager around those peak Moyes years have seen a better return from the squad he built?

'The only criticism I would have is that sometimes his innate caution would get the better of him,' recalls McParlan.

'The 2012 semi-final v Liverpool was an example. Moyes should have been far more adventurous in that game, instead his defensive strategy handed them the game.' Keoghan agrees, recalling how Moyes's 'knife to a gunfight mentality could be frustrating'.

Alternatively, it would have been interesting to see how David Moyes would have managed an increased transfer budget had the sought-after investment in Everton Football Club arrived much sooner. If there had been money to build on an existing squad consisting of the likes of Tim Cahill, Mikel Arteta and Leighton Baines, then who knows how much further Moyes could have taken Everton? Indeed, this could have been a very different book had that investment arrived around 2007/08 at the apogee of the Moyes era, when for a time it felt as if silverware was just around the corner.

Furthermore, Moyes sought a certain type of character at Everton, a player who could contribute to the dressing room in a positive way. There were few egos at Goodison Park during Moyes's reign, and even fewer players whose behaviour would disrupt the otherwise harmonious atmosphere. Any player who became disruptive was swiftly dispensed with. There was a work ethic and a clear sense of togetherness in the squad, something that has been sorely lacking in many of the squads we've had since, and credit must go to Moyes for creating such a stable environment within the club, assisting as it did with maintaining a sense of stability not seen in the years immediately before or after his appointment.

There is little doubt that Everton have a lot to be thankful for from the David Moyes era, and though the perception of the scrappy underdogs punching above their weight perpetuated by the sporting press was condescending and insulting to a club the size of Everton, the fact remains that we'd been embroiled in far too many relegation scraps in the years prior to his appointment, and it was probably a matter of time until our luck ran out. Saving Everton from the brink of oblivion is something for which I will always be grateful to Moyes. However, this reshaping by the media of 'plucky little

Everton' has persisted to this day and has at times been leant into by the club itself, even perhaps by Moyes during his time in charge, to limit the expectations of a fanbase who once again began to ambitiously look up the table, as opposed to fearfully watch the form of those at the bottom end.

Few other Premier League clubs would give a manager 11 years to build a squad in their own image, and while finances may have been limited, the support and backing of both the club and the fanbase was unwavering for David Moyes during his time at Everton. Fewer clubs still would show such patience with a manager who had not made a single addition to the trophy cabinet, despite coming close on a few occasions. For this, Moyes owes Everton a debt of gratitude. Plucked from the Championship, Moyes was given time to establish himself as one of the most consistent young managers in the English top flight over a period of 11 years, a notion practically unheard of in the modern game.

Ultimately, David Moyes was a very good manager for Everton, and his appointment back in 2002 is one of the few correct decisions that chairman Bill Kenwright has made throughout his time at the club's helm. I got my first season ticket at Goodison Park back in 1998/99, and by the time Moyes arrived at Everton, I was already in love with the place. However, I was ten years old when he took charge in 2002, and 21 at the time of his departure in 2013. Consequently, I grew up with David Moyes's Everton. Travelling around Europe with my dad and coming of age in the pubs of L4 are cherished memories. Everton may become a truly successful football club again one day, and hopefully we're around to see it, but I doubt I will ever have an emotional attachment to a squad quite like the one I had to the squad David Moyes built. As Jim Keoghan also reflects, 'Moyes gave us our pride back. He returned the sense of what Everton should be. He wasn't perfect but his achievements compare favourably to the greats of the past. We would not be where we are today without the Scot. I for one am eternally grateful he grasped the poisoned chalice that was the Everton job and breathed life back into Goodison.'

Indeed, it was a period that the ex-Everton man himself reflected upon in an exclusive March 2022 interview with Chris Beesley of the *Liverpool Echo*, 20 years on from his appointment in 2002. 'It doesn't seem like 20 years,' Moyes stated, recalling his first game in charge. 'I can still remember it all, the build-up, the day itself, going to Goodison Park ... At the time I'd never really wanted to leave Preston.

'I always remember there was a director at Blackpool, and he used to say to me: "Everton is the club for you." There was always something about Everton for me.'

On his famous 'People's Club' remark, Moyes revealed that it came to him during his first journey to Goodison Park as the area reminded him of his home city of Glasgow, 'I was being driven in ... and all the kids were in the street, out kicking a football ... and all I could see was Everton strips. That was my take on it, and it was simple.

'When I called it "The People's Club" I said that the people on the streets of Liverpool support Everton ... For some people it really took off and for Everton supporters ... they were in relegation trouble, it gave them something to hang on to.'

Moyes admitted that he struggled to sleep the night before his first game, as he pondered what kind of pre-match routine he wanted to implement at Everton. 'Because I was a young coach at Preston and we didn't have a lot of staff, I used to take the warm-ups ... But then I thought: "I've taken this big job and maybe it's not what you do?" and I couldn't sleep the night before, thinking about that. But I decided I'd just do what I'd always done ... it might have looked a bit old-fashioned but maybe it was good leadership ... showing the supporters that you're right in amongst it...

'Finding ways to win games is the all-important thing ... I told Bill Kenwright: "We'll not get relegated here, you'll be fine, we'll be good" ... I didn't care how we did it, I just cared that we'd go into the next season in the Premier League and I'd give myself a chance to build on it.'

In the second part of Moyes's exclusive *Liverpool Echo* interview, published on 17 March 2022, he revealed what inspirational words Sir Bobby Robson uttered to him after his first defeat as Everton boss, a 6-2 drubbing at St James' Park. 'Sir Bobby Robson was the manager and I remember him coming out and saying: "That result is a welcome to the Premier League for David Moyes" ... In the end we stayed up quite comfortably without it being too big an issue. It was very difficult for a young manager ... but when it came up, the Everton job was too hard to turn down ...

'I was keen to get a new, young, hungry group of players ... [and] I wanted them to know what Everton stood for in terms of their work ethic and what the supporters demanded ... The fans were great to me, and they always were, right up until my last day ... Ultimately when you're a football manager you always try to do your best. You always try to pick the best team and win every game you can. I can honestly say that's what I tried to do at Everton. Over the years I was really fortunate to have great backing from the support.

'Goodison was a brilliant, brilliant stadium when it was on its uppers. Also, I was really fortunate at the time I had great players ... The boys were so hungry to improve, they were proud to play for Everton and be part of what was an up-and-coming team.'

On being linked with a return to the Goodison Park dugout following the sudden departure of Carlo Ancelotti in the summer of 2021, Moyes stated, 'Obviously my loyalties now lie with West Ham, but Everton has played such a big part in my life ... Looking back, they were good times at Everton ... We didn't win any trophies, but we got to a cup final, which nowadays is very difficult in any competition ... I think there were much more successes than failures at Everton and I really enjoyed my time there but I'm at a new club now and I'm working hard to make them better.'

Moyes's insistence that there were more successes than failures during his time as Everton manager is another example of just how divisive his reign is among the fanbase.

Paul McParlan agrees with Moyes. 'Can his time at Everton be considered successful? In my opinion, yes. He took over a club on a downward spiral and turned them into a side that regularly challenged for a top-six finish on limited resources. He is still the only manager since Colin Harvey in 1988 to achieve a top-four place and the last since Joe Royle in '95 to reach an FA Cup Final.'

Indeed, Paul's sentiments are shared by a large number of the fanbase, but despite this there are others who remember certain moments where Moyes tarnished his legacy with his post-Everton antics. 'David Moyes's reputation at Everton will always be undermined by the absence of a trophy and the slightly tawdry way that he conducted himself when he finally became United's manager, and I'm thinking particularly of the way he tried to lowball Everton in the pursuit of Fellaini and Baines,' recalls Jim Keoghan. However, Jim continues his assessment by urging that 'this shouldn't really detract from what, within context, stands as one of the most impressive managerial tenures at Goodison. Moyes did something remarkable, resurrecting the club from the relegation-themed horror that had plagued it in the late-1990s and early 2000s.'

31

Post-Moyes Everton:
Where Are We Now?

IT HAS been almost ten years since David Moyes departed Goodison Park. A decade of such frightening uncertainty, one that so startlingly juxtaposes the stability once guaranteed by the former Everton boss, has seen calls for his return from disillusioned members of the fanbase on numerous occasions. 'In recent years, every time Everton have needed a manager, many fans wanted Moyes back. I think that is the true measure of how he is regarded at Everton,' recalls author Paul McParlan.

His 2013 successor, Roberto Martinez, initially seemed to reignite a dwindling flame of passion at Everton, with 'Bobby Brown Shoes's' brand of free-flowing, attacking football earning him countless admirers. His savvy acquisition of the experienced Gareth Barry from Manchester City, alongside loan deals for the prodigious talents of Romelu Lukaku and Gerard Deulofeu from Chelsea and Barcelona respectively, and the promotion of local lad Ross Barkley to the first team, refreshed a squad in need of a shake-up.

Securing qualification for the Europa League with a fifth-place finish on 72 points, the club's highest points tally since the title-winning 1986/87 season, Everton's new-look set-up appeared to be bearing immediate results. Furthermore, a total of 72 points would have been enough to guarantee Champions League football in every season since 1992/93, meaning that

Roberto Martinez was in fact incredibly unfortunate not to secure Everton a place in the prestigious competition for the first time since 2004/05.

Meanwhile, David Moyes's move to Manchester United proved to be ill-fated, as the Scot lasted just ten months in the Old Trafford dugout, his dismissal coming 48 hours after a 2-0 defeat to his former side Everton at Goodison Park.

In September 2014, Everton Football Club, alongside Liverpool City Council and housing association Liverpool Mutual Homes, announced plans to build a new 50,000-seater stadium in Walton Hall Park, less than a mile away from Goodison Park. With an estimated cost of £200 million, the stadium would be part-funded by a naming rights deal, and the sale of Goodison Park. Everton chairman Bill Kenwright told the *Liverpool Echo*, 'On my journey to our home games, as I pass Walton Hall Park, I inevitably think that I am only a minute away from our beloved Goodison. For several years now I've also thought, "If only it was available for our new stadium." It ticks all the boxes.'

He continued, 'It would fill me with great pride, it could be something very special for our city, the residents of north Liverpool and all Evertonians – a new home that goes beyond football and does what Everton does better than anyone else. Of course, there's enormous work to do – that again involves fixing a huge financial jigsaw – but we are certain it's an opportunity we should pursue with great commitment, endeavour, and ambition.'

Back on the pitch, a disappointing 11th-place finish in Roberto Martinez's second season at Everton raised questions among a fanbase whose expectations had once again been raised. The once renowned defensive stability implemented by Moyes appeared to be replaced with an openness that invited pressure, resulting in just seven clean sheets in the Premier League throughout the 2014/15 season. A respectable campaign in the Europa League, which ended in a 6-4 aggregate defeat to Dynamo Kyiv in the round of 16, bought Martinez time, though doubts began to creep in regarding his capacity for the role. Moyes meanwhile made the surprise move to La Liga side Real Sociedad on 10 November 2014, on an 18-month contract. Lasting just under 12 months in San Sebastian, Moyes was sacked on 9 November 2015, his second dismissal in as many years.

A second bottom-half finish, with the Blues ending the 2015/16 season in 11th place, spelled the end of Roberto Martinez's once promising tenure at Goodison Park after three years in charge. Reaching the semi-finals of both the League Cup and FA Cup afforded the Everton boss the opportunity to end the extended trophy drought, with Evertonians hoping Martinez could repeat the 2012/13 cup success he achieved at Wigan Athletic. A 4-3 aggregate defeat to Manchester City in the League Cup semi-final and a 2-1 defeat to Manchester United at the same stage of the FA Cup ended hopes of securing silverware, and the Spaniard was relieved of his duties on 12 May 2016.

With Iranian billionaire Farhad Moshiri purchasing a 49.9 per cent stake in Everton Football Club on 27 February 2016, the promise of fresh investment suggested a new era could be on the horizon. Everton's failure to re-establish themselves among the elite of English football has often been attributed to the club's limited financial clout, so the long-sought-after investment could awaken a sleeping giant of English football.

'After an exhaustive search, I believe we have found the perfect partner to take the club forward,' said chairman Bill Kenwright. 'I have got to know Farhad well over the last 18 months. His football knowledge, financial wherewithal and true-Blue spirit have convinced me he is the right man to support Everton.'

The deal brought to an end a decade-long search for fresh investment, with Kenwright first stating his preparedness to sell the club back in November 2007. With suggestions of Kenwright's ill health, there had been a growing intent in recent months to find an investor, after many years of inertia.

'I am delighted to take this opportunity to become a shareholder in Everton, with its rich heritage as one of Europe's leading clubs,' Moshiri said. 'There has never been a more level playing field in the Premier League than now. Bill Kenwright has taught me what it means to be an Evertonian, and I look forward with excitement to working with him to help deliver success for Everton in the future.' (*The Guardian*, 2016.)

With an estimated personal wealth of £1.3 billion, Evertonians could understandably feel as though their opportunity to financially compete with the wealthier Premier League sides had finally arrived in the shape of Moshiri. Furthermore, his swift dismissal of Martinez suggested Everton had a man with purpose at the wheel, with the funds to match the club's ambition. In May 2016, Everton announced their intention to scrap the proposed stadium move to Walton Hall Park, with two new sites identified by the club. On 14 June the search for a new manager concluded, as Everton appointed former Southampton boss Ronald Koeman, the Dutchman signing a three-year deal at Goodison Park.

Meanwhile, after a brief hiatus, David Moyes returned to management, taking over at Sunderland on 23 July. The 2016/17 season would be one of contrasting fortunes for Everton and their former boss, as the Blues secured Europa League football thanks to a seventh-place finish, while Sunderland's relegation to the EFL Championship, the first relegation in Moyes's managerial career, prompted the Scot to resign after just one season in charge of the Black Cats.

In March 2017, Everton Football Club took a significant step towards building a new stadium on the city of Liverpool's famous waterfront, with the club agreeing a deal with Peel Holdings to acquire the land at the Bramley-Moore Dock, the site now destined to be the home of the new stadium, designed by architectural heavyweight Dan Meis. After the deal was reached, the then mayor of Liverpool, Joe Anderson, remarked, 'It is the first step and for that reason it is a special moment in the city's – and Everton's – long, illustrious history. The proposed new stadium will be a landmark for the city's spectacular north Liverpool waterfront and a powerful statement of intent for the club and the city of Liverpool that will resonate globally.'

Everton's then chief executive, Robert Elstone, stated, 'We can now move forward into the next phase of work with much greater confidence. Clearly, it is vital we have clarity on cost, and we have to recognise that the stadium will be significantly more expensive at Bramley-Moore Dock. To get that certainty, and ensure the stadium is affordable, we need to confirm stadium design, capacity, and configuration.'

He continued, 'We're keen to stress not only the scale of the work ahead but also the remaining risks and uncertainties. We're delighted we've secured the site and we're equally delighted the mayor is continuing to support our financing model, but significant hurdles remain, not least the preparation and submission of a detailed planning application. Receipt of a successful planning approval at some point early next year will be the most significant step towards bringing the stadium to life.' (Kirkbride, *Liverpool Echo*, 2017.)

The summer of 2017 saw Ronald Koeman splash an estimated £150 million on new players, the largest transfer budget in the history of the club. It was a summer of excitement for Evertonians, as 'Mosh the Dosh', as Farhad Moshiri had become affectionately known, cashed cheque after cheque for Ronald Koeman's new-look side. Wayne Rooney returned to Goodison Park, as Romelu Lukaku departed for Old Trafford, for £75 million. Despite the summer spending spree, however, Koeman was sacked just two months into the 2017/18 season after a disappointing start to the campaign. Over a month after the dismissal, Everton appointed Sam Allardyce as manager (taking over from interim coach David Unsworth), after they failed to agree a deal with Watford for prime target Marco Silva.

Signed on an 18-month contract, Allardyce's appointment was met with almost universal disapproval among Evertonians. His negative style of play frustrated a fanbase that was becoming increasingly disillusioned with Farhad Moshiri, with an apparent lack of a coherent long-term strategy the primary concern. Crashing out of the Europa League group stage with one win out of six, Everton were out of Europe by Christmas 2017. The departure of Ross Barkley to Chelsea in January 2018 for £15 million after he refused to sign a new contract intensified the overall dissatisfaction with the running of the club.

Barkley had in fact almost completed a £30 million move to Chelsea the previous summer, though an agreement failed to materialise due to the midfielder suffering from a long-term injury at the time. Consequently, the January 2018 transfer was referred to Merseyside police by the then mayor of Liverpool and Evertonian Joe Anderson, due to accusations of fraud. No fraud was found upon investigation, though it remains one of the most contentious transfers in the recent history of Everton Football Club.

Allardyce ultimately guided Everton to eighth place in the Premier League, five points off Europa League qualification. However, Everton ranked 20th in the league for total shots under Allardyce's management, 19th for shots on target, 16th for passing accuracy and 17th for shots faced. Everton and Allardyce parted ways on 16 May 2018, as the Blues once again went in search of a new manager.

The 2017/18 season also marked a return to Premier League management for David Moyes, who replaced Slaven Bilic at West Ham United on 7 November 2017, due to the Hammers' poor start to the season. With the club sitting 18th in the league on nine points having played 11 games, Moyes accepted a six-month contract at the London Stadium, eventually steering West Ham to Premier League safety with a 13th-place finish on 42 points.

Meanwhile, Marco Silva was dismissed by Watford on 21 January 2018, with the club citing the 'unwarranted approach by a Premier League rival' that caused 'significant deterioration in both focus and results to the point where the long-term future of Watford FC has been jeopardised'. (Jones, *Liverpool Echo*, 2018.) In response to this claim, Everton agreed to pay Watford £4 million in February 2018 and the

Portuguese manager was eventually unveiled at Goodison Park on 31 May, signing a three-year deal.

The Blues once again spent big in the summer transfer window, with Silva bringing in Brazilian star Richarlison from his former club Watford for an initial fee of £35 million, alongside the high-profile signings of Lucas Digne and Yerry Mina from Barcelona. Silva's first game in charge of Everton was a 22-0 pre-season friendly victory over Austrian amateurs ATV Irdning.

Though the quality of the football improved under Marco Silva, another eighth-place finish in the Premier League concluded the 2018/19 season, as the Blues once again missed out on European football, ending the campaign three points shy of a place in the Europa League. A poor start to the 2019/20 season saw Everton part ways with their fourth permanent manager since David Moyes's departure, with Marco Silva relieved of his duties on 4 December, following a 5-2 Merseyside derby defeat at Anfield. Duncan Ferguson was placed in temporary charge of Everton while the club conducted a search for a permanent replacement, with the former Everton forward taking five points out of an available nine against Chelsea, Manchester United and Arsenal. On 21 December, Everton appointed Carlo Ancelotti as manager on a four-and-a-half-year deal. Ancelotti's first game in charge was a 1-0 victory over Burnley on Boxing Day, with Everton ending the 2019/20 season in 12th place in the Premier League.

Of course, the Covid-19 pandemic meant that for much of Ancelotti's time in the Goodison Park dugout, his side were playing in an empty stadium, with fans unable to attend. However, with the high-profile acquisition of James Rodriguez from Real Madrid in the summer of 2020, a cautious optimism gripped Evertonians as it appeared that the investment of majority shareholder Farhad Moshiri would finally bring success back to Goodison Park. Despite an excellent start to the campaign, Everton finished the season in tenth place and by the summer of 2021, Ancelotti had made an unexpected return to the Bernabeu, as the often-injured Rodriguez made the switch to Qatari side Al-Rayyan.

On 30 June 2021, Everton made the grossly unpopular decision to appoint ex-Liverpool coach Rafael Benitez as manager, the Spaniard signing a three-year contract. There was strong opposition to the controversial appointment among Evertonians, with Benitez subject to threats in the days leading up to him signing the contract, with a banner left near his home, reading: 'We know where you live. Don't sign.'

Following a horrendous run of form amid further protests against both the management and the board of the football club, Everton sacked Benitez on 16 January 2022, with the Blues in 15th place in the Premier League, six points above the relegation zone, having lost nine of the previous 13 games. Benitez became the fifth manager to lose his job at Everton in six years, with Duncan Ferguson once again tasked with managing the side on an interim basis.

Meanwhile, David Moyes's stalling career got back on track following a return to West Ham United in December 2019. They finished 16th at the end of the 2019/20 season, but with a sixth-place finish in the 2020/21 campaign, the Hammers qualified for the Europa League, subsequently reaching the semi-finals, with Moyes's rapid progress at an ailing side echoing his early success at Goodison Park.

In March 2022, Everton Football Club announced a loss of £120.9 million for the 2020/21 season, bringing the combined losses over a three-year period to a staggering £372 million. Furthermore, the club suspended sponsorship deals with USM and Megafon, companies owned or part-owned by Alisher Usmanov, the oligarch business associate of Farhad Moshiri, following sanctions on the Uzbeki-born billionaire due to Russia's invasion of Ukraine.

However, in April 2022, Everton took another significant step in the development of the new stadium at Bramley-Moore Dock by signing a main construction contract with Laing O'Rourke. The deal will see the company complete the work on-site and it locks in costs for the club, preventing the final bill from spiralling. With foundations and other remedial work completed by Laing O'Rourke since signing a pre-contract services agreement, the main construction contract committed the company to the full delivery of the project, with Everton chief executive Denise Barrett-Baxendale stating, 'This is an important agreement at a crucial time for the club and the stadium project. We are now able to lock in construction costs, while also benefiting from Laing O'Rourke's economies of scale in what is an ever-fluctuating marketplace.'

In an email to Everton supporters, the CEO added, 'The agreement ensures the work on bringing our new home to reality will continue apace. To explain the significance, this agreement means we have renewed clarity over the costs for the remaining stages of the project – and that clarity is in line with our budget and cost planning. In short – we have certainty in these uncertain times. Our accounts, released last month, revealed the profound scale of the impact the pandemic has had, and continues to have, on our club. They also demonstrated, though, the scale of investment we have already made in our new stadium – and the unwavering commitment of our owner [Farhad Moshiri] to finish what he has started.' (Hunter, *The Guardian*, 2022.)

A little over two weeks after the sacking of Rafael Benitez, Everton appointed ex-Derby County and Chelsea coach Frank Lampard as manager, the former England midfielder signing a two-and-a-half-year contract, until June 2024. Lampard arrived at Goodison Park with Everton positioned precariously in 16th place in the league, four points above the relegation zone, with just one win out of the previous 14 league games. With an immediate priority of securing Premier League safety, comparisons can easily be made between the appointment of a young, ambitious David Moyes midway through the 2001/12 season, and Frank Lampard almost 20 years later.

Of his appointment as manager of Everton, Lampard said, 'It is a huge honour for me to represent and manage a club with the size and tradition of Everton Football Club. I'm very hungry to get started. After speaking to the owner, chairman, and the board, I very much felt their passion and ambition. I hope they felt my ambition and how hard I want to work to bring it together. You can feel the passion Everton fans have for their club. That will be hugely important. As a team – the competitive level that the Premier League brings and the position we are in the table – we certainly need that.'

He continued, 'It's a two-way thing. I think Everton is a unique club in that you can really understand what the fans want to see. The first thing they want is fight and desire and that must always be our baseline. My first message to the players will be that we have to do this together. We'll try to do our job and I know the fans will be there backing us.'

Indeed, Lampard no doubt expected Evertonians to back the team, familiar as he will have been with the passion of the Goodison crowd, having played in the stadium many times throughout his career. However, few could have anticipated a reaction so visceral as supporters' groups mobilised, presenting a united front for a fanbase that had been fractured for so long. It was a turning point in the season, when even those resigned to the fate of relegation once again had fire in their bellies, determined to drag Everton back from the point of no return. At that moment, Evertonians came together to save the club, or at the very least, ensure we didn't go down without a fight.

There can be little doubt that the penultimate game of the 2021/22 season against Crystal Palace was one of the most important fixtures in Everton's modern history. While it did not quite have the 'great escape' significance of Wimbledon in 1994, or Coventry in 1998, owing to those matches being the final game of the season, it certainly had the feeling that it was our last realistic chance to ensure safety. Had Everton suffered defeat against Patrick Vieira's Crystal Palace, it would not have guaranteed relegation, with a trip to the Emirates on the final day still to be played, though with just two victories away at Arsenal in the preceding 30 years, few would have fancied our chances of survival should we have needed a win against the Gunners.

Scheduled for a Thursday evening, I remember being in work the day of the Palace game and the emotional weight of the fixture was almost too much to bear. With Everton's relocation to the new stadium at the Bramley-Moore Dock scheduled for the 2024/25 season, it dawned on me that, should we lose to Palace, it could be our last top-flight game at Goodison Park. Such a historic stadium deserved so much better than to bow out in such ignominious circumstances, and as I stood outside its doors with thousands of fellow Evertonians, singing 'The Goodison Gang' amidst a sea of blue smoke, there was a defiance among us that Premier League football would once again be played there the following season.

However, Everton seldom do things the easy way, and with two opportunities to secure Premier League safety already squandered in recent weeks, away at already-relegated Watford and at home to Brentford, the final home game of the season would be the most emotionally polarising two hours that I have ever experienced. Goodison Park was a cauldron at kick-off, with raw emotion echoing off each corner of the ground, but as Palace raced into a 2-0 lead inside 36 minutes, defiance quickly gave way to despair.

I slumped in my seat at the interval, my dad sat next to me as he has been at every match since 1998 and, unable to summon fitting words for what had been a disastrous 45 minutes, we sat in silence. I overheard someone nearby state that we had been 2-0 down at half-time against Wimbledon in 1994 and went on to win 3-2 to avoid the drop, so we could do it again. It's true we had been in similar situations before and dug our way out of them, but had we ridden our luck on one too many occasions? Perhaps a goal early in the second half might swing the momentum of the game our way, but with so few chances created in the opening period, I was doubtful we could create three opportunities, and even if we did, who would score them?

Nine minutes into the second half, Everton clawed their way back into the game, with a goal from the unlikeliest of sources in defender Michael Keane, who produced a finish that a centre-forward would have been proud of. Keane has had his critics during his time at Everton, me among them, and while his performances failed to meet expectations, this goal must have felt like a moment of redemption for the former England international. No doubt, the fan I overheard at half-time suggesting that an early second-half goal could ignite a comeback will have been starting to believe his unlikely prediction might just come true, as was I.

The half-time introduction of Dele Alli had galvanised Everton and a Richarlison equaliser with 15 minutes remaining, followed by a diving Dominic Calvert-Lewin header to settle the tie on 85 minutes, meant Goodison Park swelled into a cacophony of noise the likes of which I have never witnessed, nor would I want to again under such circumstances. The full-time whistle was met with a mass pitch invasion and indeed, I was one of the fans who ran on to the playing surface: not out of celebration, but out of sheer relief that the season was over, and we had survived. I grabbed a handful of turf from the 18-yard box in front of the Gwladys Street, roughly from where Dominic Calvert-Lewin would have been standing before his diving header secured the most precious of three points. No doubt it'll become a treasured keepsake when Goodison Park is no longer standing, but for now I keep it as a reminder not to take our status in the top flight of English football for granted.

'It is one of the greatest moments of my footballing life and career,' Lampard said of keeping Everton in the Premier League. 'I have been very fortunate to have amazing times, especially at Chelsea as a player and a coach. But when you feel the feelings and desperation of what relegation brings to the table, it is different. I thought I might cry [at full time]; I thought I might jump out of my body. Nobody can question the celebrations at the end. It is easy to say, "but you haven't won anything". You know what, come and work at this club for a few months and see the difficulties and what it means to people to stay in this league. It is a special night in Everton's history.' (Jones, *Liverpool Echo*, 2022.)

Lampard continued, eager to reiterate the importance of rebuilding, 'Now is the time to take stock, enjoy the moment and then make sure we are not here again next year, because there are reasons for it. We have to find every way to improve the squad, the club and ourselves. Everton fans can know as long as we are at this club myself and the staff will give everything.'

'It's pure relief,' said Michael Keane, the man who started the comeback early in the second half. 'It has been a hard season, but we are so proud of how the club has come together in the last six weeks and built a platform to make sure it never happens again. We've had our mentality questioned and how much we care. It hurt. We care about this club more than anything else in the world. We have let the fans down a lot this season. But you could see out there what it means to all the players. We did not want to take this club down.'

* * *

Everton Football Club is once again in a period of decline as I write this, and ultimately almost all of the progress made under David Moyes has been undone, despite Farhad Moshiri's investment and business acumen, which were supposed to take Everton to the next level – to smash the Premier League glass ceiling that we had on occasion fractured in the years prior, ultimately lacking the necessary tools to break through. However, the stadium move to the Bramley-Moore Dock is an example of the club investing well in its own future, as the scheduled 2024/25 relocation will no doubt enhance Everton's potential revenue streams and ensure a world-class infrastructure for many decades to come. Indeed, it is an exciting prospect.

Everton are now in a position where clubs we may consider to be our contemporaries on the pitch, can cherry-pick our better players, with the players themselves concurring that their prospects of success are better elsewhere. Moshiri's investment suggested that the days of Everton having to sell our best players could finally be over. I remember feeling there could be a change in attitude at the club back in 2016 when Everton rejected Chelsea's advances for John Stones, prompting the Goodison crowd to sing, 'Money Can't Buy You Stones' to the tune of The Beatles' hit 'Money Can't Buy You Love'. Of course, the Yorkshire-born centre-half departed for Pep Guardiola's Manchester City 12 months later.

Romelu Lukaku's transfer to Manchester United in the summer of 2017 was yet another example of the club losing one of Europe's top young talents, with academy graduate Ross Barkley making the switch to Chelsea the following January, and replacements for both players yet to be found many years later. Indeed, at the time of writing, Everton are on their seventh permanent manager since David Moyes's departure, and the third director of football. Consequently, an inconsistent recruitment strategy has resulted in a squad of highly paid individuals on long-term contracts, incapable of performing to the standard that both their transfer fee and salary would suggest. Their exorbitant wages provide little incentive for them to improve, nor are we able to offload such players, with few clubs prepared to offer similar terms, and the players themselves reluctant to take a wage cut, naturally.

Indeed, the 4-1 defeat at home to Brighton & Hove Albion in January 2023 saw Everton end the game with players purchased by three directors of football and eight different managers, including David Moyes. With this in mind, it is hardly surprising that there is a distinct lack of cohesion within the squad, or indeed a recognisable identity. Consequently, the few players we have that are worthy of the shirt inevitably seek opportunities elsewhere, understandably unwilling to see their potential and ambition go unfulfilled at a club who have become little more than an also-ran. Richarlison's 2022 transfer to Antonio Conte's Spurs is the latest example of a key player sold by Everton, and not sufficiently replaced.

Financial losses in the hundreds of millions have seen Everton fortunate to avoid financial fair play sanctions, and we

POST-MOYES EVERTON: WHERE ARE WE NOW?

once again have little choice but to sell our best and brightest. There are echoes of the Peter Johnson era of the 1990s, a period of such instability that the club is yet to recover from, and perhaps never truly will. Farhad Moshiri insisted back in 2017 that Everton Football Club did not want to be a museum, that we had to rediscover our competitive edge to compete once more among the elite. However, a museum is exactly what we have become, a relic of the past in a culture where footballing history seems to count for less with each passing year.

Nostalgia is entrenched in Everton's modern identity, but in the absence of the restoration of the club to its former status, there is merely a wistful reflection that we were once a grand old team. We long as a club for the success of the 1980s, the Holy Trinity, School of Science, and the days of Dixie Dean. There's also a nostalgia for Joe Royle's Dogs of War, perhaps owing to the fact that they were the last team to put a trophy on the table. However, I believe we have become a club that lives solely in our past, held hostage by our heritage; once renowned for setting the standard, we now seem unable to find our place in the modern footballing world. The past decade has seen the club regress from the Premier League's best-of-the-rest to over-spending relegation candidates. As if to underline how far Everton Football Club have fallen, there is already a nostalgia for the David Moyes era of 2002–13, a period that ultimately did not bring success back to the club.

Without silverware, it is difficult to describe a manager in charge of Everton for 11 years as successful. However, David Moyes was successful in providing Everton with an on-the-pitch identity, with a group of players that fans were willing to get behind, something that for the most part, the club have sorely lacked since. Where Moyes's shrewd eye for a player on a tight budget once provided Everton with a squad filled with fan favourites, the club's subsequent transfer strategy has left us with an expensively assembled group of mismatched individuals. The last decade has seen the club undo much of the good work achieved the decade before, emphasised by the countless protests orchestrated by concerned fans over recent years, with chants of 'sack the board' now a regular feature of the Goodison matchday experience.

Everton Football Club have become a well-rehearsed disaster, though it is always darkest before the dawn, as the saying goes. The 2021/22 season provided some of the darkest moments I have experienced in my 24 years as a season-ticket holder, but out of the worry, out of the sleepless nights and anxiety, out of the anger and frustration emerged something beautiful: a fanbase united. Evertonians have always had a strong identity. It's a little insular, and occasionally a little self-deprecating but always passionate. However, I have always found it to be fractured, generationally speaking. Often, the ambition of older fans, no doubt a reflection of the success of the club in decades gone by, contrasts with that of anyone under the age of 40, with younger fans perhaps conditioned to accept failure, or at best mediocrity. The lineage of this trend can be traced back to the altered perception of Everton in the media in the 1990s, when we went from an elite club going through a rough patch, to one in serious decline.

As the 2021/22 campaign progressed, however, Evertonians came together and did what was necessary to save the club from relegation. Goodison Park is famed for its atmosphere, but there have always been differing ideas of what a Goodison atmosphere should consist of, and what would be considered 'Kopite behaviour'. Consequently, this has limited the participation in modern fan culture, with flags, flares and coach greetings deemed un-Evertonian for many years. Thankfully, these attitudes are changing, with fans embracing such ideas wholeheartedly, and while the origins of such a shift in attitude may have been born out of the direst of circumstances, the outcome was quite spectacular: marching down Goodison Road, blue smoke bombs filling the air, flags and banners hung from bedroom windows, lampposts, and scaffolding. If these are to be our final years at Goodison Park, then let's make them memorable – the place deserves to go out with a bang, as opposed to a whimper.

Growing up supporting Everton was an education in patience. It can leave you at once sick of football, and completely in love with it. I'm fortunate enough to be a part of a genuine Everton family: a multi-generational group of Blues whose origins can be traced back many decades. They have been part of my Everton experience since my very first game, back in 1998, and there is barely a season that goes by when we don't welcome new members into the fold. Their company makes the dark times a little more tolerable, and our brighter days shine that bit brighter.

David Moyes became almost intertwined with Everton's identity while I was growing up, and though he was ultimately unsuccessful in bringing silverware back to Goodison, some of my fondest match day memories were formed during his tenure. Going to the match with my dad, our mates – these are memories that I cherish, and hold on to tighter the older we all get. Players and managers come and go, but we as fans are a constant. Indeed, writing this book allowed me to reflect upon an era that had such an effect on me, as no doubt it did many others, particularly those of a similar age. My only regret is that I was unsuccessful in obtaining an interview with Moyes or any player who shared their time with him at the club, despite numerous attempts. I don't know if their reluctance to speak about that time holds any significance, but countless attempts at contact were ignored.

For many, David Moyes's departure left them with fear and loathing, and a decade after his exit, we're just as brittle as we were the day he walked through the door, with it looking like a tightrope walk for the foreseeable future. The circuitous narrative of our modern history has been one of decline, recovery, progression, stagnation, and rapid decline once more. Once a paragon of stability, Everton have become a club in chaos as a conveyor belt of managers collect their P45s and our players become increasingly well versed in rallying cries. As fans, our reward for giving everything is nothing, and I can only hope that we continue to demand a culture change at Everton Football Club, before it's too late.

UTFT

Lou Reed Foster

Bibliography

Books
Keane, R., *The Second Half,* 2015, Weidenfeld & Nicolson
Howard, T., *The Keeper: A Life of Saving Goals and Achieving Them,* 2014, Harper

Publications
The Guardian
Bryant, T., 'Everton executive behind Kirkby move stands down'
(2008) The Guardian
https://www.theguardian.com/football/2008/jul/30/everton.premierleague
Burnton, S, Fotheringham, W., 'Everton call off China tour because of Sars'
(2003) *The Guardian* https://www.theguardian.com/football/2003/apr/08/
newsstory.sport8
Chase, G., 'Moyes calls on supporters to raise the roof and lift Everton'
(2008) *The Guardian*
https://www.theguardian.com/football/2008/mar/12/newsstory.uefa
Fifield, D., 'Mind games give Moyes dream start' (2002) *The Guardian*
https://www.theguardian.com/football/2002/mar/18/match.sport1
Fifield, D., 'Moyes and Hoddle go back to the future' (2002) *The Guardian*
https://www.theguardian.com/football/2002/aug/19/match.sport5
Fifield, D., 'Youngest goalscorer gets into the habit of wrecking records'
(2002) *The Guardian*
https://www.theguardian.com/football/2002/oct/21/match.sport
Fifield, D., 'Rooney signs Everton deal and starts on £13,000 a week'
(2003) *The Guardian*
https://www.theguardian.com/football/2003/jan/18/newsstory.sport2
Fifield, D., 'Everton fall beyond consolation' (2003) *The Guardian*
https://www.theguardian.com/football/2003/may/12/match.everton
Fifield, D., 'Moyes banking on Rooney staying' (2004) *The Guardian*
https://www.theguardian.com/football/2004/jul/08/sport.dominicfifield
Fifield, D., 'Birch walks out of Everton after six weeks in job'
(2004) *The Guardian*
https://www.theguardian.com/football/2004/jul/17/newsstory.sport2
Fifield, D., 'Reds to make Everton sweat over Rooney move'
(2004) *The Guardian*
https://www.theguardian.com/football/2004/aug/27/newsstory.sport3
Fifield, D., 'Gravesen set to sign for Real today' (2005) *The Guardian*
https://www.theguardian.com/football/2005/jan/14/newsstory.sport4
Fifield, D., 'Arteta's Everton tip-off' (2005) *The Guardian*
https://www.theguardian.com/football/2005/feb/02/newsstory.sport1

[""]

Fifield, D., 'Everton confront new Spanish force' (2005) *The Guardian*
https://www.theguardian.com/football/2005/jul/30/newsstory.sport

Fifield, D., 'Everton's day finally dawns' (2005) *The Guardian*
https://www.theguardian.com/football/2005/aug/09/newsstory.sport1

Fifield, D., 'Everton rail at the arrogance of Collina' (2005) *The Guardian*
https://www.theguardian.com/football/2005/aug/26/newsstory.sport4

Fifield, D., 'Johnson takes derby shortcut to hero status' (2006) *The Guardian*
https://www.theguardian.com/football/2006/sep/11/match.sport7

Fifield, D., 'Everton may sue Mourinho' (2006) *The Guardian*
https://www.theguardian.com/football/2006/dec/19/newsstory.sport5

Fifield, D., 'Benítez slur raises Everton hackles and is as short of guile as his team' (2007) *The Guardian*
https://www.theguardian.com/football/2007/feb/05/match.sport13

Gaunt, K., 'Vaughan lifts high-flying Everton' (2007) *The Guardian*
https://www.theguardian.com/football/2007/dec/21/match.everton

Gaunt, K., 'Tim Cahill seals comeback victory for Everton in Minsk' (2009) *The Guardian*
https://www.theguardian.com/football/2009/oct/01/europa-league-bate-borisov-everton

Gaunt, K., 'Jack Rodwell injury adds to David Moyes woes as Everton youngsters toil' (2009) *The Guardian*
https://www.theguardian.com/football/2009/dec/17/everton-bate-borisov-europa-league

Gibson, O., 'Kirkby rejection forces Everton to consider Liverpool ground-share' (2009) *The Guardian*
https://www.theguardian.com/football/2009/nov/26/everton-liverpool-stadium-share

Hunter, A., 'Voodoo still has a hold on Moyes' (2007) *The Guardian*
https://www.theguardian.com/football/2007/sep/20/newsstory.sport5

Hunter, A., 'Everton fans under Uefa scrutiny after illicit online ticket buys' (2007) *The Guardian*
https://www.theguardian.com/football/2007/nov/07/newsstory.everton

Hunter, A., 'Moyes appeals for calm as ticketless fans heighten fears' (2007) *The Guardian*
https://www.theguardian.com/football/2007/nov/08/newsstory.sport6

Hunter, A., 'Anichebe cameo drives Everton ahead' (2007) *The Guardian*
https://www.theguardian.com/football/2007/nov/09/match.everton

Hunter, A., 'Opportunist Cahill profits from Zenit misfortune to send Everton through' (2007) *The Guardian*
https://www.theguardian.com/football/2007/dec/06/match.everton

Hunter, A., 'Moyes wary as he plots to extend Everton renaissance in Florence' (2008) *The Guardian*
https://www.theguardian.com/football/2008/mar/06/newsstory.fiorentina

Hunter, A., 'Howard alone gives feeble Everton chance of progress' (2008) *The Guardian*
https://www.theguardian.com/football/2008/mar/07/match.everton

Hunter, A., 'Everton pay penalty after brave fightback' (2008) *The Guardian*
https://www.theguardian.com/football/2008/mar/07/match.everton

Hunter, A., 'Record signing Fellaini ready to get physical for Everton's cause' (2008) *The Guardian*

BIBLIOGRAPHY

https://www.theguardian.com/football/2008/sep/13/everton.
premierleague

Hunter, A, Taylor, D., 'Moyes ends Everton uncertainty by signing £16.9m contract' (2008) *The Guardian*
https://www.theguardian.com/football/2008/oct/15/everton-premierleague

Hunter, A., 'Everton preparing smash and grab on Anfield, says Howard' (2009) *The Guardian*
https://www.theguardian.com/football/2009/jan/16/everton-liverpool-tim-howard-merseyside-derby-premier-league

Hunter, A., 'Benítez reignites 'small club' row after Everton frustrate Liverpool again' (2009) *The Guardian*
https://www.theguardian.com/football/2009/jan/25/everton-liverpool-fa-cup-anfield-rafael-benitez-david-moyes

Hunter, A., 'Proud' Moyes hails Everton Cup hero Gosling' (2009) *The Guardian*
https://www.theguardian.com/football/2009/feb/05/david-moyes-everton-dan-gosling

Hunter, A., 'Moyes puts down 'small club' concerns to focus on the big stage' (2009) *The Guardian*
https://www.theguardian.com/football/2009/apr/18/david-moyes-everton-manchester-united-fa-cup

Hunter, A., 'Phil Jagielka sends Everton through and denies Manchester United quintuple' (2009) *The Guardian*
https://www.theguardian.com/football/2009/apr/19/everton-manchester-united-fa-cup-david-moyes-sir-alex-ferguson

Hunter, A., 'Moyes believes it's time for Everton to close the gap on the Big Four' (2009) *The Guardian*
https://www.theguardian.com/football/2009/may/30/everton-fa-cup-final-david-moyes

Hunter, A., *'Wembley defeat will inspire Everton to break glass ceiling",* *The Guardian,*
https://www.theguardian.com/football/2009/jun/01/david-moyes-everton-fa-cup

Hunter, A., 'Unsettled Joleon Lescott strikes at the heart of Everton's unity' (2009) *The Guardian*
https://www.theguardian.com/football/2009/aug/16/everton-arsenal-match-report

Hunter, A., 'Officials got it wrong over Louis Saha's red card, fumes David Moyes' (2009) *The Guardian*
https://www.theguardian.com/football/2009/sep/17/europa-league-everton-aek-athens1?CMP=gu_com

Hunter, A., 'Everton humbled by Benfica once more fumes David Moyes' (2009) *The Guardian*
https://www.theguardian.com/football/2009/nov/05/europa-league-everton-benfica

Hunter, A., 'Tim Cahill admits Everton 'couldn't hit a barn door at the moment" (2009) *The Guardian*
https://www.theguardian.com/football/2009/nov/30/tim-cahill-everton

Hunter, A., 'David Moyes names young Everton team with Uefa's blessing' (2009) *The Guardian*

https://www.theguardian.com/football/2009/dec/17/david-moyes-
everton-bate-borisov

Hunter, A., 'Everton's plan for new stadium in Kirkby rejected by the
government' (2009) *The Guardian*
https://www.theguardian.com/football/2009/nov/25/everton-stadium-
plan-rejected

Hunter, A., 'David Moyes pledges his loyalty to Everton and pleads for new
investment' (2009) *The Guardian*
https://www.theguardian.com/football/2009/nov/28/david-moyes-everton-
rafael-benitez-liverpool

Hunter, A., 'David Moyes says Everton can still qualify for Europe'
(2010) *The Guardian*
https://www.theguardian.com/football/2010/jan/30/david-moyes-everton

Hunter, A., 'Jack Rodwell and Sylvain Distin's blunder undermines Everton'
(2010) *The Guardian*
https://www.theguardian.com/football/2010/feb/16/everton-sporting-europa-
league-match-report

Hunter, A, James, S., 'Roberto Mancini clashes with David Moyes as
Manchester City slump' (2010) *The Guardian*
https://www.theguardian.com/football/2010/mar/25/roberto-
mancini-david-moyes

Hunter, A., 'David Moyes to complain to Belgian FA over Marouane Fellaini
injury' (2010) *The Guardian*
https://www.theguardian.com/football/2010/oct/16/david-moyes-belgian-fa-
marouane-fellaini

Hunter, A., 'Liverpool spent their own way into trouble, says Everton's Tim
Cahill' (2010) *The Guardian*
https://www.theguardian.com/football/2010/oct/16/tim-cahill-
everton-liverpool

Hunter, A., 'Everton finances stretched to the limit, admits chairman Bill
Kenwright' (2011) *The Guardian*
https://www.theguardian.com/football/2011/aug/18/everton-finances-
chairman-bill-kenwright#:~:text=Kenwright%20reveals%3A%20
%22What%20do%20you,your%20bank%2C%20daily%20for%20me.

Hunter, A., 'Everton keen to show positive intent to end winless run at
Liverpool' (2011) *The Guardian*
https://www.theguardian.com/football/2011/jan/15/everton-liverpool-
premier-league

Hunter, A., 'Everton supporters' group the Blue Union to hold protest march'
(2011) *The Guardian*
https://www.theguardian.com/football/2011/sep/07/everton-blue-
union-protest-march

Hunter, A., 'David Moyes welcomes unity at Everton but not parity with Aston
Villa' (2011) *The Guardian*
https://www.theguardian.com/football/2011/sep/11/david-moyes-
everton-aston-villa

Hunter, A., 'Everton manager worried about message sent out by sale of Mikel
Arteta' (2011) *The Guardian*
https://www.theguardian.com/football/2011/sep/14/everton-david-
moyes-bank-arteta

BIBLIOGRAPHY

Hunter, A., 'Everton's David Moyes points finger at referee in defeat to Liverpool' (2011) *The Guardian* https://www.theguardian.com/football/2011/oct/01/everton-david-moyes-referee-liverpool

Hunter, A., 'Phil Jagielka: 'It was difficult to see Mikel Arteta leave Everton ' (2011) *The Guardian* https://www.theguardian.com/football/2011/dec/30/phil-jagielka-mikel-arteta-everton

Hunter, A., 'Everton left in shade by Tottenham's improvement, says David Moyes' (2012) *The Guardian* https://www.theguardian.com/football/2012/jan/10/everton-tottenham-david-moyes

Hunter, A., 'Steven Pienaar eager to show Everton fans he deserves to be forgiven' (2012) *The Guardian* https://www.theguardian.com/football/2012/feb/02/steven-pienaar-everton-tottenham-hotspur

Hunter, A., 'Landon Donovan on way out of Everton but he wants David Moyes to stay' (2012) *The Guardian* https://www.theguardian.com/football/2012/feb/17/landon-donovan-everton-david-moyes

Hunter, A., 'David Moyes: 'Ten years at a club like Everton takes some doing'' (2012) *The Guardian* https://www.theguardian.com/football/2012/mar/09/david-moyes-10-years-everton

Hunter, A., *'David Moyes says Everton will attract neutrals in FA Cup semi-final' (2012) The Guardian* https://www.theguardian.com/football/2012/apr/13/david-moyes-everton-neutrals-fa-cup

Hunter, A., 'David Moyes says Europe dream gives Everton Cup semi-final incentive' *(2012) The Guardian* https://www.theguardian.com/football/2012/mar/30/david-moyes-europe-everton-fa-cup

Hunter, A., 'Royston Drenthe told to stay away by Everton after discipline breach' (2012) *The Guardian* https://www.theguardian.com/football/2012/apr/15/royston-drenthe-everton-real-madrid#:~:text=%22It%20didn't%20seem%20as,do%20that%20to%20beat%20us

Hunter, A., 'David Moyes wants 'chink of light' before new Everton deal' (2012) *The Guardian* https://www.theguardian.com/football/2012/may/11/david-moyes-everton-deal

Hunter, A., 'Wayne Rooney asked to play for Everton in Tony Hibbert's testimonial' (2012) *The Guardian* https://www.theguardian.com/football/2012/aug/07/wayne-rooney-everton-tony-hibbert

Hunter, A., 'Liverpool's Luis Suárez has a history of diving, says David Moyes' (2012) *The Guardian* https://www.theguardian.com/football/2012/oct/26/everton-david-moyes-liverpool-luis-suarez

Hunter, A., 'Everton manager comes out fighting in face of criticism from Liverpool' (2012) *The Guardian* https://www.theguardian.com/football/2012/nov/02/everton-david-moyes-criticism-liverpool

Hunter, A., 'David Moyes delays Everton contract talks until after transfer window' (2012) *The Guardian* https://www.theguardian.com/football/2012/nov/27/david-moyes-everton-contract

Hunter, A., 'Liverpool and Everton draw blank as Sylvain Distin effort is ruled out' (2013) *The Guardian* https://www.theguardian.com/football/2013/may/05/liverpool-everton-premier-league

Hunter, A., 'Overwhelmed David Moyes offers to help Everton find his successor' (2013) *The Guardian* https://www.theguardian.com/football/2013/may/12/everton-david-moyes-west-ham-finale

Hunter, A., 'We know where you live': police investigate banner near Benítez home' (2021) *The Guardian* https://www.theguardian.com/football/2021/jun/28/banner-near-benitez-home-as-everton-deal-looms-manager-we-know-where-you-live

Hunter, A., 'Everton sign contract to complete new stadium construction' (2022) *The Guardian* https://www.theguardian.com/football/2022/apr/13/everton-sign-contract-to-complete-new-stadium-construction

Jackson, J., 'Liverpool and Everton 'must' share new ground, council says' *(2009) The Guardian* https://www.theguardian.com/football/2009/jun/07/liverpool-everton-stadium-share

Jackson, J., 'David Moyes quits as Everton manager to take over at Manchester United' *(2013) The Guardian* https://www.theguardian.com/football/2013/may/09/david-moyes-quits-everton-manchester-united

Keeling, P.,'Cahill crackles as Everton lose count' (2007) *The Guardian* https://www.theguardian.com/football/2007/nov/25/match.everton

Lovejoy, J., 'David Moyes left shell-shocked by Everton's implosion against Wigan' (2013) *The Guardian* https://www.theguardian.com/football/2013/mar/10/david-moyes-everton-wigan-fa-cup

Lovejoy, J., 'Manchester City's hopes crushed anew by Everton's Osman and Jelavic' (2013) *The Guardian* https://www.theguardian.com/football/2013/mar/16/everton-manchester-city-premier-league

Rich, T., 'Depleted Everton fall prey to the brilliance of Benfica's Angel Di María' (2009) *The Guardian* https://www.theguardian.com/football/2009/oct/22/europa-league-benfica-everton#:~:text=%22I%20would%20like%20to%20play,difficult%20circumstances%2C%22%20continued%20Moyes

Rich, T., 'David Moyes fumes at Everton's teatime Europa League kick-off' (2010) *The Guardian* https://www.theguardian.com/football/2010/feb/15/david-moyes-everton-europa-league

Rich, T., 'Sporting Lisbon send Everton tumbling out of Europa League' (2010) *The Guardian* https://www.theguardian.com/football/2010/feb/25/sporting-lisbon-everton-europa-league

Rich, T., 'David Moyes: Liverpool have spent considerably more money than Everton' (2011) *The Guardian* https://www.theguardian.com/football/2011/sep/30/david-moyes-everton-liverpool

Rich, T., 'Luis Suárez shows sense of humour but is destined to remain a villain' (2012) *The Guardian* https://www.theguardian.com/football/2012/oct/28/luis-suarez-humour-liverpool-everton

Scott, M., 'ITV apologises after cameras miss only goal in Merseyside derby' (2009) *The Guardian* https://www.theguardian.com/football/2009/feb/05/itv-fa-cup-coverage

Tallentire, M., 'Everton announce plan for new stadium in nearby Walton Hall Park' (2014) *The Guardian*

BIBLIOGRAPHY

https://www.theguardian.com/football/2014/sep/15/everton-new-stadium-walton-hall-park-goodison

Taylor, L., 'Everton descend into disarray' (2004) *The Guardian* https://www.theguardian.com/football/2004/jul/22/sport.comment2

Taylor, L., 'Everton's faulty choreography leaves Moyes at lowest point' (2005) *The Guardian* https://www.theguardian.com/football/2005/sep/16/match.sport2

Taylor, L., 'Everton comeback banishes memories of Bucharest' (2007) *The Guardian* https://www.theguardian.com/football/2007/oct/05/match.everton

Taylor, D., 'Phil Neville, Goodison's Stepson, revels in return to his home from home' (2013) *The Guardian* https://www.theguardian.com/football/2013/dec/03/phil-neville-interview-manchester-united-everton

The Observer., 'Everton confirm sale of 49.9% of club to former Arsenal shareholder Farhad Moshiri' (2016) *The Guardian* https://www.theguardian.com/football/2016/feb/27/everton-takeover-arsenal-shareholder-farhad-moshiri

The Press Association., 'Everton: 'Rooney is going nowhere' (2003) *The Guardian* https://www.theguardian.com/football/2003/oct/16/newsstory.premierleague200304

The Press Association., 'Everton hit out at 'terrible tackle' that ended Marouane Fellaini's season' (2010) *The Guardian* https://www.theguardian.com/football/2010/feb/17/david-moyes-marouane-fellani-everton

The Press Association., 'David Moyes admits Everton deserved to lose Sporting Lisbon tie' (2010) *The Guardian* https://www.theguardian.com/football/2010/feb/26/david-moyes-everton-sporting-lisbon

The Press Association., 'It was our own fault today,' admits Everton manager David Moyes' (2012) *The Guardian* https://www.theguardian.com/football/2012/apr/14/david-moyes-everton-fa-cup

Walker, P., 'Everton box clever with Rocky in the stands' (2007) *The Guardian* https://www.theguardian.com/football/2007/jan/11/newsstory.sport8

Widdicombe, J., 'Fiorentina 2-0 Everton' (2008) *The Guardian* https://www.theguardian.com/football/2008/mar/06/minutebyminute.everton

Wilson, P, 'Moyes the merrier after Carsley seals derby victory' (2004) *The Guardian* https://www.theguardian.com/football/2004/dec/12/match.sport3

Wilson, P, 'Everton's defensive wall Stubbs out talk of title' (2007) *The Guardian* https://www.theguardian.com/football/2007/feb/04/match.sport1

Wilson, P, 'Dan Gosling strikes to help Everton seal victory over Manchester United' (2010) *The Guardian* https://www.theguardian.com/football/2010/feb/20/everton-manchester-united-premier-league

Wilson, P, 'Wayne Rooney is spared the pain – but Manchester United aren't' (2010) *The Guardian* https://www.theguardian.com/football/2010/sep/11/wayne-rooney-everton-manchester-united

Winrow, I., 'Rooney delay in signing new contract' (2002) *The Guardian* https://www.theguardian.com/football/2002/oct/22/newsstory.sport2

Winrow, I., 'Hard graft as good as hard currency says David Moyes' (2009) *The Guardian* https://www.theguardian.com/global/2009/apr/21/everton-david-moyes-easyjet-fa-cup

'Rooney going nowhere unless price is right: Moyes' (2004) *The Guardian* https://www.theguardian.com/football/2004/aug/27/newsstory.everton

'United make bid for Rooney' (2004) *The Guardian* https://www.theguardian.com/football/2004/aug/25/newsstory.sport15

'Moyes backs Beattie to rock the nation' (2005) *The Guardian* https://www.theguardian.com/football/2005/jan/05/newsstory.sport11

'Mourinho apologises to Johnson over diving insinuation' (2006) *The Guardian* https://www.theguardian.com/football/2006/dec/20/newsstory.sport8

'Everton crack down on Van Der Meyde' (2007) *The Guardian* https://www.theguardian.com/football/2007/aug/17/newsstory.everton

'Cup is still half full for Moyes despite his losing gamble' (2008) *The Guardian* https://www.theguardian.com/football/2008/jan/08/newsstory.everton

'FA 'hypocritical' over Cup final ticket allocation, says David Moyes' (2009) *The Guardian* https://www.theguardian.com/football/2009/may/01/andy-burnham-fa-cup-football

'Steven Pienaar to miss Everton's Europa League match in Minsk' (2009) *The Guardian* https://www.theguardian.com/football/2009/sep/29/steven-pienaar-everton-europa-league

'Everton to consider joint stadium with Liverpool after Kirkby snub' (2009) *The Guardian* https://www.theguardian.com/football/2009/nov/26/everton-liverpool

The Liverpool Echo

Beesley, C., 'How Everton became 'The People's Club' – David Moyes lifts the lid on iconic moment' (2019) *The Liverpool Echo* https://www.liverpoolecho.co.uk/sport/football/football-news/how-everton-became-the-peoples-15987931

Beesley, C., "EXCLUSIVE: 'There was always something about Everton' – David Moyes reveals 'People's Club' inspiration and what kept him up night before first game", (2022) *The Liverpool Echo* https://www.liverpoolecho.co.uk/sport/football/football-news/david-moyes-everton-peoples-club-23396659

Beesley, C., "EXCLUSIVE: David Moyes makes 'incredible' Everton admission and sends West Ham message", (2022) *The Liverpool Echo* https://www.liverpoolecho.co.uk/sport/football/football-news/david-moyes-everton-breaking-23397061

Carroll, S., 'Everton, Villarreal and the great Pierluigi Collina mistake that altered the course of David Moyes' reign' (2019) *The Liverpool Echo* https://www.liverpoolecho.co.uk/sport/football/football-news/everton-villarreal-great-pierluigi-collina-16784869

Carsley, L., 'Lee Carsley: Everton FC fans were the real stars in Lille' (2014) *The Liverpool Echo* https://www.liverpoolecho.co.uk/sport/football/football-news/lee-carsley-everton-fc-fans-8000517

BIBLIOGRAPHY

Jones, A., 'Worst 15 minutes ever' – Jimmy Bullard explains unseen aspect of Duncan Ferguson Everton clash' (2020) *The Liverpool Echo*
https://www.liverpoolecho.co.uk/sport/football/football-news/worst-15-minutes-ever-jimmy-18124300

Jones, A., 'Watford sack Marco Silva – and is an 'unwarranted approach' by Everton to blame?' (2018) *The Liverpool Echo*
https://www.liverpoolecho.co.uk/sport/football/football-news/watford-sack-marco-silva-unwarranted-14183475

Jones, A., 'I might cry' – Frank Lampard reacts to stunning Everton comeback against Crystal Palace' (2022) *The Liverpool Echo*
https://www.liverpoolecho.co.uk/sport/football/football-news/everton-frank-lampard-breaking-24004298

Kay, D., 'Self-made Everton 'ratter' sparked iconic Goodison pile-on before helping shape England's football future' (2022) *The Liverpool Echo*
https://www.liverpoolecho.co.uk/sport/football/football-news/everton-iconic-goodison-england-future-25704501

Kirkbride, P., ''Everton new stadium – Blues vow to consult fans on design and capacity' (2017) *The Liverpool Echo*
https://www.liverpoolecho.co.uk/sport/football/football-news/everton-stadium-blues-vow-consult-12787491

O'Neill, C., ''I made a mistake' – Rafa Benitez has already clarified his Everton 'small club' comments' (2019) *The Liverpool Echo*
https://www.liverpoolecho.co.uk/sport/football/football-news/rafa-benitez-everton-mistake-comments-20835720

Pearce, J., 'David Moyes calls for a final push from his Everton troops' (2009) *The Liverpool Echo*
https://www.liverpoolecho.co.uk/sport/football/football-news/david-moyes-calls-final-push-3453702

Pearce, J., 'The last 10 Merseyside derbies' (2011) *The Liverpool Echo*
https://www.liverpoolecho.co.uk/sport/football/football-news/the-last-10-merseyside-derbies-3473316

Prentice, D., 'Remember the name Wayne Rooney? Clive Tyldesley recalls the day an Everton hero announced his arrival' (2017) *The Liverpool Echo*
https://www.liverpoolecho.co.uk/sport/football/football-news/remember-name-wayne-rooney-clive-13780645

Prentice, D., 'Dave Prentice: The painfully short memory of Arsene Wenger' (2011) *The Liverpool Echo*
https://www.liverpoolecho.co.uk/sport/football/football-news/dave-prentice-painfully-short-memory-3382029

Prentice, D., 'Argentinian playmaker Juan Roman Riquelme will now NEVER play for Everton' (2015) *The Liverpool Echo*
https://www.liverpoolecho.co.uk/sport/football/football-news/argentinian-playmaker-who-now-never-8520095

Prentice, D., 'Everton v Fiorentina: David Moyes calls for Goodison payback' (2008) *The Liverpool Echo*
https://www.liverpoolecho.co.uk/sport/football/football-news/everton-v-fiorentina-david-moyes-3491023

Prentice, D., 'David Moyes delighted as Landon Donovan agrees to return to Everton FC on loan' (2011) *The Liverpool Echo*
https://www.liverpoolecho.co.uk/sport/football/football-news/david-moyes-delighted-landon-donovan-3357837

Prentice, D., 'Brendan Rodgers: Liverpool FC will discipline Luis Suarez over 'unacceptable' comments on diving (VIDEO)' (2013) *The Liverpool Echo*
https://www.liverpoolecho.co.uk/sport/football/football-news/brendan-rodgers-liverpool-fc-discipline-3325089

Thompson, J., 'I'd love to sign forever, says Johnson' (2007) *The Liverpool Echo*
https://www.liverpoolecho.co.uk/sport/football/football-news/id-love-sign-ever-says-3512798

'Moyes blasts Toon over Rooney bid' (2004) *The Liverpool Echo*
https://www.liverpoolecho.co.uk/sport/football/football-news/moyes-blasts-toon-over-rooney-3541309

'Cahill sending off sparks FIFA probe' (2004) *The Liverpool Echo*
https://www.liverpoolecho.co.uk/sport/football/football-news/cahill-sending-sparks-fifa-probe-3539753

'Everton FC fans told "tickets all gone" for Nuremberg clash' (2007) *The Liverpool Echo*
https://www.liverpoolecho.co.uk/news/liverpool-news/everton-fc-fans-told-tickets-3498337

'Bill Kenwright: Everton fans deserve compo' (2007) *The Liverpool Echo*
https://www.liverpoolecho.co.uk/news/liverpool-news/bill-kenwright-everton-fans-deserve-3498663

'Fresh injuries sober up Everton after Europa League win in Athens' (2009) *The Liverpool Echo*
https://www.liverpoolecho.co.uk/sport/football/football-news/fresh-injuries-sober-up-everton-3435555

'David Moyes delighted with "fantastic" Jermaine Beckford strike to rescue point for Everton FC against Bolton' (2009) *The Liverpool Echo* https://www.liverpoolecho.co.uk/sport/football/football-news/david-moyes-delighted-fantastic-jermaine-3390169

'David Moyes and Roberto Mancini make peace after Everton's win at Manchester City' (2010) *The Liverpool Echo*
https://www.liverpoolecho.co.uk/sport/football/football-news/david-moyes-roberto-mancini-make-3429444

'Angry Everton FC say Blue Union showed a lack of respect following recording of Bill Kenwright talks' (2011) *The Liverpool Echo*
https://www.liverpoolecho.co.uk/sport/football/football-news/angry-everton-fc-say-blue-3368146

'Mikel Arteta leaves Everton FC to join Arsenal (GALLERY)' (2011) *The Liverpool Echo*
https://www.liverpoolecho.co.uk/sport/football/football-news/mikel-arteta-leaves-everton-fc-3364149

'Blues youngsters will ensure bright future at Everton FC says Tim Cahill' (2011) *The Liverpool Echo*
https://www.liverpoolecho.co.uk/sport/football/football-news/blues-youngsters-ensure-bright-future-3364987

'I'll always be an Evertonian, says departing Tim Cahill as he is unveiled as a New York Red Bulls players' (2012) *The Liverpool Echo*
https://www.liverpoolecho.co.uk/sport/football/football-news/ill-always-evertonian-says-departing-3340903

'Everton FC boss David Moyes surprised by Tony Hibbert's set-piece prowess' (2012) *The Liverpool Echo*
https://www.liverpoolecho.co.uk/sport/football/football-news/everton-fc-boss-david-moyes-3337035

'Everton FC: David Moyes takes his share of the blame for Blues' FA Cup exit' (2013) *The Liverpool Echo* https://www.liverpoolecho.co.uk/sport/football/football-news/everton-fc-david-moyes-takes-3009357

BBC Sports
Burnett, M., 'West Ham 0-2 Everton' (2007) *BBC Sports* http://news.bbc.co.uk/sport1/hi/football/eng_prem/7134154.stm
Cheese, C., 'AZ Alkmaar 2-3 Everton' (2007) *BBC Sports* http://news.bbc.co.uk/sport1/hi/football/europe/7145803.stm
Chowdhury, S., 'Derby 0-2 Everton' (2007) *BBC Sports* http://news.bbc.co.uk/sport1/hi/football/eng_prem/7054070.stm
Fletcher, P, 'Everton 0-2 Benfica' (2009) *BBC Sports* http://news.bbc.co.uk/sport1/hi/football/europe/8342599.stm
Hughes, I., 'Blackburn 2-3 Everton' (2010) *BBC Sports* http://news.bbc.co.uk/sport1/hi/football/eng_prem/8619900.stm
Lewis, A., Everton 6-1 SK Brann' (2008) *BBC Sports* http://news.bbc.co.uk/sport1/hi/football/europe/7254725.stm
Lyon, S., 'Man Utd 2-1 Everton' (2007) *BBC Sports* http://news.bbc.co.uk/sport1/hi/football/eng_prem/7145754.stm
Mercer, N., 'Everton 3-1 Larissa' (2007) *BBC Sports* http://news.bbc.co.uk/sport1/hi/football/europe/7054188.stm
McNulty, P., 'Everton 2-1 Wigan' (2007) *BBC Sports* http://news.bbc.co.uk/sport1/hi/football/eng_prem/6602877.stm
McNulty, P., 'Bolton 1-2 Everton' (2007) *BBC Sports* http://news.bbc.co.uk/sport1/hi/football/eng_prem/6963699.stm
McNulty, P., 'Everton 1-2 Liverpool' (2007) *BBC Sports* http://news.bbc.co.uk/sport1/hi/football/eng_prem/7043002.stm
McNulty, P., 'Everton 7-1 Sunderland' (2007) *BBC Sports* http://news.bbc.co.uk/sport1/hi/football/eng_prem/7099691.stm
McNulty, P., 'Everton 3-0 Fulham' (2007) *BBC Sports* http://news.bbc.co.uk/sport1/hi/football/eng_prem/7122774.stm
Phillips, O., 'Chelsea 2-1 Everton' (2013) https://www.bbc.co.uk/sport/football/22499152
Rej, A., 'Everton 1-1 Sunderland' (2011) *BBC Sports* http://news.bbc.co.uk/sport1/hi/football/eng_prem/8660310.stm
Rose, G., Sunderland 1-0 Everton (2013) *BBC Sports* https://www.bbc.co.uk/sport/football/22133512
Shea, J., 'Everton 1-0 Portsmouth' (2010) *BBC Sports* http://news.bbc.co.uk/sport1/hi/football/eng_prem/8660310.stm
Sheringham, S., 'Everton 2-1 Sporting' (2010) *BBC Sports* http://news.bbc.co.uk/sport1/hi/football/europe/8516353.stm
Smith, B., Everton 2-2 Liverpool (2012) *BBC Sports* https://www.bbc.co.uk/sport/football/20020076
Soni, P., 'Chelsea 1-1 Everton' (2007) *BBC Sports* https://www.bbc.co.uk/news/sport1/hi/football/eng_prem/7076647.stm
Stevenson, J., 'Nuremberg 0-2 Everton' (2007) *BBC Sports* http://news.bbc.co.uk/sport1/hi/football/europe/7076600.stm
Stevenson, J., 'Everton 1-1 FC Metalist Kharkiv' (2007) *BBC Sports* http://news.bbc.co.uk/sport1/hi/football/europe/6996451.stm

sitive after freak injury' (2003) *BBC Sports*
http://news.bbc.co.uk/sport1/hi/football/teams/e/everton/2995404.stm
'Radzinski backs Rooney exit' (2004) *BBC Sports*
http://news.bbc.co.uk/sport1/hi/football/teams/e/everton/3880385.stm
'Wyness takes Everton post' (2004) *BBC Sports*
http://news.bbc.co.uk/sport1/hi/football/teams/e/everton/3640234.stm
'Everton 1-1 Birmingham' (2005) *BBC Sports* http://news.bbc.co.uk/sport1/hi/
football/eng_prem/4451353.stm
'Everton 0-2 Manchester United' (2005) *BBC Sports*
http://news.bbc.co.uk/sport1/hi/football/eng_prem/4126970.stm
'Everton 0-4 Bolton' (2005) *BBC Sports* http://news.bbc.co.uk/sport1/hi/
football/eng_prem/4516330.stm
'Lescott completes Everton switch' (2006) *BBC Sports*
http://news.bbc.co.uk/sport1/hi/football/teams/e/everton/5036292.stm
'Everton 2- 1 Watford' (2006) *BBC Sports* http://news.bbc.co.uk/sport1/hi/
football/eng_prem/4786651.stm
'Tottenham 0- 2 Everton' (2006) *BBC Sports* http://news.bbc.co.uk/sport1/hi/
football/eng_prem/5266276.stm
'Everton 3-0 Liverpool' (2006) *BBC Sports*
http://news.bbc.co.uk/sport1/hi/football/eng_prem/5308190.stm
'Middlesbrough 2- 1 Everton' (2006) *BBC Sports*
http://news.bbc.co.uk/sport1/hi/football/eng_prem/5415958.stm
'Everton 0-1 Aston Villa' (2006) *BBC Sports*
http://news.bbc.co.uk/sport1/hi/football/eng_prem/6116240.stm
'Everton plan Mourinho complaint' (2006) *BBC Sports*
http://news.bbc.co.uk/sport1/hi/football/eng_prem/6192485.stm
'Everton 1-0 Blackburn' (2007) *BBC Sports*
http://news.bbc.co.uk/sport1/hi/football/eng_prem/6327075.stm
'Everton 1-0 Arsenal' (2007) *BBC Sports*
http://news.bbc.co.uk/sport1/hi/football/eng_prem/6437253.stm
'Everton 2-1 Charlton' (2007) *BBC Sports*
http://news.bbc.co.uk/sport1/hi/football/eng_prem/6534815.stm
'Everton 3-0 Portsmouth' (2007) *BBC Sports*
http://news.bbc.co.uk/sport1/hi/football/eng_prem/6602877.stm
'Chelsea 1- 1 Everton' (2007) *BBC Sports*
http://news.bbc.co.uk/sport1/hi/football/eng_prem/6627785.stm 'Tony
Hibbert: Goal in Everton testimonial "a fairytale"' (2012) *BBC Sports* https://
www.bbc.co.uk/sport/football/19192961

Everton FC Official Website
'Lampard appointed Everton Manager' (2022) *Everton FC*
https://www.evertonfc.com/news/2467281/lampard-appointed-
everton-manager
McNamara, P., 'Everton Scorers DCL and Keane on 'incredible' night'
(2022) *Everton FC*
https://www.evertonfc.com/news/2625320/everton-scorers-dcl-and-keane-on-
incredible-night

The Irish Examiner 'Wayne Rooney recalls being "fuming" before scoring
stunning winner against Arsenal in 2002' (2017) *The Irish Examiner*

https://www.irishexaminer.com/sport/soccer/arid-30810801.html
'Moyes: Rooney not too big for Goodison' (2004) *The Irish Examiner* https://
www.irishexaminer.com/sport/soccer/arid-30155361.html

The Mirror ' Moyes Scathing of Beattie Sending Off' (2005) *The Mirror*
https://www.mirror.co.uk/news/world-news/moyes-scathing-of-beattie-
sending-off-1605574
'Everton star Tim Cahill dedicates Europa League winner to Samoa tsunami
victims' (2009) *The Mirror* https://www.mirror.co.uk/sport/football/news/
everton-star-tim-cahill-dedicates-3370755

The Daily Mail 'Moyes backs down over Beattie headbutt' (2005) *The Daily
Mail* https://www.dailymail.co.uk/sport/football/article-337728/Moyes-
backs-Beattie-headbutt.html
'I had nothing to prove, says hotshot AJ' (2006) *The Daily Mail* https://www.
dailymail.co.uk/sport/football/article-404652/I-prove-says-hotshot-AJ.html
'No contact from Tottenham and I'm happy to stay at Everton, says Moyes'
(2012) *The Daily Mail* https://www.dailymail.co.uk/sport/football/
article-2160344/Tottenham-manager-news-David-Moyes-contact.html

Sky Sports Marshall, A., 'Collina explains Dunc decision' *Sky Sports*
https://www.skysports.com/football/news/11671/2354766/collina-
explains-dunc-decision

Metro
'Warnock frustrated by "gamesmanship" (2006) *Metro* https://metro.
co.uk/2006/10/22/warnock-frustrated-by-gamesmanship-302928/
'Toffees stand up for Johnson' (2006) *Metro* https://metro.co.uk/2006/11/06/
toffees-stand-up-for-johnson-348147
'Steven Pienaar 'could be sold to Spurs in January', David Moyes admits' (2010)
Metro https://metro.co.uk/2010/12/13/steven-pienaar-could-be-sold-to-
spurs-in-january-david-moyes-admits-610855/
'Luis Suarez labels Fifa vice-president a "nobody" in response to diving claim'
(2012) *Metro* 'https://metro.co.uk/2012/10/13/luis-suarez-labels-fifa-vice-
president-a-nobody-in-response-to-diving-claim-599834/

The Times
Hughes, M., 'Mourinho in no mood to apologise for Johnson accusation'
(2006) *The Times*
https://www.thetimes.co.uk/article/mourinho-in-no-mood-to-apologise-for-
johnson-accusation-0337klrfj5s

Eurosport
'What The Managers Say' (2006) *Eurosport* https://www.eurosport.
co.uk/football/premiership/2006-2007/what-the-managers-say_
sto1001255/story.shtml

I-News
Lucas, K., 'Rafael Benitez: Why he called Everton a "small club" – and if their
fans can forgive former Liverpool boss' (2021) *I-News* https://inews.co.uk/
sport/football/rafael-benitez-everton-next-manager-liverpool-1056642

The Independent
Gaunt, K., 'Moyes upbeat after Benfica lesson' (2009) *The Independent* https://www.independent.co.uk/sport/football/european/moyes-upbeat-after-benfica-lesson-1816083.html
Herbert, I., 'Benitez: I was right to call Everton a small club, (2011) *The Independent* https://www.independent.co.uk/sport/football/news/benitez-i-was-right-to-call-everton-a-small-club-2363821.html

The Independent IE
'Stoke manager Tony Pulis brands Luis Suarez dive "an embarrassment" and calls for FA action' (2012) *The Independent IE* https://www.independent.ie/sport/soccer/stoke-manager-tony-pulis-brands-luis-suarez-dive-an-embarrassment-and-calls-for-fa-action-28818696.html

North Wales Live
'Andrew Johnson delighted to sign Everton deal' (2007) *North Wales Live* https://www.dailypost.co.uk/sport/football/football-news/andrew-johnson-delighted-sign-everton-2855980
'Everton FC 2 Liverpool FC 0: We've played better and lost says David Moyes' (2010) *North Wales Live* https://www.dailypost.co.uk/sport/football/football-news/everton-fc-2-liverpool-fc-2743722

The Bolton News
Sudlow, C., 'Everton fans in Uefa ticket blow' (2007) *The Bolton News* https://www.theboltonnews.co.uk/news/1813104.everton-fans-in-uefa-ticket-blow/

Daily Post
'Everton FC baffled after 'winner' against Stoke City disallowed' (2010) *Daily Post* https://www.dailypost.co.uk/sport/football/football-news/everton-fc-baffled-after-winner-2754655

Daily Record
'Derby Sting Drives Everton' (2007) *Daily Record* https://www.dailyrecord.co.uk/sport/football/derby-sting-drives-everton-961221

Cheshire Live
'Everton FC boss David Moyes explains why prospect of going above Liverpool in the Premier League has surpassed expectations' (2011) *Cheshire Live* https://www.cheshire-live.co.uk/sport/football/football-news/everton-fc-boss-david-moyes-5181740

TalkSport
Varney, A., 'Everton confirm David Moyes exit as Manchester United prepare to unveil Scot as Sir Alex Ferguson's successor' (2012) *TalkSport* https://talksport.com/football/premier-league/94372/everton-confirm-david-moyes-exit-manchester-united-prepare-unveil-scot-s-1971/

BIBLIOGRAPHY

The Scotsman
Parkes, I., 'David Moyes still tight-lipped on future' (2013) *The Scotsman*
https://www.scotsman.com/sport/football/david-moyes-still-tight-lipped-
future-1590058

Wikipedia
Everton F.C. (2023) *Wikipedia*
https://en.wikipedia.org/wiki/Everton_F.C.
David Moyes (2023) *Wikipedia*
https://en.wikipedia.org/wiki/David_Moyes
Preston North End F.C. (2023) *Wikipedia*
https://en.wikipedia.org/wiki/Preston_North_End_F.C.
Wayne Rooney (2023) *Wikipedia*
https://en.wikipedia.org/wiki/Wayne_Rooney
2001–02 Everton F.C. Season (2022) *Wikipedia* https://en.wikipedia.org/
wiki/2001%E2%80%9302_Everton_F.C._season
2002–03 Everton F.C. Season (2022) *Wikipedia* https://en.wikipedia.org/
wiki/2002%E2%80%9303_Everton_F.C._season
2003–04 Everton F.C. Season (2022) *Wikipedia*
https://en.wikipedia.org/wiki/2003%E2%80%9304_Everton_F.C._season
2004–05 Everton F.C. Season (2022) *Wikipedia*
https://en.wikipedia.org/wiki/2004%E2%80%9305_Everton_F.C._season
2005–06 Everton F.C. Season (2022) *Wikipedia*
https://en.wikipedia.org/wiki/2005%E2%80%9306_Everton_F.C._season
2006–07 Everton F.C. Season (2022) *Wikipedia*
https://en.wikipedia.org/wiki/2006%E2%80%9307_Everton_F.C._season
2007–08 Everton F.C. Season (2022) *Wikipedia*
https://en.wikipedia.org/wiki/2007%E2%80%9308_Everton_F.C._season
2008–09 Everton F.C. Season (2022) *Wikipedia*
https://en.wikipedia.org/wiki/2008%E2%80%9309_Everton_F.C._season
2009–10 Everton F.C. Season (2022) *Wikipedia*
https://en.wikipedia.org/wiki/2009%E2%80%9310_Everton_F.C._season
2010–11 Everton F.C. Season (2022) *Wikipedia*
https://en.wikipedia.org/wiki/2010%E2%80%9311_Everton_F.C._season
2011–12 Everton F.C. Season (2022) *Wikipedia*
https://en.wikipedia.org/wiki/2011%E2%80%9312_Everton_F.C._season
2012–13 Everton F.C. Season (2022) *Wikipedia*
https://en.wikipedia.org/wiki/2012%E2%80%9313_Everton_F.C._season
The Kirby Project (2022) *Wikipedia*
https://en.wikipedia.org/wiki/The_Kirkby_Project#CABE

Podcasts
Episode 34: Mark Clattenburg – *The Greatest Game with Jamie Carragher*
https://www.spreaker.com/user/13203969/8-clattenburg-master (2021)

Videos
Toffee TV, (2022), "Wayne Rooney Exclusive Interview PT.1", available at:
https://www.youtube.com/watch?v=fwUpgfpK9Ds
TheBlueUnion1878, (2012), "Kenwright: The Blue Union have betrayed this
club", available at: https://www.youtube.com/watch?v=c-BklwScNYs